Cavalcade of American Horses

Books by Pers Crowell

BEAU DARE
SIX GOOD FRIENDS
THE FIRST HORSEMAN
CAVALCADE OF AMERICAN HORSES

Cavalcade of
AMERICAN
HORSES

PERS
CROWELL

Bonanza Books　　　New York

THIS EDITION PUBLISHED BY BONANZA BOOKS
A DIVISION OF CROWN PUBLISHERS, INC.
BY ARRANGEMENT WITH MCGRAW-HILL BOOK COMPANY, INC.

Library of Congress Catalog Card Number: 51-12662

PRINTED IN THE UNITED STATES OF AMERICA

Preface

The story of how man developed the horse from a wild, untamed animal to its present high degree of usefulness is an intriguing one. Down through the ages the horse has been not only a close companion to man, but one of the most useful animals in the advance of civilization. It is this background of history and legend, as well as the story of individual breeds, that I have attempted to tell in this book.

All the breeds represented here, except two, are of American origin. The two exceptions are the Thoroughbred and the Arabian. However, the Thoroughbred's development in America parallels the best accomplishments made for the breed in any other country; and even though the Arabian is not a true child of America, he has been adopted as a beloved son. Also, because of the importance of the Arabian's influence on other breeds, he cannot be excluded from a book on American horses.

It has been said that the American wilderness could not have been settled without the horse and that the winning of the West was virtually accomplished on horseback. Indeed, the horse has been part and parcel of America's whole colorful history. Each breed has contributed its part to our heritage of great racers, trotters, riding horses, carriage teams, show horses, cow ponies, cavalry mounts, and plain utilitarian horses of all kinds. Out of this "cavalcade" I have attempted to present the romance, bloodlines, training, records, and anecdotes about great horses of the past in each breed.

There is a real need for a cementing of fellowship among all horse folk, regardless of the breed they favor. I sincerely believe that every horseman should "look beyond the ears of his own horse so that he may see the good in the other man's," and I hope that this volume will create a better understanding of all breeds and bring closer together all horse lovers.

When a horseman begins to feel that he knows "all about horses," he ceases to be a horseman. Therefore, it is with humbleness that I present these facts, anecdotes, surmises, and theories. Even during the printing of this book, of course, some records will have been bettered and some standards may have changed. There may be some who will not agree with everything set down here, but I have tried to be as objective as it is possible to be in presenting so comprehensive a subject.

With sincere gratitude I thank the scientists, breed associations, and numerous trainers and horsemen with whom I have discussed horses in compiling this record. Without their generous cooperation it would have been an insurmountable task. Also credit must be given to the fine horses of all breeds which served as models for the illustrations.

Also I wish to thank the authors and publishers from whose works historical and other data were quoted, as follows: *Evolution of the Horse,* Leaflet Guide Series No. 36, American Museum of Natural History; letters to the author from Dr. George Gaylord Simpson of the American Museum of Natural History; article by Dr. Samuel H. Chubb in *Natural History,* Vol. XXIX, No. 5, published by American Museum of Natural History; *The Last of the Mohicans* by James Fenimore Cooper; *America Dissected* by James McSparran; *American Horse Shows Rules Book,* published by American Horse Shows Association; article by Herbert J. Krum in *Mexico Ledger,* Mexico, Mo.; *The Authentic Arabian Horse* by Lady Wentworth; *Gleanings from the Desert of Arabia* by R. D. Upton; *American Quarter Horse Official Stud Book and Registry; Famous Saddle Horses* by Suzanne; *The Horse of America* by John H. Wallace; *Horses and Americans* by Phil Stong, Garden City Publishing Company, Inc.; speech by Dr. C. D. Parks, *The Western Horseman;* article in *Wallace's Monthly,* 1882, by James D. Ladd; article on the Morgan horse by W. H. Gocher, Historian of *American Trotter and Pacer; Drivers Up* by Dwight Akers, G. P. Putnam's Sons; letters to the author from J. J. Murray; "Which Way Are We Going?" by B. C. Hunter, *Tennessee Walking Horse;* "Sum of the Past" by Stanley Harrison, *Thoroughbred Record; The Grand National* by David Hoadley Monroe, Huntington Press; *"El indomable caballo cuarto de milla"* by Dan Casement, reprinted in *The Western Horseman;* "Cow Sense Can Be Developed" by Wallace Reames, *The Western Horseman.*

Helpful information was also gathered from the following sources: American Quarter Horse Association; American Quarter Racing Association; United States Trotting Association; Tennessee Walking Horse Association of America; *Horse of the Americas* by Robert Moorman Denhardt, University of Oklahoma Press; *History and Romance of the Horse* by Arthur Vernon, Waverly House; *Down the Stretch* by Colonel Matt J. Winn as told to Frank G. Menke, Smith & Durrell, Inc.; Pinto Horse Society; Appaloosa Horse Club of America; the Morgan Horse Club, Inc.; and *The Horse of the Desert* by William Robinson Brown.

Pers Crowell

Contents

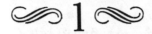

Prehistoric Men and Horses

"Among all of the animals of the past and present there is none so deserving of our interest and affection as the horse. It is the most useful of the domestic animals and has played the largest part in the development of civilization. Since the dawn of recorded history the man with the horse has been in the forefront of progress. Whether leading the military civilization of the past or breaking ground for the industrial civilization of the present, the pioneer and leaders of progress have always made large use of the noble animal.

"It is not too much to say that without his help our ancestors in the Old World might have advanced but little further on the road of civilization than did the inhabitants of the ancient semi-civilized states of Peru and Mexico where the horse was unknown, and travel, agriculture and military success were limited by the capacity of unaided human strength.

"From another point of view, the horse is of peculiar interest. It is one of the most perfect machines for swift running that exists among living animals and displays throughout its organization the most exact and finished mechanism adapted to this purpose. It is perhaps the finest example of what nature, acting through millions of years, has been able to accomplish in the way of adapting a large quadruped to speed over long distances and likewise of the extent to which man, during the few thousands of years that he has controlled its development, has been able to improve upon nature, in the sense of adapting it to serve more exactly his own purpose."

The above is one of the finest tributes to the horse that has ever been written. If it had been said by a horseman, we might suspect that sentiment had prompted it. The fact that it was written by scientists who deal in facts makes it richer and more respected. It is a quotation from the Leaflet Guide Series, Number 36, *Evolution of the Horse,* published by the American Museum of Natural History in 1921.

Many volumes about the horse give lengthy explanations of the evolution of prehistoric horses that roamed the earth before the existence of man. Though it is an interesting subject, we shall sketch here but briefly the development of the earliest horses and shall bring the discussion quickly to the point in prehistory where human beings and horses were contemporary.

PREHISTORIC HORSES

The dawn horse *Eohippus* was approximately twelve inches high and lived some forty-five million years ago, during the Eocene period. He was among the earliest mammals to grace the earth. At that time, the tiny creature had four toes on each front foot and three on each hind foot. He was a far cry from the horse we know today, but his structure and that of his descendants fits into a long chain of progress that leads to the present horse (*Equus caballus*).

Steadily increasing in size, the little horse developed, during the Oligocene period, into the early three-toed *Mesohippus* (middle horse) and then into the later three-toed *Merychippus,* during the Miocene period. This horse ran upon the center toe of his foot and the other two hung uselessly at the sides. The Miocene period ended approximately seven million years ago.

The Pliocene period in Europe closed with a moist, warm temperate climate and widespread forests and meadows favorable to grazing animals. During the middle and late Pliocene times, true horses (*Equus stenonis*) of remote North American origin arrived in Europe along with the first true cattle (*Leptobos elatus*) from southern Asia. *Equus stenonis* was a full-fledged horse, having only one toe. It is probable that he migrated over the land bridge of what is now known as the Bering Straits and through Asia to Europe and Africa. The Pliocene period ended, as nearly as can be estimated, about one million years ago.

The old Stone Age of man was contemporaneous with the early Pleistocene, or Ice Age, and it was at this time that men undoubtedly first glimpsed the horse, which, it is interesting to note, was quite similar to the *Equus caballus* of today, except that he was smaller.

Early Types

From fossil remains and the earliest cave art of the Cro-Magnons, men of Aurignacian times, we can deduce that there were three general types of horses in contemporary existence with human beings. They were the forest type (sometimes called Nordic horses), the steppe type, and the plateau or desert type (sometimes called the Celtic type).

STEPPE TYPE   CELTIC OR DESERT TYPE   NORDIC OR FOREST TYPE

The Nordic horse, or forest type, was the largest of the three. Evidence proves him to have been an animal with a large head, convex face line, and a rough coat. He was coarse in structure. In all probability, he was short-legged, clumsy, and without much speed. This prehistoric type is generally conceded to have been the predominating strain in the heavy horse used by the knights of the Age of Chivalry and in the draft horse of modern times, although the present-day horse has been increased in size by long and careful breeding.

The steppe type was somewhere between the Nordic and the plateau types, with short neck, large head, and fairly fine legs, and not as large as the forest horse. It is a curious fact that there exists today a wild species that seems to resemble very closely the ancient steppe type. This is the Przewalski horse (*Equus przewalskii*), to be found on the wild steppes of Turkestan. This animal is about the size of a pony, with a short, thick neck, large head, and small ears. In color it is light reddish brown, with a near-white muzzle and dark points (mane, tail, and legs). There is no forelock, and the mane stands upright, in a similar way to that of the horses pictured by cave men. The hair of the tail is sparse.

The plateau, or desert, type was the finest of the three ancient types. Representations in early Cro-Magnon art and fossil remains prove that he was smaller and possessed a more spirited air than the other two. While there is considerable disagreement among students of paleontology, some believe this type to have been the progenitor of the Arab-type horse.

It is believed by some students that all modern horses were derived from this trio of general species. Furthermore, a great many conflicting attempts have been made to correlate certain wild breeds, or apportion certain percentages of their blood, with domestic breeds of modern times. As has been indicated, the forest, steppe, and plateau horses were types within a main species; also, there were many varieties and subtypes within the three general groups. The horses of Mauer (*E. mauerensis*), Mosbach (*E. mosbachensis*), and Sussenborn (*E. sussenbornensis*) were larger and more specialized in character than Steno's horse of First Interglacial times. These first-mentioned species occurred in the Second Interglacial period. As will be explained presently, the animals of all groups, some more than others owing to certain traveling qualities, in all likelihood roamed and migrated from one area to another. Interbreeding created many subtypes and at the same time aided the upward evolution of the animals involved while they were in a feral state.

Migration Routes

During the early Pleistocene, especially the period of the First Interglacial stage, the land of Europe, Asia, and Africa was extremely elevated. This caused natural land bridges between Europe and Africa at Gibraltar and the Sicilian area. With these two land connections and the connection of Africa with lower Asia at the isthmus of the Dardanelles, there were three natural migration routes for animal and human races north and south.

GENERAL MIGRATION ROUTES OF PREHISTORIC HORSES

Great Britain appears to have been continuously elevated through the Third Interglacial, Fourth Glacial and Post Glacial stages and was a part of the Continent as well, affording east and west migration of men and animals. It is known that the Lower Paleolithic peoples wandered back and forth between the valleys of the Somme and the Thames, interchanging their weapons and inventions. Ancient horses undoubtedly roamed in the same manner to seek better pastures and to avoid the hunters who pursued them.

The connection between the North American continent and Asia over what is now called the Bering Straits has been in existence from the earliest epochs

A factor that had much to do with the migration of men and animals during the Pleistocene was the Glacial and Interglacial periods. Changing conditions of temperature and humidity, and the accompanying changes in the flora, determined great movements of men and beasts.

We know from the discoveries of geologists that there is no portion of Europe or hardly any part of the world, with the possible exception of Australia, where the fossil remains of horses have not been discovered.

From his earliest origin in North America, the horse has been a wanderer. In his earliest form, he traveled from North America to Asia and thence to Europe. In his more true horse form, he again journeyed from North America to Asia and Europe and down into Africa. Some of the African varieties wound up as zebras—true horses in all but their color markings—and Nubian and Somaliland wild asses. Others lingered in Asia to become different types of asses known as onagers and kiangs.

Though many of the different branches of horses prospered in the continents to which they migrated, it is a strange fact that they did not persist on the North American continent, scene of their original development. All the ancient horses of North and South America passed into extinction before the coming of the white man. One theory is that ancient hunters might have played a part in the extinction, not by killing all of them but perhaps by disturbing their habits and opportunities to graze and by driving them away from their feeding grounds. Competition caused by the increase of bison and antelope may have been another cause. Continued draught or a devastating disease are other possible causes for their complete extermination on the New World continents.

Adaptability of the Horse

Two qualities in the horse seem to stand out as reasons for his survival through millions of years. The first of these is his great speed. Even the tiny *Eohippus* was able to evade his enemies by scampering through the ancient forests, but as time went on, the horse achieved more power and swiftness of movement in his legs with the change from joints that swiveled in all directions to pulley-wheel joints which were grooved to allow only forward and backward motion. The change from toes to the single hoof also added to his speed over plains and rocks.

The language of the earliest people attested to their admiration of the horse's speed. The word for horse in the ancient Sanskrit tongue was *asva*. The sound *as* in this language meant sharp, swift, or speedy. The word *equus* itself is a corrupted form of the Icelandic word *ekvus,* meaning to run.

The other favorable factor in the survival of the horse was the superiority of his teeth. In the beginning, the dawn horse's teeth were not used for grazing but for nibbling the leaves of the forest. Gradually these teeth developed into an increasingly complex denture until they became amazingly perfect self-sharpening tools which enabled the animals to survive on the toughest grasses.

Thus through the ages the horse has shown a persistence and tenacity to cope with an ever-changing world. This creature that is distinguished from all other animals now living by the fact that he has but one toe on each foot, was so adaptable that in a wild state the whole world seemed to be his domain. As a domestic animal, the horse is to be found almost everywhere that man can live.

Man's First Use of the Horse

The first use of horses by man was undoubtedly for food. Scientists establish facts about the early existence of man and animals in various ways. One method is the discovery of man's implements, combined with the knowledge gathered from fossil remains of the mammals existing at the time. There are many indications that the ancient people of Lower Paleolithic times used the horse for food over one hundred thousand years ago.

As the industry of the early races progressed and finer tools of stone were developed, many animals, including the horse, were taken not only for their flesh but for their hides and furs as well.

Implements of the Late Acheulean industry of the Neanderthal race exhibited a great advance in workmanship. There were stone daggers and ovaloid instruments that had been worked into fine sharp blades. These, in all probability, were used like butcher knives for dismembering the carcasses of game as well as for cutting up the pelts into desired shapes. Almond- and disk-shaped implements of stone may have been used as scrapers in preparing the animal skins for use as clothing.

Throughout Mousterian times, at the close of the Lower Paleolithic, Neanderthal man hunted in the open country. His most common game was the wild horse, wild ox, and reindeer. It is believed that both pelts and flesh were used and that the larger bones were split for their marrow at the bone anvils. Fire was used by men, as indicated by the ancient hearths.

According to geologists, the Cro-Magnon appeared at the opening of the Upper Paleolithic period. With a fairly reasonable degree of accuracy, this more modern type of Homo sapiens can be recorded as having entered western Europe between twenty-five and thirty thousand years ago.

We must credit the Cro-Magnon men of the Upper Paleolithic for our first glimpse of the horse. From paintings and sculpture on the walls of their caves and small slabs of stone, from engravings on bone and horn and decorations on ceremonial pieces, geologists have discovered forms depicting horses and other mammals of those times. All three general types of early horses are profusely represented. There is no positive indication in these drawings that the horse was used for anything except food and clothing.

That the Cro-Magnons used the horse extensively for food is proved quite conclusively by the findings of geologists around the Aurignacian camp at Solutré. Accumulated there in a wide circle around the ancient camp are the remains of not less than one hundred thousand horses. A great majority of these belonged to the short-legged, coarse-headed northern type. For some curious reason these horses averaged from five to seven years of age.

Another interesting fact to note is that they measured about 13 hands 2 inches high, which would be about the size of our existing ponies. There is no evidence that the people of Aurignacian times either bred or raised any of these animals; it seems that they pursued them only for food. However, there is belief that discovery of the horse as an animal of transport might have been taking place at approximately this time in far eastern Asia.

This brings us to the very close of the Stone Age and the beginning of the Neolithic period, believed to have been between ten and seven thousand years before the present era. We know that the horse had been used for food and that possibly his hide was used for clothing. Furthermore, there is the remote possibility that his true use as an animal of transportation might have been in the process of discovery. There are indications that in the vast stretches of Asia men might have been considerably ahead of the Europeans in their culture.

Domestication of Animals

The Neolithic period in Europe ushered in great changes in the human way of life. In certain localities, nomadic modes of life were abandoned. Polished-stone implements found their way gradually into western Europe giving evidence of the economic change caused by the growing, but still rudimentary, knowledge these people had of agriculture. Use of a variety of plants and seeds required new implements for preparing the soil and harvesting crops, although some implements of the chase were still used in acquiring certain food and clothing.

The oldest Neolithic findings, however, show no trace of the horse as an object of food. Many students consider this an indication that he was being used during those times as an animal of transport. If we are correct in our assumption that earlier nomadic peoples had discovered a better use of the horse than for food, the tribes migrating to the west in early Neolithic times were undoubtedly attracted by the great number of forest and Celtic types which had survived from the Upper Paleolithic period.

Migrating westward, Neolithic peoples brought with them and selected from the forests a great variety of animals similar to the domesticated types of today, such as horses, cattle, sheep, goats and swine, thus merging plant agriculture with animal husbandry.

Speculations on First Domestication of the Horse

A subject that has always intrigued me is the manner in which horses were first used by men. A number of writers have pointed out that the first horses were harnessed and hitched to vehicles of some sort, and support their claims by the ancient drawings of Assyria and Egypt that picture the horse pulling crude chariots. As further substantiation, they assert that the early horse was too small for man to ride.

While it may have no bearing on our discussion of the present use of the horse, it is interesting to pursue the question a little further. Being a saddle-horse enthusiast, perhaps I am biased in my belief that horses were first ridden and later driven.

It is difficult for me to believe that men of the Upper Paleolithic or early Neolithic period went to the trouble of devising complex harnesses and vehicles to use in conquering and training a wild horse. Furthermore, a vehicle riding upon a wheel and axle would have been extremely cumbersome and slow over wild terrain. It is also doubtful that primitive people waited until the invention of the wheel before enlisting the aid of the horse. It is easier to imagine that the first horseman threw a leg over the back of one of these animals and, grasping a handful of mane, took what came, as in a prehistoric rodeo.

Undoubtedly, primitive men realized the strength of horses as they watched them being leaped upon by carnivorous beasts in quest of food. Perhaps they themselves, armed with a stone dagger instead of tooth and claw, had attacked a wild horse for the same reason. From these physical encounters they may have become experienced in riding.

The North American Indians, at the time of discovery by the white man, were in a state of Stone Age culture comparable, perhaps, to the early Neolithic period. While the horse was, in a way, introduced to them by white men, it is interesting to observe how the Indians used the horse, which may or may not have been the method used by people thousands of years earlier.

First of all, the Indians rode the horses. Certain tribes, to break the horses, would drive them into water deep enough to force them to swim and then the Indians would get upon their backs. By the time the animals reached land, they were sufficiently subdued to be ridden without great difficulty.

INDIAN METHOD OF BREAKING HORSES

In other tribes, the horse would be led about with an inanimate weight upon its back. Later an Indian would mount the animal and allow another Indian to lead it. The primitive Indian's caution was extreme, and it was usually quite some time before an animal in training was ridden and guided by a lone rider.

The nearest the Indians came to harnessing horses to a vehicle was in their use of the travois, a draglike arrangement. The travois had been used earlier with dogs as the beasts of burden. Two or more tepee poles were crossed over the horse's neck in the vicinity of the withers and secured with a surcingle or bellyband. The poles fanned outward behind the animal. Platforms or grids of rawhide were lashed between the poles, and the luggage, wrapped in buffalo skins or cases, was piled on top of the grids.

The braves would have nothing to do with the travois horses. This was the work of squaws, who sometimes would mount the horse and ride with their legs on the outside of the tepee poles.

The belief that a horse must attain great size before he can be ridden seems to be a fairly modern English and American idea. Perhaps it is impelled by pride rather than actual necessity, or it may be a carry-over from the days of knights when large horses were a necessity owing to the weight of armor. Orientals have for centuries ridden horses of pony stature. Arabian horses have always been small but capable of carrying their masters over the worst possible terrain at great speed and for long distances. Some of these horses are scarcely larger than the horses of Solutré which, as we have already noted, measured 13 hands 2 inches.

The present-day horsemen of Mongolia literally live on the backs of their horses which are the size of mere ponies.

One writer has stated that primitive man did not ride the horses because his feet would have dragged the ground. My belief is that high saddles of the type that perch the riders above the back of the horse were of extremely antique invention.

MONGOLIAN HORSEMAN

As to the strength, speed, and endurance of prehistoric horses we have living proof. Early in March, 1922, Roy Chapman Andrews headed the National Geographic Association's Central Asiatic Expedition to Mongolia for the purpose of delving into the geologic history of central Asia and to ascertain whether or not the area had been the nursery of many of the dominant groups of animals, including the human race. The expedition traveled by motorcar supported by advance camel caravans.

At Tsagan Nor, the expedition had an excellent opportunity to study a species of wild ass (*Equus h. hemionus*), a mammal new to the men of the expedition and but little known to the scientific world. These Tibetan asses are said to be about 52 inches high, or in horse terms 13 hands at the shoulder. They resemble a fine-bodied mule in structure, and a yellow fawn color shades beautifully downward into a pure-white belly and rump. Their manes are dark brown, and a meridian line of dark chocolate runs along the spine into a mulelike tufted tail. These asses, like the Przewalski horses, are wild and untamable. In short, they resemble very closely ancient horses of the steppe type.

The interesting discovery regarding these animals was their extreme speed and stamina. One day, two members of the expedition saw a fine stallion of the species well up on the plain near Tsagan Nor. Chasing the animal by motor, they were amazed to discover he was able to maintain a top speed of

40 miles per hour as far as a furlong. During the chase, the ass traveled 29 miles without a single rest or breathing spell before it became exhausted. The first 16 miles were covered at an average speed of 30 miles per hour!

We can say with certainty that animals of similar or even superior quality existed during the closing stages of the Upper Paleolithic period.

There seems to be no evidence of just how the first horses were domesticated. It may have taken place in different sections and at different times, in various ways. In a letter addressed to me, Dr. George Gaylord Simpson, Curator of Fossil Mammals and Birds of the American Museum of Natural History, gives another highly plausible explanation of how horses might first have been put into use as a servant of mankind. The letter reads, in part, as follows:

> I agree with you that it seems probable that the earliest domestic horses were ridden rather than driven, but I do not know that there is any very good direct evidence one way or the other. The usual evidence for the statement that horses were driven first is that the oldest near-eastern representations of horses usually show them pulling chariots. This may have been the usual use among the Egyptians and Assyrians, but I suspect that the more nomadic peoples had been riding horses long before this. There is really nothing conclusive about the place or method of domestication although it does seem likely that domestication started somewhere in the region north or northeast of the Caucasus. One can only speculate as to the method. My own guess is that colts were raised as pets and that then some boy discovered that he could ride these animals.

We can well imagine, in the earliest domestication of animals, the happy thought one day striking a man that he could herd a band of wild cattle into a box canyon and hold it there until such time as he would need the meat more urgently. No doubt he brought food to these animals to sustain them while they were in live storage. From this beginning he possibly realized that it would be easier to herd them from one grazing area to another than to feed them himself.

While purely speculative, it is my theory that nomadic peoples eventually learned to use the horse as a mount to assist them in driving their flocks and herds from upland pastures to lower winter quarters.

These nomadic peoples undoubtedly shifted annually north and south, rather rapidly, to avoid cold and stormy weather. Always in their minds was the thought of suitable pastures for their herds. Owing to the great distances traveled each year, the horse must have been extremely helpful in this early struggle for existence. Such activity may have taken place on the grassy steppe lands of central Asia over ten thousand years ago.

ANCIENT NOMAD

While many historians maintain that the first horses were domesticated to draw chariots, in my opinion, oxen were the first animals to feel the strain of a yoke. It is known that draft oxen were used in Egypt centuries before the horse was introduced there. The cattle were slower and less excitable, thus being easier to train. I do not believe that horses in any large number were hitched to vehicles until the advent of organized warfare and sports events, where speed and recklessness abounded.

Wild Breeds and Domestic Types

Though the idea probably originated farther east, the wild horse of prehistoric Europe was domesticated by man. This fact is established by the discovery of crude drawings sketched on bone or ivory by men of the Neolithic, or polished-stone, period. One authority states that the domesticated horses now in use are derived chiefly from the Asiatic and African species, although it is probable that in some breeds there is a considerable strain of the shaggy, short-legged European race.

In summarizing man's earliest uses of the horse, three general conclusions may be drawn, for which there is much evidence:

1. During and after the Glacial period, many thousands of years ago, prehistoric men hunted and killed wild horses, using their flesh for food and their skins for clothing.

2. Following this period, wild horses were captured and broken to ride and drive.

3. The earliest phases of domestication passed into the last, which was

artificial development, during which the horse was modified for standards of use. This phase is still continuing at the present time.

From what specific wild sources has our modern horse evolved? we may ask. Students have reached diverse and totally conflicting conclusions. Some think that at one time the horse was domesticated in a restricted locality and that all breeds developed from this single original stock. Others think that there were two (light and heavy, or hot- and cold-blooded, etc.), three (desert-Celtic, steppe, or forest-Nordic), or even six or more ancestral groups of wild horses (Skorkowski who cites Mosbach, Abel's, Gutsen's, Ewart's, Krakow, and Nordic types). Gromova identified twelve or more distinctly different types in Eurasia, although it must be understood that all these were not living at the same time and certainly all of them could not have contributed to the domestic horse.

There are some students who believe the domestic breeds can be divided into broad types, each corresponding with one particular group of wild horses. Others believe the domestic breeds to be hybrids between wild types and even between different wild species. The latter was Ewart's view. Some of those who hold such views maintain that the segregation in the domestic breeds cannot be correlated in this way with wild races, while others think they can characterize domestic breeds by actual percentages of blood of this, that, or the other wild races. One student goes so far as to state that he can clearly distinguish three different wild races among Arabian horses alone!

To be sure, this is confusing, none of it is conclusive, and much of it, with due respect to the serious students who evolved it, is nonsense. We know, of course, that there were light and heavy, or light, medium, and heavy wild horses of varying sizes, just as there are light, medium, and heavy domestic horses of varying sizes today. There is no absolute evidence that this makes a natural two- or threefold breeding classification of wild horses or that present-day horses had a double or triple origin corresponding to these various classes of body build. To the practical horseman it is interesting but not important.

As previously stated, in early recent times there were wild horses all over Europe, Asia, and North Africa. These animals most likely avoided the desert areas because of their inability to exist in barren places. These probably all belonged to one species; all interbred to some extent with their neighbors. We will realize, of course, that there were differences between local groups. If all their remains were at hand for examination, doubtless a hundred or more local types could be distinguished, although these, too, would intergrade and change. For instance, a light horse in Asia was of the same *physical type* as a light horse in Europe, but was not of the same local subspecies or race.

As the idea of domestication spread over the land, men must have domesticated a great many different local groups throughout the various regions. It would be impossible to say how many. At an early date, man commenced to crossbreed the horses of different localities, probably on a wider scale than had taken place in the voluntary crossbreeding of wild local races. As will be explained later, Thracian and Thessalian horses were purposely crossbred by the ancient Greeks to serve their specific standards better. The ancient Egyptians also crossbred horses of widely different origins.

In a broad sense, man thus took over a large pool of varying groups for his early stock, reshuffled this, and finally used it to produce particular types which were suitable to his varying standards of performance. Some of these resemble wild physical types, to be sure, but this does not necessarily indicate a correspondence between domestic breeds, as such, and the true wild races or subspecies that we may distinguish from fossil remains.

Biblical References to the Earliest Horses

We know from the Bible that Abraham received as a transfer of property sheep, oxen, asses, camels, and servants. The horse is not mentioned, but if other animals, particularly asses, were domesticated at that time, it is reasonable to believe that horses might have been, even if in other localities.

There is an indirect reference to the horse in the biblical statement that Anah discovered the mule in the wilderness. The earliest actual reference to the domesticated horse is made in Genesis 47:17:

> . . . and Joseph gave them bread in exchange for horses, and for the flocks, and for the cattle of the herds, and for the asses.

There is a reference earlier in the Bible which indicates that horses were being used. It is contained in Genesis 41:43:

> And he made him [Joseph] to ride in the second chariot which he had;

Later in the same story there is a statement which leads us to suspect that horses were being ridden as well as driven. This passage occurs after the death of Jacob, Joseph's father, Genesis 50:9:

> And there went up with him chariots and horsemen: and it was a very great company.

Later, in Exodus 14:23, there is another passage which gives us reason to believe horses were ridden:

And the Egyptians pursued, and went in after them to the midst of the sea, *even* all Pharaoh's horses, his chariots, and his horsemen.

If we still doubt that there were riding horses in this company, let us read the account of the same scene as related by the Prophetess Miriam in Exodus 15:21:

And Miriam answered them, Sing ye to the Lord; for he hath triumphed gloriously; the horse and his rider hath he thrown into the sea.

Further recordings that the horse was used early as a saddle mount and for the purposes of war are contained in the book of Job 39:19–25. We quote as follows and call particular attention to the passage which reads, "The quiver rattleth against him. . . .":

Hast thou given the horse strength? hast thou clothed his neck with thunder? Canst thou make him afraid as a grasshopper? the glory of his nostrils *is* terrible.
He paweth in the valley, and rejoiceth in *his* strength: he goeth on to meet the armed men.
He mocketh at fear, and is not affrighted; neither turneth he back from the sword.
The quiver rattleth against him, the glittering spear and the shield.
He swalloweth the ground with fierceness and rage: neither believeth he that *it is* the sound of the trumpet.
He saith among the trumpets, Ha, ha; and he smelleth the battle from afar off, the thunder of the captains, and the shouting.

The first pages of the Bible are difficult to correlate with geological periods and epochs, but the period in prehistory believed by some to mark the beginning of domestication for the horse is contained in the first few pages of the Bible. The absence of the word "horse" within those pages does not necessarily refute its existence.

We note from the earliest biblical writings that asses, the blood relatives of horses, are mentioned frequently. There is evidence that herds of asses were kept for their milk. This type of domestication might have been developed before the animals were used as beasts of burden, though it seems unlikely in view of the many references to them as pack animals plus the fact that in order to use them in this manner they would first have to be tamed and possibly used for breeding purposes.

It is an interesting fact that the milk of mares is used by some races even today. At certain seasons of the year, some Mongol and Turkic nomadic tribes subsist mainly on kumiss, a product of mare's milk. Two or three times a day the animals are milked—when they come in from the pasture to suckle the foals, which are tied to a picket line near the nomads' dwellings.

The kumiss is made by pouring the whole milk into a sheep or colt skin. Remaining in the skin for about twenty-four hours, the mares' milk is stirred or churned by the women of the tribe several times each day. The solids form a thick white curd which settles to the bottom, and the thin upper layer is drawn off ready to drink the following day. The curds are used in the process of tanning hides.

Despite the scarcity of facts concerning primitive man's domestication of the horse, no one can deny that it has been one of the greatest single factors in helping man on his upward climb on the ladder of civilization. Man's power of imagination together with this unique animal has certainly been a combination with a strong influence on progress through the centuries.

During the first days of the horse's use in a savage world it may have been the only living thing that primitive man could trust. Certainly it made his tasks easier. It is not difficult to imagine the horse as man's first source of relaxation and diversion. This companionship has endured through the ages to the present time.

~ 2 ~

Man Develops the Ancient Horse

In order to trace domesticated horses from their earliest stages to the present day it is necessary to have a knowledge of the migrations of the people they served through almost countless centuries. Naturally, their paths are dimmed by time and in places completely broken.

The Age of Cultivation began ten or twelve thousand years ago. The more progressive people of those times became aware of the possible use of objects of nature. They began to develop their implements, to tame and domesticate wild animals, and to learn something about agriculture. This early Neolithic state marked a turning point in primitive man's thinking.

While at first his agriculture was the taking of snatch crops, this practice later developed into a basic knowledge of the time for sowing and for harvesting.

Language began to form on man's savage tongue and aided him in passing on his accumulated knowledge to others. In a limited way he was able to count his possessions. With childlike curiosity he was thinking and wondering about the many things around him. How could he use this or that? What was beyond the mountains, and where did the sun go when it set? His clock and calendar were the sun and the moon.

Tradition, legend, and superstition also grew out of speech, and the tribal, or clan, system was evolved. Nomadic families roamed far and wide with the seasons. Horses were no longer used for food. Although there is no definite proof, it seems reasonable to believe this to be an indication that horses were being used to help with the herds. Undoubtedly there were clashes between clans over grazing grounds, and in this way the horse was pressed into his first service as a war animal. Man perceived that one horse was better suited to his purposes than another, and, because of this, selective breeding was commenced. Furthermore, it was easier to tame camp-bred horses than to capture wild ones. We can imagine that one clan vied with another to produce better stock. A reverent attitude toward the horse emerged early in man's history.

Another type of civilization—the settlers—was contemporary with the nomads. Certain conditions caused Neolithic man to settle down. He had to find a place where there was an ample year-round supply of water and food for himself and his animals, as well as material with which to build a permanent home. Once the wanderer discovered such a place, the need for seasonal migrations ended and community life began. No doubt many such isolated communities existed in widely separated Asiatic and European valleys. The early Swiss lake dwellers have been cited as one instance of this type of living. Such civilizations grew at an early date in the Mesopotamian and Egyptian areas, which were ideal for the raising and harvesting of crops.

It is not likely that the horse was used to any great extent in these earliest communities. The people had no place to go, no empires to conquer. The sedentary life required no rapid shifting from one far-flung pasture to another. If such people had previously been nomadic and used horses, they probably now abandoned and forgot them. It is more likely that the lowly, plodding ox was better suited to the necessary work of tillers of the soil. The development of a solid axle and wheels from a rough-hewn log probably led to the invention of slightly less cumbersome carts drawn by easily controlled cattle.

The chariot was yet to be devised; it must wait for more clever inventiveness. War was not yet waged on a grandiose scale, and the sport of racing with horse-drawn vehicles was unthought of. It is said that the Sumerians who lived about 7000 B.C. had cattle, asses, sheep, and goats, but no horses.

There were unquestionably battles in the form of light skirmishes. The shifting paths of the nomads undoubtedly brought them to the villages, and in lean years they must have coveted the stores that the settlers had laid away. With lightninglike thrusts, such mounted groups of men must have taken from the slower, settled men what they needed.

As the centuries rolled onward, the more aggressive nomadic peoples swept out of the vast unknown stretches to subdue the unwarlike villagers. While at first the skirmishes had been border raids and the small attacking clans could steal but could not stay, eventually the leader of a warring clan gained sufficient power to induce other tribes to join him in his attacks. Such united efforts would break the back of the established communities and the conquerors would settle on the conquered land, only to be treated, generations later, in like manner by newly formed nomadic armies.

Then, as the settled people became more entrenched and their numbers gave them strength, they began to use the horse to defend themselves. The oxcart was improved to accommodate horses, and thus defensive armies probably went out from the cities to meet the attacking cavalry.

The absorption of the nomadic tribes into cities introduced fresh ideas, and the horse was one of them. Leisure prompted new uses for the horse. Hunting expeditions, with chariots drawn by horses, were sent out to the hunting field, and upon the racecourses thundered the hoofs of horses, drawing light chariots and reckless charioteers.

MYTH, LEGEND, AND ART

Although Pegasus was a creature of myth, he is important because he was the first recorded horse of ancient times. We know that the wings of this steed could not have been real, but they must have been a symbol of man's early admiration for the superb speed and gracefulness of the horse.

PEGASUS

One of the earliest works of literature, the Greek *Iliad,* was recited by storytellers a thousand years before Christ. In its concluding passages it tells of Hector, son of King Priam of Troy:

And so horse-taming Hector's rites gave up his soul to rest.

If we believe Pegasus was not flesh and blood and think that Hector's horse-taming activities are vague, then let us turn for a look at graphic representations of real horses. Countless examples present themselves—the royal Assyrian chariot horses carved in stone relief, cavalry horses on the Greek Parthenon, the Tang war horses, Chinese stone-sculptured horses.

GREEK HORSES

Almost twelve centuries before Christ, crossbred Thracian and Thessalian horses were being raced in harness to light chariots. They are among the first horses of recorded history. A favored place for such races was on the island of Chios, protected by the island kings as a place of sport. The Mercury Temple was built in 1200 B.C. by Greek citizens, who dedicated it to Hermes in the belief they were paying homage to the god of speed.

Foot races and water sports were held on Chios, but most popular was the horse racing, for which Thracian stallions of strong bone were crossed on the small but swift mares from the plains of Thessaly.

It is recorded that the chariots used were astoundingly light and fragile, one day's grueling racing being all they could endure. Frequently it was necessary to weight the vehicles, drawn by two or three fleet horses, to keep them on the ground in their headlong plunge down the courseways.

The Thracian stallions which sired the chariot race horses were sought after by conquerors from other lands. Many were taken in raids from people of the distant lands and thus found their way into Turkey and perhaps even Outer Mongolia.

ASSYRIAN HORSES

War Horses

Almost a thousand years before the hoofs of racing horses pounded over the courses at Chios, raiding nomads from the East were invading Babylonia, bringing with them the war horse and war chariot. The centuries that followed saw the Assyrians at last adopt the horse and chariot and develop the military art to a high degree. Power swayed back and forth between the warring Assyrians and Babylonians.

Perhaps even earlier the Greeks had used horses to draw crude fighting chariots into the field of battle. If these ancient people did use horses in battle, the horses were probably novel enough to terrorize those who were being attacked. In any case, from the *Iliad,* we do know that oxen and the hybrid mule were employed for ordinary draft purposes.

The first Assyrian chariots were top-heavy contrivances drawn by a pair of horses, with an extra horse running alongside in case of casualty. The floor boards were high above the wheel base, with the axle line directly beneath the center of the body. The small wheels probably left much to be desired in riding comfort as they went jolting and careening across the battlefield. The earlier models were devoid of any facilities for carrying arrows or spears. The crew that piled onto this ancient vehicle of war consisted of a driver, a warrior who did the fighting, and one or two assistants with shields to protect the soldier.

While the first chariots were an improvement on previous methods of warfare, it is likely that dangerous spills and jostlings motivated the Assyrians to invent the improved models that were used later. Wheels were made larger, for smoother travel over rough terrain. The body of the vehicle was lowered until the floor boards rested on the axle, thereby lowering the center of gravity. The axle line, instead of being placed in the center, was put at the aft end of the platform, thus lessening the danger of the occupants' being thrown out the back. More weight rested on the horses, which stabilized the whole chariot. Quivers for arrows and a sheath for the warrior's spear became standard equipment. The sides and front of the body were amply high to protect the charioteers.

The Assyrians were fond of color and fancy trappings. They wore great beards and long ringleted hair. On their heads were tall caps. This love of decoration was also lavished on the war horse, as if to impress the enemy. The bridle was an elaborate piece with a fancy bit and many straps about the cheeks, neck, nose, and brow. In addition, tassels, rosettes, and plumes adorned the horse's head. The collar and harness were equally decorative.

The lighter cavalry horses were less profusely decorated, but even they did not escape entirely the fancy adornments about the head. These horses were ridden without saddles or stirrups, and probably the archers paid little attention to the reins in the heat of battle.

In all probability, the Assyrians gave careful thought to improving their horses, through selective breeding, to serve their needs better. Their activities in war must have required larger and heavier animals. The vast majority of their war horses seem to have been stallions. Fierceness was a quality greatly desired, and animals of such nature were probably used as breeding stock to perpetuate and intensify the trait. The purpose of the chariot war horse was to trample, run down, and kill everything that happened to be in its path. The animals themselves were as much warriors as the soldiers were, and much more destructive.

In battle, a solid mass of chariots formed a frontal line, wheel to wheel. Behind this came the phalanx of foot soldiers in close formation. At the sides of the main battle hosts rode the cavalry horsemen to close in on the sides of the enemy forces. To open the battle, an array of archers and stone throwers ran forward to dispatch their ammunition. Then the chariot horses were goaded into a terrorizing frenzy. Once the horses started their forward plunge, they stampeded head on into the enemy, grinding and pulverizing them into the dust of the battle plain.

Horses in Sport

To Assurbanipal (called Sardanapalus by the Greeks), one of the last of the Assyrian monarchs (667 B.C.), we owe much of our knowledge of the history and customs of Assyria. He was a fervent collector of clay documents, and his library is now one of the most valuable sources of historical information. From these documents we know that Assyrian horses were also used for less gory purposes than war. Assurbanipal enjoyed the sport of the hunt and the chase, and his horses were used in this hobby.

A hunting expedition of this young monarch was indeed a colossal entourage. The party consisted of many chariots, horses, mounted lancers, servants, dogs, pack mules, and edible supplies in the form of live goats and cattle.

ASSURBANIPAL

The monarch rode in grand style in a chariot of state attended by slaves. Each night of encampment necessitated the building of a temporary palace in addition to suitable stables for the royal horses and shelters for the cattle.

Animals of great ferocity were singled out for the monarch's hunting pleasure. If a wild ox was chosen as worthy prey, the beast was partially wounded by mounted horsemen, and then the driver of the royal chariot would give chase. As Assurbanipal drew his vehicle alongside the ill-fated animal, he would take hold of one of its horns and kill it with a dagger. If he hunted the lion, it is recorded, the monarch, on the back of a horse, would chase the beast until it was thoroughly exhausted, whereupon an attendant would hand Assurbanipal a lance with which to kill it.

THE OLYMPIAN GAMES

An outcome of the Hellenic union of the Greeks was the inauguration of the Olympian games in 776 B.C. They were held once every four years and continued regularly for over a thousand years, doing much to maintain a sense of common unity and to transcend the petty politics of the city states. Among the chief sports were foot racing, boxing, wrestling, javelin throwing, quoit throwing, jumping, and chariot and horse racing.

GREEK GAMES

The horse events became so popular that a separate arena was built to stage them. This was called the "hippodrome," which means a course for horses.

The first chariot races were feats of endurance, with the horses running 4 miles. Later, in their thirst for skill and physical prowess, the Greeks introduced variations of the straight running races in which was demanded more than outright speed. One of these was a novelty race in which the rider began with four bareback horses. At appointed places he would free one of the horses and leap from it to the next in line—all at top running speed. When only one horse remained, the rider would leap down and run beside the horse, grasping the bridle, the last half mile to the finish.

Other equine games involved strategy and skill similar to that needed in modern polo. The period saw many great strides in horse management and horsemanship. Thus, under the Greeks, horses reached a pinnacle in sports.

CAVALRY HORSES

The historian Herodotus has given us one of the early records of the use of cavalry in Western civilization in his description of Croesus, the Lydian king, who, about 550 B.C., was alarmed by the threat of Cyrus and the strength of his Persians. Croesus and Cyrus first fought an indecisive battle from which the Lydian king retreated. The chief strength of the Lydians presumably lay in their cavalry, though they were undisciplined horsemen who fought with long spears. After their battle at Pteria, Cyrus followed Croesus and again fought him outside of Sardis. Cyrus must have known a considerable amount about horse nature, as evidenced by the neat trick he devised against the Lydian army, reported as follows by Herodotus:

> Cyrus, when he saw the Lydians being arrayed for battle, fearing their horse-men, did on the suggestion of Harpagos, a Mede, as follows: All the camels which were in the train of his army carrying provisions and baggage he gathered together and he took off their burdens and set men upon them provided with the equipment of the cavalry; and, having thus furnished them, forth he appointed them to go in front of the rest of the army towards the horsemen of Croesus; and after the camel-troop he ordered the infantry to follow; and behind the infantry he placed his whole force of cavalry. Then, when all his men had been placed in their several positions, he charged them to spare none of the other Lydians, slaying all who might come in their way, but Croesus himself they were not to slay, not even if he should make re-sistance when he was being captured. Such was his charge: and he set the camels opposite the horsemen for this reason—because the horse has a fear of the camel and cannot endure either to see his form or to scent his smell: for this reason then the trick had been devised, in order that the cavalry of Croesus might be useless, that very force wherewith the Lydian king was expecting most to shine. And as they were coming together to the battle, so soon as the horses scented the camels and saw them, they turned away back, and the hopes of Croesus were at once brought to nought.

In 401 B.C., about one hundred and fifty years after the subjection of Croesus by Cyrus, Xenophon immortalized, in his personal war book, the *Anabasis,* the retreat of the ten thousand Greeks from Babylonia to the coast. Horsemen, particularly, are indebted to Xenophon for more than this. He is reputed to have been the originator of the curb bit. Also, through his writings, he gives us a description of the ideal riding horse of his times. That Xenophon was aware of an advanced theory of horsemanship is evidenced by several remarks in his writings. We must realize that riders of that day were not mere passengers but were horsemen who exercised control over the animals through extreme collection and principles of horsemanship— which have persisted to modern times. Furthermore, we may assume from his remarks that horses were being bred for quality to meet high standards of performance. Xenophon's description follows:

On examining the feet, it is benefiting first to look to the horny portion of the hoofs, for those horses which have the horn thick are far superior in their feet to those which have it thin. Nor will it be well, if one fails next to observe whether the hoof be upright both before and behind, or low and flat to the ground; for high hoofs keep the frog at a distance from the earth, while the flat tread with an equal pressure on the soft and hard parts of the foot, as in the case of bandy-legged men. And Simon justly observes that well-footed horses can be known by the sound of their tramp, for the hollow hoof rings like a cymbal when it strikes the solid earth. But having begun from below, let us ascend to the upper parts of the body. It is needful then that the parts above the hoof and below the fetlock be not too erect like those of a goat, for legs of this kind, being stiff and inflexible, are apt to jar the rider, and are more liable to inflammation. The bones must not, however, be too low and springy, for in that case the fetlocks are liable to be abraded and wounded if the horse be galloped over clods and stones. The bones of the shank should be thick, for these are the columns which support the body, but they should not have the flesh and veins thick likewise; for if they have, when the horse shall be galloped in difficult ground, they will necessarily be filled with blood, and will become varicose, so that the shanks shall be thickened, and the skin distended and relaxed from the bone; and when this is the case, it often follows that the back sinew gives away and renders the horse lame. But if the horse, when in action, bends his knees flexibly at the walk, you may judge that he will have his legs flexible when in full canter; for all horses as they increase in years increase in the flexibility of the knee, and flexible goers are esteemed highly, and with justice, for such horses are much less liable to blunder or to stumble than those which have rigid unbending joints. But if the arms below the shoulder blades be thick and muscular, they appear stronger and handsomer, as is also the case with man. The breast also should be broad as well for beauty as for strength, and because it gives a handsomer action of the forelegs, which do not then interfere, but are carried wide apart. And again the neck ought not to be set on like that of a boar, horizontally from the chest, but like that of a game cock should be upright toward the crest, and slack toward the flexture; and the head being long, should have a small and narrow jaw bone, so that the neck shall be in front of the rider, and the eye shall look down on what is before the feet. A horse thus made will be the least likely to run violently away, even if he be very high-spirited, for horses do not attempt to run away by bringing in, but by thrusting out their heads and necks. It is also very necessary to observe whether the mouth be fine or hard on both sides, or on one or the other. For horses which have not both sides equally sensitive, are likely to be hard mouthed on one side or the other; and it is better that the horse should have prominent than hollow eyes, for such will see a greater distance. And widely opened nostrils are far better for respiration than narrow, and they give a horse a fiercer aspect; for when one stallion is enraged against another, or if he becomes angry while ridden, he expands his nostrils to their full width. And the loftier the crest, and the smaller the ears, the more horselike and handsome is the head rendered; while lofty withers give a rider a surer seat and produce a firmer adhesion between body and shoulder. A double loin is also softer to sit upon, and pleasanter to look at, than if it be single; and a deep side rounded toward the belly renders the horse easier to sit, and stronger and more easy to keep in condition. The shorter and broader the loin, the more easily will the horse raise his fore-quarters, and collect his hind quarters under him in going. These points more-over cause the belly to appear smaller, which, if it be large, at once injures the appearance of the animal, and renders him weak and less manageable. The quarters should be broad and fleshy, in order to correspond with the sides and chest; and should they be entirely firm and solid, they would be the lighter in the gallop, and the horse would be speedier. But if he should have his but-tocks separated under his tail by a broad line, he will bring his hind legs under him with a wider space between them, and so doing he will have a prouder and stronger gait and action, and will in all respects be better on them.

The Horses of Philip of Macedon

Almost two centuries after the battle between Croesus and Cyrus, cavalry warfare was improved by Philip of Macedon, who was made king of Macedonia in 359 B.C. Though Philip's son, Alexander the Great, was later to amass a great empire by conquest, Philip must be credited with making such conquering armies possible.

Before Philip's time, most of the fighting was done with massed chariots and a phalanx of foot soldiers. The Assyrians developed this battle formation to a high degree, but such battering rams of soldiers and horse flesh had very slight maneuverability. None of the close-order chariot or infantry formations were flexible enough to withstand a flank or rear attack. The mounted cavalry soldiers attending such forces were mere accessories to the main battle; unorganized, they fought in a scattered fashion, each man performing his individual feats.

Philip of Macedon devoted the first years of his kingship to organizing and disciplining his army. Revolutionary changes were put into effect, one of them being the use of charging cavalry. The Macedonian phalanx and the massed cavalry worked together as a team for the first time under Philip's tutelage. The phalanx advanced in the center and held the enemy's main body in a frontal attack, while on one wing or the other the cavalry action brushed away the enemy cavalry and, in organized formation, swept across and around to attack the flank and rear of the enemy's main battle phalanx. The enemy's main battle organization was thus broken up.

With this new and intelligent use of the horse, Philip held in his hand an effective battle instrument. With it he first turned his attention to the north and then later sent his conquering expeditions into Illyria and to the Danube, as well as spreading his power along the coast as far as the Hellespont.

Philip was one of the few monarchs in history to give much thought to his successor. His son Alexander was educated expressly for the empire. Aristotle was but one of the few able tutors chosen to educate him. At the age of sixteen, he was entrusted with authority and, it is recorded, was placed in command of the great cavalry at Chaeronea under Philip's guidance.

Alexander the Great

Alexander was undoubtedly one of the truest horsemen that ever lived. His intelligent use of horses, a skill gained from his father, created one of the greatest empires the world has ever known. Though the vain Alexander was ruthless to his enemies, he possessed a genuine love for horses and treated them humanely, and removed them from the dreadful type of chariot warfare that had been their fate since before the time of the Assyrians.

Bucephalus, Alexander's beloved war horse, was presented to him when he was a boy of thirteen. Believed to be Scythian-bred because of its large size, this imposing black stallion was untamable by the officers of Philip's cavalry. Attesting to Alexander's intelligent and kind horsemanship, despite his tender age, is the fact that he alone was able to tame the stallion and claim him for his own.

Through most of Alexander's conquests Bucephalus served him well. One of these conflicts was the Battle of Arbela, October 1, 331 B.C. In the spring of that year, Alexander started a long march toward Assyria, passing the Syrian Desert on his right. Near the crumbling ruins of Nineveh he came upon a great Persian army led by Darius III. Still relying on the antiquated war chariots, the Persians had equipped two hundred of them with sharp scythes attached to the wheels, pole, and body. Four horses were hitched to each chariot, the two outside animals serving as buffers for the pole horses. Such an array of vehicles seemed to be invincible, but Darius made the mistake of flinging them against Alexander's cavalry and light infantry. Only a few of them reached their objective, and these were quickly demolished.

After some maneuvering for position, the well-drilled Macedonians moved obliquely across the enemy's front lines, keeping good order. The Persians followed this movement to the flank and consequently left gaps in their array. Suddenly Alexander's crack cavalry charged at one of these weakened places and struck at the heart of the Persian phalanx. With the Macedonian infantry taking advantage of the opening, the center and left of the Persian forces crumpled. For a short time, the Persian's right light cavalry made some headway against Alexander's left but were soon cut to ribbons by the Macedonian's allies, the Thessalian cavalry. Soon the Persians, led by Darius, were reduced to a panic-stricken multitude of beaten fugitives, fleeing across the plain toward Arbela.

Bucephalus remained with Alexander the Great through his years of conquest with the Macedonian army as it moved north and east of the then known world. Together they traveled the shores of the Caspian, eastward across western Turkestan, and thence down into India by way of the Khyber Pass.

Alexander fought a great battle on the upper Indus against Porus, in which the Macedonians encountered and were victorious over an array of fighting elephants.

It was in the strange land of India that Bucephalus died at the age of thirty. So greatly did Alexander love his faithful old war horse that he built and named a city, Bucephala, after the animal. Bucephalus's memory was honored by the erection, in the center of the market place, of a circular tomb of alabaster tiles faced with pure gold leaf. This monument was called Bucephalum.

THE HORSES OF ROME

Of all the ancient nations of the world it would seem that Rome would have had the greatest opportunity to study and improve the horse through selective breeding. In 98 B.C., during the time of Trajan, the Roman Empire extended to nearly every great horse-raising nation in the then known world. Macedonia and Thrace lay within her borders. Persia, Mesopotamia, and Egypt lay to the east and south, and Numidia was a stone's throw across the Mediterranean. All these countries contained expert horsemen and good horses.

Despite these opportunities, there was a national neglect of horses during almost the entire existence of the Roman Empire. It is true that horses existed there and were used to a certain extent, but in a broad sense, the horse was not permitted to aid the Romans as it did other nations prior and subsequent to the rise of Roman power.

It is interesting to examine the reasons for this situation. Before 1200 B.C., Italy and Spain were populated with dark white people of the Iberian or Mediterranean race. Then the ancient Aryans moved from northern to central Italy and intermarried with their darker predecessors. These earliest Aryan peoples of the Neolithic period were not horsemen and it is not likely that they brought horses in any great numbers with them when they settled down on their boot-shaped land. Rome was founded in 735 B.C., and when the Gauls invaded north Italy in the fifth century B.C., they subdued the Etruscans but were repulsed by the Romans.

The point of contrast to be made here with other settled peoples, especially those that lay across the Adriatic Sea, is that the fresh injections of conquering nomadic horsemen tribes did not influence the Romans. The first Aryan settlers were never subdued by outsiders. The Gauls tried it in 500 B.C., but failed. Later, in 390 B.C., Rome was sacked by the Gauls, but in 367 B.C. internal dissensions were ended, and by 275 B.C. all of Italy was being unified. In her early days, Rome could give and take. Though rugged horse peoples did not lie within her borders, her power lay in the fact that she understood the value of such allies and used them.

The Romans were repeatedly repulsed in wars with kingdoms that made use of war horses. A noted example occurred in the time of Pyrrhus, a kinsman of Alexander the Great. Pyrrhus's army included all the established military devices of the time—an infantry phalanx, Thessalian cavalry, and twenty fighting elephants from the East. In 280 B.C., he routed the Romans at Heraclea and, pursuing them, again defeated them at Ausculum (279 B.C.).

The events of the Roman Empire might have taken a different turn had not Pyrrhus at this point entered into a truce so that unhampered he could cast a covetous eye toward Sicily.

Hannibal pushed the Romans around considerably until Scipio defeated him at the Battle of Zama near Carthage. It is interesting to note, however, that in this instance the Romans secured as allies the Numidians, who were expert horsemen and who gave them for the first time in their battles with Hannibal a superior cavalry. This stroke of good fortune also placed Spain under the Romans' control.

The offensive efforts to enlarge the empire met with defeat when they encountered opposing soldiers who rode horses. An example of the futility with which Roman foot soldiers fought mounted cavalry is contained in the experiences of Crassus when he crossed the Euphrates into Persia (53 B.C.). The Roman commander did not anticipate encountering such mobile horsemen tribes as the Parthians. They were excellent bowmen with unusual bows that discharged high-speed arrows. This campaign ended in complete disaster. Laboriously the Roman foot soldiers trudged through the sand, futilely charging an enemy which continually evaded and rode around them, shooting their ranks to pieces. Twenty thousand Romans were killed and upward of ten thousand were taken eastward into Iran as prisoners.

Likewise, Rome was never able to subjugate or thrust back the nomadic horsemen tribes that lay in a huge arc from the Rhine to the Euphrates, north of the Alps, the Danube, and the Black Sea. The Mongolic and Hunnish nomads were continuously a threat to the Romans.

While Rome was concerned with its intrigue, its politics, and its pleasures from 200 B.C. to A.D. 200, a great movement of nomadic peoples was welling up in central Asia, pushing in waves toward the Baltic to the west and southwestward toward the Black Sea. These Hunnish peoples were horse masters of the first degree. Their ancient ancestors had been the first to attend their flocks mounted on the backs of horses. They had grown up with the horse. The bit, the saddle, and the stirrup were not new to them; they were common necessities in the lives of men and horses who had to keep moving great distances over the vast steppelands. Such westward-drifting peoples were in a broad sense the ones who finally and indirectly broke the back of Roman power.

Yet, two hundred years after Caesar's time, the Romans seemed not to have learned the value of cavalry from their previous disastrous experiences at the hands of Hannibal or the Parthians at Carrhae. They persisted in marching on foot and, as always, were easily encircled and shot to pieces. Completely oblivious to the vitality of the horsemen peoples surrounding them, they remained stupidly vain and unimaginative in their methods of offensive warfare.

At least two prominent Romans showed their dislike for horses by their actions and remarks. One was Marcus Porcius Cato, born about 234 B.C., who distinguished himself as a Roman army commander in Spain through his harsh cruelties. Loyal horsemen will forever hold Cato in contempt for leaving behind, on the pretext of saving freight, the war horse which had carried him faithfully through his Spanish campaigns.

The other was Emperor Claudius, who repulsed the Goths at Nish in A.D. 269. Contemptuously he wrote: "I will not have the beasts [horses] near me—mean, truculent little spiders that they are."

The Roman Horse in Sport

While the Romans never mastered the war horse, they conducted equine sports—although I hasten to explain that the word "sport" is used loosely here. In 60 B.C., Julius Caesar published the proceedings of the Senate by having them written upon bulletin boards (albums). Professional letter writers copied these reports and sent them by special messengers to rich country correspondents. They, in turn, recopied the news upon the album. It is interesting to note that Cicero, while governor in Cilicia, complained bitterly that the correspondents seemed to be preoccupied with the chariot races and other sports and that the report contained too much of such things and not enough of the political situation.

Unlike the skillful horse games of the Greeks, the Roman races were

ROMAN CHARIOT HORSES

grisly affairs. What the audience seemed to want more than anything else was uncontrolled speed and action, with complete disregard for the safety of horses and drivers.

A wealthy Roman named Herodes Atticus amused himself by making huge donations to various cities for sporting events. Among these was a racecourse at Athens and another at Delphi. The Circus Maximus, of course, was one of the greatest stadiums for such bloodthirsty events.

The Roman hitch consisted of four or six horses abreast. The chariots afforded no protection to the charioteers who stood up with the reins tied around their waists. From the moment the horses were whipped into a white-hot frenzy at the start of the race, it was a continuous round of bloodcurdling excitement in which chariots were smashed and drivers dragged and killed, usually ending in a brutal scene of writhing masses of horseflesh.

It is only fair to admit that there were a few sane Romans who practiced the noble art of horse training, as evidenced in the following quotation from John Lawrence, a noted historian who wrote in the early nineteenth century concerning horses of Roman times:

> In forming the paces, if the colt was not naturally of a proud and lofty action, like the Spanish or Persian horses, wooden rollers and weights were bound to their pastern joints, which gave them the habit of lifting up their feet. This method, also, was practiced in teaching them the ambulatura, or amble, perhaps universally the common traveling pace of the Romans.
>
> The natural and most excellent pace, the trot, seems to have been very little prized or attended to by the ancients and was, indeed, by the Romans held in a kind of contempt, or aversion, as is demonstrated by the terms which served to describe it. A trotting horse was called by them successator, or shaker, and sometimes cruciator, or tormentor, which bad terms, it may be presumed, were applied specially to those which in these days we dignify with the expressive appellation of "bonesetters."

HORSES OF EGYPT

From the discussion thus far it would appear that the idea of horse domestication originated in the steppelands of Asia and moved southward into India, down between the Caspian and Red seas, and westward into all parts of Europe. While it is impossible to say with certainty that such was the case, the evidence seems to support such a conjecture.

But the question also arises: What about the horses of north Africa and Arabia? In an attempt to answer this question, let us examine the known facts.

Fourteen thousand years ago, the rains, which for centuries had fallen upon the lush green tableland of northeast Africa, commenced to fail. As a result, the game which was hunted by the ancestors of the ancient Egyptians became scarce, forcing the people to abandon their nomadic scheme of existence and settle down as cultivators of the soil along the Nile River.

At the beginning of the Neolithic period in North Africa, about 5000 B.C., new types of tools and weapons were invented, pottery vessels were manufactured, and permanent homes of wood, reed, and mud were constructed. The cultivation and storage of grain began in this period, and the idea of domesticating useful animals developed. Oxen were used to till the soil and asses seem to have been servants of the Egyptians at an early period, but the horse was absent from the everyday scene.

The ancient civilizations of Sumeria and Egypt ran parallel in much of their development. Babylonia lay open on every side to invasion, but Egypt, on the other hand, was protected by desert to the west and desert and sea to the east and, to the south, had only the Negro peoples to contend with. Owing to this fact, her history is less interrupted by invasions of foreign races. But through this isolation she was deprived, for a long period, of new ideas, among which was the domestic use of the horse.

The story of early Egypt is largely an internal history until the first traces of the Hyksos appear about 1900 B.C. They filtered into Egypt from Palestine, which lay to the north, and by the eighteenth century B.C., these foreigners were in power and horses appeared in great numbers. The Hyksos, known as the "Princes of the Uplands," were, beyond a doubt, the ones who introduced the domesticated horse into Egypt.

The origin of the Hyksos is an unsolved mystery, though it seems fairly clear that they were basically of Semitic stock. It is estimated that their invasion took place about the time of the first Babylonian Empire of Hammurabi. For more than a century, two Hyksos kings ruled Egypt with absolute authority. Then gradually the true Egyptians turned from only mildly resisting vassals to more vigorous protestors. In the Seventeenth Dynasty, the native "Princes of the Southern City" began to fight back in earnest. The Egyptians, taking a lesson from the Hyksos, began to import horses from Asia. These importations may have been through Persia and farther east, indicating Oriental types. Also, the horses owned by the Hyksos may have been of similar origin. The Egyptian chariot division added a deadly branch to the army which, through its mobility and efficiency, finally subdued the hated Hyksos and transformed the former peace-loving Egyptians into world conquerors.

The remains of an ancient Egyptian horse were uncovered near an Eighteenth Dynasty tomb, dating about 1490 B.C. The manner of burial proves that the animal was esteemed highly and merited great honor. This horse, it is believed, was of Arab or Oriental type. Although interred with its saddle, the indications are that the Egyptians were not enthusiastic about riding horses but used them largely to draw chariots.

The Egyptian chariots were in some principles similar to those developed by the Assyrians, though they never reached the size of the latter. The floor boards were level with the axle, which was attached at the back of the carriage.

Chariots were used in a different manner, however, serving solely as movable platforms from which expert archers could rain murderous onslaughts of arrows upon their less mobile enemies. The vehicles were strong but lightly constructed, which made them capable of extreme speed and maneuverability when drawn by two fast horses. Thus, instead of serving as an artillery vehicle, the Egyptian chariot served more the intents and purposes of cavalry.

EGYPTIAN WAR HORSES

One of these ancient vehicles now rests in the Metropolitan Museum of Art. Light in weight, graceful, and with the body sheathed in embossed leather, it is a masterpiece of refinement. The wheels contain six light spokes and the rims are banded with tires of rawhide.

In 1478 B.C., under the guidance of Thutmose III, the Egyptian army descended from the heights of Carmel and struck at the Syrian allies (the biblical Battle of Armageddon) on the plain of Esdraelon, driving them into the heavily fortified city of Megiddo where the defenders were forced to surrender. Lack of military strategy on the part of Thutmose III was more than compensated for by the efficiency of the Egyptian war chariots.

During the first years of the New Kingdom, each warrior managed his own chariot. Later, the vehicles carried a crew of two men—a charioteer to drive the horses and a fighter who could devote his entire attention to the battle.

Though always conservative and reluctant to change her traditions, Egypt became less and less isolated. Eventually, she enlarged the sphere of her worldly acquaintanceship and commerce to include the entire eastern Mediterranean area. With interchange of ideas, the fine Egyptian horses undoubtedly spread out in all directions. The Libyans and Numidians possibly procured some of their stock more or less directly from Egypt.

THE ARABIAN HORSE

The earliest history of Arabian horses is obscure. Investigators have been unable as yet to discover satisfactory knowledge concerning their origin. It is probable that Arabia was one of the last Asiatic countries to use and train domesticated horses. Records show that Xerxes, who died in 465 B.C., used a number of Arabian soldiers in his army, none of them horsemen.

Until archaeology divulges more specific data on the period in history when horses were first used in Arabia, it will be impossible to say from whence they came. However, there are four peoples from whom Arabia may have received its original stock—the Egyptians, Persians, Parthians, and Scythians.

One authority asserts that the Arabs obtained horses through Egypt from the Libyan tribes of northern Africa. If this could be proved as a fact, such horses would necessarily have originated in one or more of three ways. First, they might have been from wild stock indigenous to the region; second, they could have been descendants of the first horses to arrive in Egypt, brought there by the ancient Hyksos invaders, and of the horses procured from Asia by the Egyptians to combat the Hyksos kings; and third, they may have been derived from stock landed on the north African coast by the early Phoenician traders. In each case, except the first, such animals were probably of Oriental type, originating in Persia and farther east.

A point worth noting is that many of the antique breeds possessed at least a few of the Arab horse characteristics. For instance, many of the horses of Greek sculpture bear a striking resemblance to what we recognize today as the Arab type. The truth probably is that the ancestors of both breeds were of similar conformation. The Arabs no doubt intensified such strains of beauty through their wise breeding programs. Nonetheless, the general type existed previous to Arab pedigrees.

As the Moslem Empire spread in the seventh and eighth centuries, the Arabian horse's sphere of influence settled over a large area from Turkestan and Persian, across the North African coast to Morocco, and up into Spain. From that time onward, the Arabian horse contributed a great share to the improvement of all domestic horses.

It may never be known from what specific breeds the Arabian horse developed. Perhaps there are many ancient bloods flowing in his veins. In any case, the Arabian was developed to a high degree and the breed has influenced more strongly the horses of the entire world than any other strain of recent early horses.

PERSIAN HORSES

Before the time of Xerxes, Persian horses were widely known for their proud, aristocratic beauty. They were sleek, nervous, and fleet, though not noted for great endurance. Persian horses drew chariots as well as being ridden. While they were known to be extremely nervous and high-strung, their gaits were greatly admired. It is recorded that they were endowed with a graceful pace, smooth and rhythmic, which the rider could endure for hours on end with extreme comfort. This may be an indication that the Persian breed was one of the earliest forerunners of the present-day gaited horse. A Persian's wealth was measured in terms of the number and quality of horses he owned. These people so greatly admired their horses that they endowed them with the name "wind-foot."

PARTHIAN HORSES

The name "Parthian" means horseman in the Chaldean language. Parthian horses were less noble in appearance than Persian horses. Their owners bred them for useful purposes to a greater extent than did the Persians. They were trained in a manner that caused them to lift their legs in high action to make them more sure-footed and useful over rough, uneven ground. They were able to travel great distances without food or water. Parthian horses were one of the most serviceable of ancient horse breeds. It will be remembered that the Parthians were the horsemen with "twanging" bows who so efficiently defeated the Roman foot soldiers of Crassus at Carrhae in 53 B.C.

SCYTHIAN HORSES

Scythian horses, among the most ancient of domesticated horses, were admired for their greater size. They were offered as sacrifices by the early Scythians in a most gruesome manner, which, however, attests to the reverent attitude with which their owners contemplated them. We find the Scythian horse's influence in many areas during ancient times. We have already mentioned that Bucephalus, the war horse of Alexander the Great, was believed to have been Scythian. While Thracian horses are reputed to be represented on the Parthenon frieze depicting the youth of the Athenian cavalry during the Peloponnesian wars, it is likely that Scythian blood was present in these beautiful animals. Many fine Scythian horses were taken by conquest into Turkey. The Tang war horses show a resemblance to the Scythians.

If the Scythian horse was popular enough to be desired by so many countries, it is reasonable to believe that he traveled down from his home above the Caspian and Black seas to influence, later, the desert steeds of the Bedouins.

HORSES OF BRITAIN AND WESTERN EUROPE

When the Romans advanced the western boundary of their empire by invading and annexing the southern half of Britain around the middle of the first century B.C., they found the natives in possession of horses. These animals were reputed to be small but hardy, and horsemanship was executed with considerable skill. The small size of the animals may have been due to the manner in which they were fostered. The herds received no care, being left to forage for themselves. Occasionally, they were rounded up and certain ones selected for use. Because of the lack of a concerted breeding program, the animals naturally remained undeveloped and of miniature size. Many students point out that the various pony breeds originating in the British Isles are the descendants of this earliest foundation stock.

The use of horses as saddle mounts was not widely adopted until nearly the seventh century. According to the Roman legions who invaded Britain, the natives used horses hitched to battle chariots to transport foot soldiers quickly to points of battle.

It would be difficult to say with any certainty how the first domestic horses got to Britain. From the countless fossil remains discovered, we know that prehistoric wild horses migrated there before the waters of the English Channel arose to cut off passage between Britain and the Continent. It is possible that these wild species were tamed and domesticated by the ancient inhabitants in the same way that took place in other parts of the world.

Another wholly different explanation has been advanced for the existence of domestic horses in the British Isles. As intimated previously, the ancient Phoenicians were known to have visited Mediterranean and Atlantic ports of Spain several hundred years before the Christian era. Horses were one of the principal items among their cargoes. There is a strong possibility that in the course of barter such horses found their way into Britain.

The question also arises as to where the Britons obtained the sizable horses that later carried their heavy armor. It is not definitely known what type of blood was used to build up the Great Horse, but at the time of the Romans' western European invasion, heavy Belgian and Flemish types were discovered. It is highly probable that such horses were used by the islanders to infuse size into their native stock. The present-day English Shires are believed to be the descendants of the Great Horse of English knighthood and chivalry.

"Great" Horses

The Frankish kingdoms lying to the north of the old Roman Empire had horses in the eighth century A.D. For centuries they had been hunting and raiding horsemen. Western Europe at that time was a land without law or administration. Men were forced to link themselves to one another for protection. Out of this condition grew feudalism. The horsemen or horse owners received higher positions in the ranks of their lords than did those without horses. The horse in this way became the cause and symbol of noble rank among men.

Western Europe appears to be the region in which horses of immense size were developed. One explanation is that when the most ancient nomadic horse peoples moved westward into Europe they discovered the survival of the wild forest, or Nordic, horse species. It is likely that their lighter horses were crossed upon these large forest varieties, thereby producing horses of larger size than had been used previously.

The modern Belgian horse is believed to have descended from the early Flemish. Much of the size of the early western European horses must have been bred into them as the feudal system took hold of those countries and the need grew for horses that could carry the heavy armor and equipment necessary for successful knighthood.

Much more could have been said in this chapter about specific deeds of real horses. The wars and conquests might have been more fully explained. We have not touched upon the noble animals that served the Crusaders and but briefly upon the horses that carried the "knights of old." The purpose of this chapter, however, has been to sketch broadly the great movements of ancient horse domestication from the time horses were first used until they became generally common in the world of antiquity as animals of domestic usefulness.

In summary, it is interesting to note that from their first use horses gave man a power without which he probably would not have progressed very far. Always the vigor of the horseman influenced civilizations to new and better things, even though war was the frequent medium for such improvement.

This chapter, of course, does not complete the history of man's improvement of the horse, nor does it tell the whole story of the horse's value to mankind. Those are things which will be related more specifically in the chapters that follow. Up to this point, we have attempted to create stepping-stones which will enable us to understand more fully the modern light horses that exist around us with so much popularity in America.

3

Gaits and Their Importance

When a man walks or runs, he does so by treading the earth first with one foot and then the other. Because he has but two legs, the variation in the pattern of his footfalls is limited.

The horse, however, can place his four feet in many combinations in forward movement. Because of this, many fine horse movements have arisen and developed, causing some men to prefer one type of horse and others another. Peculiarly smooth gaits, as we have already noted, distinguished the mounts of the Persians from the swift chariot steeds of the early Greeks. The gait of the knight's charger was different from that of his courser. The desert mounts of the Arabs traveled in a different manner from the mounts of the early nomadic herders.

Gaits are interesting and important because they generally determine an animal's use.

EXPERIMENTATION

Before the invention of the camera, artists frequently pictured the running horse with both front feet stretched forward and the hind feet backward, suspended in the air. We know now that this was not a true-to-life depiction and that when the horse travels in the gallop he does so with at least one foot on the ground, except for a short moment at that phase of his stride when the feet are gathered under him. The camera gave us the proof of this fact.

During the latter part of the nineteenth century, Leland Stanford, California millionaire, experimented with the subject. Are all the feet of a rapidly trotting horse off the ground at any time in his stride? This was one of the many questions that Stanford sought to answer. Eadweard Muybridge, a San Francisco photographer, was employed to try to throw some light on the subject. After the exposure of many negatives as Stanford's trotter Occident moved past his camera, it was proved that all four feet do leave the ground at a certain fleeting moment during the trotting gait.

The late Dr. Samuel H. Chubb, as Associate Curator of Comparative Anatomy at the American Museum of Natural History, made exhaustive studies of the laws governing animal locomotion. At the museum, a hall of "living skeletons" has been created where anyone interested in the subject may come and observe. In this hall is an important collection of specimens of members of the Equidae, or horse family. These skeletons have been carefully prepared and mounted to show the true action of different breeds or types of horses. Sysonby, one of America's great running horses, forms a part of this exhibit, as well as Lee Axworthy, who for many years held the world's record for trotting stallions with a mark of 1:58¼ for the mile.

Dr. Chubb's findings were supported in part by careful observations of living animals on the race tracks and study of a great many photographs of animals moving at top speed in their respective gaits. The pictures were taken with cameras that exposed the film at $\frac{1}{1000}$ of a second in order to "freeze" the exact position of every anatomical part of the subject during extreme bursts of speed.

The object of the exhibits is not only to show the function and behavior of the bones during intensely speedy action but also to call attention to rules of locomotion which are strictly adhered to by all mammals.

According to Dr. Chubb's findings, there are minor variations in the methods of locomotion among different animals. The dog, being a smaller animal, yet almost equaling the speed of the horse, must necessarily assume a greater degree of action to attain such great speed. For instance, when the legs of a running horse are gathered together, the spine is slightly arched. The dog's back acquires a much sharper curve to duplicate the horse's speed. At the moment of maximum flexure, with the horse's feet gathered under him, the hind toe comes approximately in line with and under the front pastern, whereas a dog in the same flexure will almost cross the knee of the hind leg and the elbow of the front leg.

The dog, perhaps owing to his lightness, runs more nearly like the horses in early paintings. In other words, there are two moments in the dog's stride when all four feet leave the ground. One is at the moment of extreme flexure

and the other when the forelegs are stretched forward and the hind ones
backward.

Owing to these two differences in locomotion, it was discovered that the
horse, when at full speed, is entirely free from contact with the earth approximately one-fourth of the time—that being the moment when his limbs are
drawn together—whereas the dog is suspended in the air about one-half the
time.

One technical difference, however, between the running action of the horse
and that of the dog involves the succession, or order, of footfalls. The dog runs
with *rotary* action, whereas the horse runs with *diagonal* action. The me-
chanics of rotary and diagonal action are shown in the charts below.

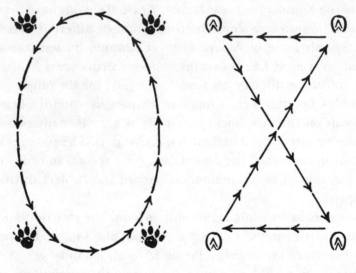

A. Rotary Gallop   B. Diagonal Gallop

It is difficult to understand exactly why certain animals employ the diagonal system and others the rotary. The Equidae family, and the cow,
buffalo, goat, and bear use the diagonal, while dogs, deer, antelope, and elk
run according to the rotary. At first, we might suspect that only lighter animals use the rotary system and heavier ones the diagonal. However, this is
untrue, because in the diagonal classification we find the goat, which is a
comparatively light animal, and in the rotary system the elk, which is fairly
heavy. Also there are ruminants, or cud-chewing animals, in both groups.

Chart *A* shows the rotary action of the dog. The succession of footfalls
is right rear foot first, right fore second, left fore third, and left rear fourth.
The rotation can be changed to left rear, left fore, right fore, and right rear,
but the gait is basically the same.

Chart *B* explains the order of footfalls in the diagonal action of the galloping horse. Here, by studying the chart, we discover that if the off hind foot strikes first, the near hind will strike second; then the action crosses over to the off fore, which will strike third, and the near fore, which will strike fourth. In horsemen's phraseology, this indicates that the horse is leading on the "left hand." If the action is started on the left rear and progresses to right rear, left fore, and right fore, the horse is galloping on the "right hand," or leading to the right.

It is fortunate for the human race that the horse uses the diagonal system of running. Occasionally a horse will take what horsemen call a "false lead" or "cross canter." In the light of the above explanation, the horse in such cases accidentally changes his way of traveling to a *rotary* action. The unpleasantness resulting from this has been experienced by most horsemen; there is a twisting sensation that makes for a most uncomfortable ride.

The fact that a horse moves forward on an absolutely straight line, even at an extremely slow canter, may be attributed to his use of the diagonal system.

Another amazing law of progressive movement which all four-legged animals seem obliged to obey is the manner in which front and hind feet pass each other at the moment of extreme flexure. As the hind feet move forward to start a new stride, they always pass, not toward the median line but toward the *outside* of the front feet. Science has not yet discovered the answer to the question: Why is it imperative that a creature must pass his hind feet in a course lateral to his front feet?

To show how strict is this law of nature I quote a paragraph from *Natural History*, Volume XXIX, Number 5, published by the American Museum of Natural History, written by the late Dr. Chubb:

There is one very striking example of the universal application of this law which has come to my notice. The English bull dog, poor creature, has been so distorted by man's breeding and selection that he can hardly be called a normal animal. His measurement through the shoulders is two or three times that of the hips, and as he stands, the distance between front feet bears a similar proportion to that of the hind, so that we might suppose it to be quite impossible for him to reverse the measurement between front and hind feet in any position that he assumes. Yet, when he can be induced to run with sufficient speed to bring his hind feet in any proximity to his front feet, he follows the well established and time honored traditions of his ancestors, passing his hind feet outside of his front—a most interesting example of the way that exacting old "Dame Nature" demands observance of certain rules which might seem to us quite arbitrary.

I was so interested in Dr. Chubb's findings that I sought more information. His answer to my letter brought to light another law of locomotion—which will possibly be doubted by many horsemen. Dr. Chubb's letter read, in part, as follows:

There is but one point in your letter to which I must take exception. That is in regard to the trot and pace of the horse. Every horseman will say exactly as you have stated in your letter (that the trot and pace are square two-beat gaits), but this is undoubtedly due to the fact that the difference in footfalls is so slight that it is not apparent to the eye. It is a most interesting fact that there seems to be a law governing animal locomotion that *no two feet shall move simultaneously.* The trot is the most nearly simultaneous movement and yet the hind foot strikes the ground a minute fraction of a second *before* the front of the opposite side. Again, in the pace the hind foot strikes the ground slightly *before* the front of the same side. The walk is practically a slow pace but the succession of footfalls is the same. Why this law prohibiting simultaneous movements should be so exacting is hard to say, but I know of no exceptions among the mammals.

In order to prepare skeletons to represent progressive action correctly, I have taken thousands of photographs with exposures of $\frac{1}{1000}$ of a second, which faithfully record the facts. I know of no publication that has been so helpful in making these studies as *Animals in Motion* by Eadweard Muybridge. It was completed in 1885 when rapid photography was in its infancy and the photographs are not of the very best quality but they are nonetheless authentic.

To Dr. Chubb's findings I might add in his support that during my studies and observations of horses' gaits I have taken many high-speed photographs of horses in action, and they almost all bear out the law of locomotion that he has mentioned. One other observation might be mentioned that has come to my attention. While my photographs showed the rear foot of the trot and pace to strike the ground first, when the horse was "going away" at speed, when the animal commenced to slow up or stop, it was interesting to note, the *front* foot struck the ground first as if to brake the speed.

Another interesting point is the manner in which a horse propels himself. At almost every gait the hind legs furnish the power for forward movement. The exception would be in the case of the fast running walk, where the forelegs are used as a propelling force, though not so greatly as the rear legs.

The forelegs are used to guide the animal and also act as a balance. They also serve as a brake. It is an interesting fact that nature has provided for quicker growth of the hind toes to aid in propelling and of the heels of the fore hoofs because this part of the front foot is worn away in the action of stopping.

RUDIMENTS OF GAITS

What constitutes a gait? Is it a technical difference in the pattern of foot-falls, and does speed enter into it?

We have all seen horses that perform three gaits, which are perhaps the most common. Most of us have seen five-gaited horses in action.

If we were to believe that different patterns of footfalls are the only factors that determine gaits, then we might agree that it is impossible for a horse to execute more than four gaits. These would be:

1. The walk: an evenly spaced four-beat gait.
2. The trot: a diagonal two-beat gait.
3. The pace: a lateral two-beat gait.
4. The gallop: an unevenly spaced four-beat gait.

If, however, we decide to take a broader view and include such factors as speed, form, and appearance, we can increase the gaits to a much larger number.

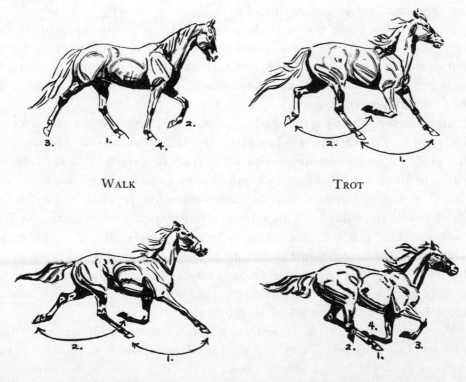

WALK   TROT

PACE   GALLOP

POSSIBLE ORIGIN OF GAITS

It has been said that the only basically natural gaits of the horse are the walk and the run and that the trot is merely an intermediate gait to enable the animal to gain speed so that he can easily break into the run. I shall neither agree nor disagree with this theory except to say that if such is the case the theorists should add the pacing gait to their assertion.

The walk, of course, is the slow manner in which horses move either when they are grazing or going unhurriedly from one point to another. The run, clearly, is their main escape protection from danger because of its great speed.

Everyone knows that all sound horses can walk and run. As for the two intermediate gaits, it appears that a few horses cannot trot and many of them cannot pace. Some horses will do both.

Many theories have been advanced as to the reasons for the pacing and trotting tendencies. We can be certain that neither of them has been added to the horse's gaits in recent years. In all probability, these methods of traveling were learned many thousands of years before man knew of them. Just why only certain horses should be blessed (or cursed) with these traits is unanswerable. Some horsemen believe that the determining factor is the body conformation of the horse. This has some validity, as it has been noticed that pacing or easy-gaited horses have certain distinguishing characteristics. Such body conformation, however, may have resulted from practice extending over thousands of years.

An interesting theory is that pacing horses were created by the character of the terrain on which they lived and traveled. The advocates of this explanation point to the ancient steppe-type horse and call to mind that the land in which he lived was rolling and smooth. As the animal walked down the inclines, he may have commenced to shuffle, and when he came to the flat he may likewise have lined out in a full-fledged swinging pacing gait. As Dr. Chubb pointed out, the pace seems to be most closely related to the walk.

Trainers, today, often start their colts in the saddle gaits by working them down a slight grade. The pace in its early stages gives the impression that the horse is bracing himself in front and carrying weight on his haunches, which might be his action when traveling downhill.

Horses with a strong pacing tendency seem to show its influence in their walk and canter as well. Tennessee Walking Horses, which have a dominant pacing trait, often have a "pacy" canter in the beginning of their training. In other words, the lateral legs seem to move almost together as they gallop.

The fact that the ability to "gait" is an inherent trait in the brain and fiber of some horses is clearly illustrated by this breed. A foal only a few hours old will break into a running walk or a pace as it hurries after the dam. This is observed in some colts of American Saddle and Standard Bred breeding, although to a lesser degree.

The smoothness of the terrain in certain localities during ancient times may have kept pacing horses from developing a natural high action, and rather, made their legs, moving in lateral pairs, seem to swing together, literally skimming the ground.

Another writer believes that the trot and pace may have been perfected in the same species and was an interchangeable gait. This group of horses may have developed the two medium-speed gaits because there was not frequent necessity for quick bursts of speed in escaping from their enemies. Perhaps they lived in open country where it was not possible for predatory animals to lurk before making sudden attacks.

All the foregoing is substantiated, to a great extent, by the fact that typical running horses do not excel at the trot and very few of them are able to pace at all. Running horses may possibly be traced to the ancient plateau, or Celtic, type. Most running horses of today show finer structure than that of the trotters and pacers.

Arabians and Barbs are excellent gallopers. The breed that stemmed from them, the Thoroughbred, is noted for one thing: the ability to run. These horses can trot, but it is not an outstanding gait with them. A few have gaiting tendencies, but these are exceptions to the rule.

Whether or not today's horses trace directly to ancient wild types is a highly dubious question. Scientists as eminent as Ewart, Skorgowski, and Gromova have taken different points of view. Of one thing we can be certain: The Oriental, or so-called "hot-blooded," horse is the opposite of the northern "cold-bloods" in the matter of gaits, the former being runners exclusively. The latter group, I believe can be divided into two classifications with respect to gaits—one in which the trotting gait is dominant and the other in which the pacing tendency is stronger. Double-gaited horses, those that trot and pace as well, are probably the result of crosses in breeding, first in the early wild state and later when domesticated.

While I favor the theory that the rudimentary gaits (walk, trot, pace, and gallop) were present before domestication, there is much to be said for the idea that ancient man may have done much to develop and enhance certain gaits and to cause others to deteriorate through disuse.

For instance, the Arabian horse may have developed a rapid, flat walk and a fast gallop through the Bedouins' interchangeable use of the camel and the horse as animals of transportation. The Arabian was used as a war or raiding animal, whereas the camel was used for travel at medium speed. Perhaps the Arab's trot was not highly perfected, or perhaps his pacing or easy-gaiting tendency, if he possessed one, was allowed to erase itself from his instincts through centuries of disuse.

A modern horse in which this process is taking place is the Tennessee Walker. It is easy to imagine that training in which the trot is not used, if persisted in over a period of centuries, might cause the animal eventually to lose his trotting tendency entirely, or at least to develop an inferior trotting gait. The disuse of the trot would, of course, be hastened by selective breeding as animals with predominant pacing tendencies were selected.

DESCRIPTION OF GAITS

The Walk

The walk is the slowest gait used by horses. The rhythmic sound of the footfalls is four evenly spaced beats. Each of the four legs works separately and at a time distinctly different from the other three. There are always at least two feet on the ground. When only two feet are on the ground, one must be the fore and one the hind. In a true walk, each foot is placed flat and solidly on the ground.

The successive order of the footfalls is as follows: (1) left hind; (2) left fore; (3) right hind; (4) right fore.

In viewing the horse at a walk, we notice that his head nods up and down. This is for balance, much the same as a human being swings his arms when he walks. If we watch closely, we may perceive that the head of the horse reaches its lowest point at approximately the moment when one of the hind feet hits the ground and as the foreleg on the same side rises. The head rises and falls twice during each stride cycle.

Another characteristic peculiar only to the walking gait is that the legs exert no lift to the body of the horse. Once a foot is placed solidly on the ground, the muscles are used solely to push that foot backward. The weight of the animal is evenly placed on both the front and hind legs.

Length of stride is the distance between two tracks of the same foot. In other words, if the left front foot is watched from the time it leaves the ground until it again touches the ground, the distance between the two tracks is the measurement of stride. This varies with different horses, but good stride is desirable in all horses.

If we examine the tracks of a horse that has walked past us, we will discover that the imprint of the hind hoof will nearly touch that of the fore. Some horses place their hind track squarely in the fore track, while others may step just short of it or slightly past it. When viewed from the side, the hind foot, as it swings forward, almost touches the front foot of the same side as it leaves the ground.

The Trot

The trot is a two-beat gait in which, for all practical purposes, the diagonally opposed feet strike the ground simultaneously.

An early definition of the trotting gait was written by Sieur Guillet in his *Les Arts de l'homme d' épée:*

> The trot is the Pace or Going of a Horse in which the Motion is Two Legs in the Air and Two upon the Ground crosswise, in the form of a St. Andrews cross, continuing alternately to raise at once the Hind-leg of one side and the Fore-leg of the other. A horse puts himself to a Trot when, upon a walk, he makes haste or quickens his Pace; and if he be assisted by the Switch or Heels he takes it yet better.

The only thing that can be added to Guillet's definition is to call attention again to the Stanford-Muybridge experiment which showed that, instead of "Two Legs in the Air and Two upon the Ground," all four are in suspension at the interval between beats.

When a horse strikes this gait, he appears to spring up slightly as he moves forward. Although remaining horizontal, the backbone rises and falls with each stride. There is very little or no motion of the head at this gait.

If all history could be surveyed and summed up, it would undoubtedly be found that the trotting gait has never been favored by travelers who rode upon the backs of horses because of the jarring caused by the rise and fall of the trot. The ancients who rode without stirrups must have held a great contempt for this gait. But with the aid of stirrups and the present-day horseman's use of the posting technique, much of the discomfort has been removed. There was a current saying in eighteenth-century England that "a butcher rides a trotter."

Viewed in profile, the legs of a trotting horse generally have height of action. The Frisian horses of Holland have been credited with contributing much to the blood of famous trotting breeds, among which are the Russian Orloff, the English Hackney, and the American Standard Bred. The Frisian horses, it is said, originated among the marshes of north Holland, where they were obliged to develop a high, speedy trot because of the muddy, water-covered land.

The armor-clad knights of England employed a large and powerful "trottynge" horse because of his high trot. Such horses were sure-footed, and their masters did not fear that the animals would stumble and fall on uneven ground.

Although the trotting horse was held in disfavor as a saddle animal, he was quickly adopted when roads were constructed and wheeled vehicles used. As a harness horse, he is without peer. Horses that trot are possessed of a powerful stride and a smooth speed, ideal for roadwork. Furthermore, the trot has more style and airiness than the pace.

For pure trotting speed the Standard Bred Horse is one of the most outstanding. Greyhound, one of these, holds the record for trotting the mile with a mark of 1:56.

The Gallop

The gallop is the speediest gait of all horses. Essentially it is a leaping motion wherein the legs are gathered under the body and then violently extended to push the animal rapidly forward in great strides. The hind legs furnish the propelling energy. The forelegs are used to balance, support, and guide the animal.

To the ear, the galloper issues a sound of four rapid, distinct beats and then a pause while the legs regather for another drive. According to the findings of Dr. Chubb, the sound of the four beats should occupy three-fourths and the interval one-fourth of the time consumed by a complete stride cycle.

Owing to the exertion required, a running horse should be kept at a gallop for only a short time—notwithstanding the fact that the horses in current "horse operas" seem to gallop incessantly without tiring.

The Jog and Dogtrot

These gaits are simply slower movements of the extended trot.

The Canter and Lope

The canter and lope are slower versions of the gallop. The pattern of footfalls is the same. The lope is a swinging, ground-consuming gait that is less tiring to the horse and more comfortable for the rider. The lope is a prescribed gait for Western-type horses. High action is not in evidence.

The canter is slower than the lope, and there is more rise and fall fore and aft when the horse executes it. Properly done, it presents a beautifully rhythmic rocking-chair action, with a comfortable sensation to the rider. The purpose of the two gaits is somewhat different. The lope is used to go from one point to another as rapidly as possible without undue fatigue to the horse and without stress to the rider. The canter may be called a "diversionary" gait. Those who would dispute this are reminded that either a good brisk trot or a racking gait are faster than a desirably slow canter. The canter is a prescribed gait for pleasure hacks and show horses.

The Pace

The pace is a nearly true two-beat gait in which the lateral legs work together. As the chart on page 45 will show, the left rear and left fore strike the ground almost simultaneously, followed by the right rear and right fore. As in the trot, although not so pronounced, there are intervals, particularly at high speed, when all four feet are off the ground.

The true pacing gait may not be as pleasing to watch as the trot, which is more "airy" and square. There is, however, a peculiar fascination about its rhythm as the "side-wheeler" swings along. The up-and-down movement of the trot is absent, but the body and head seem to swing in unison with the lateral pairs of legs.

As a speed gait on a race track, the pace compares favorably with the trot. In fact, some pacer enthusiasts declare that it is a faster gait, and it must be admitted that the record for the fastest mile in harness is held by Billy Direct, a pacer with an official mark of 1:55¼. Dan Patch, the immortal horse, in 1906 paced a mile in 1:55 at the Minnesota State Fair, though the record is not officially recognized because of the use of running pacemakers.

Aside from the pacer's use as a race horse, his great contribution to the horse world is his ability to produce multiple-gaited horses.

The "Easy" Gaits

We shall discuss each of these gaits separately, but because of similarities and overlapping characteristics among them it may be necessary for the reader to refer back and forth. Horses that do a good running walk, for example, are frequently accused of doing a "slow gait." A "fox trot" is often mistaken for a running walk. All the slow gaits are delicately balanced, and their intricacies have made them difficult to analyze and understand.

In the category of easy gaits are the three that were formerly known as the "slow gaits." These were the running walk, the fox trot, and the stepping pace. When the slow gait was called for in the old-time horse shows, it was permissible for the entrants to perform any one of these three. In more recent years, however, the stepping pace has come to be recognized as the acceptable slow gait. Thus the stepping pace and the slow gait have become synonymous.

The Running Walk

The true running walk is no more and no less than an accelerated flat walk. It is often referred to as an "extension" of the flat-footed walk.

Many people have a misconception of this gait. The error may be in the naming of it, for it has no connection with the run, nor does it even approach that gait in speed. It is not comparable to either the trot or the pace as a speed gait, although a good running walker will invariably force another horse to break into a slow trot to stay with him.

While there are horses of other breeds known to perform the running walk, the Tennessee Walking Horse is the king of them all at this gait. Further, in connection with the question of speed, I quote a paragraph of a letter from the late J. J. Murray, who was the founder and publisher of the *Tennessee Walking Horse Magazine:*

> The greatest trouble now afflicting our breed is the fact that new owners disregard the fact that the running walk is not for speed. It has been perfected for a medium fast equine gait from four to eight miles an hour and for a long ride not over five would be my suggestion. Walking Horses are being ridden entirely too fast in most of the shows, even in Tennessee and in 1945 they were slowed down to a natural gait. . . .

The association sponsoring the Tennessee Walking Horse breed always states that the speed of the running walk is from 6 to 8 miles an hour.

The only way in which the running walk differs from the flat walk is that the legs move more rapidly and the stride is longer. In this connection it is interesting to note that the track of the hind foot is placed a considerable distance ahead of the front one. In a few cases, this "overstride," or "overreach," has been measured at 34 inches.

The running walk is one of the most comfortable of all gaits, for it carries the rider steadily forward in a smooth gliding manner without a jar.

The Fox Trot

Assuming the reader understands the primary gaits illustrated on page 45, the fox trot is best described as being somewhat related to both the trot and the walk. It is a four-beat gait, but not as evenly spaced as the walk.

When a horse changes from a trot to a walk, his pattern of footfalls naturally changes from a square two-beat to a square four-beat. The fox trot is somewhere between these two gaits. The left hind foot strikes the ground, followed quickly by the diagonal, or right forefoot, then a slight pause, after which the right hind strikes, quickly followed by the left fore. In musical terms the sound of the rear foot would precede the sound of the diagonal front foot somewhat like a grace note or appoggiatura. Instead of the evenly spaced one—two—one—two of the trot, we would have a one-two—one-two rhythm.

The fox trot presents an appearance quite similar to a rapid walk, and the head nods, but not so vigorously. There is one absolute method by which it can be detected. The rear quarters will jog up and down slightly as in the trotting movement. The reason for this is that the legs are exerting a slight upward exertion before the foot leaves the ground. As a result, the fox trot does not have as much stride as the running walk; neither does it have as much speed.

In early Plantation Horse classes, the fox trot was an acceptable substitute for the running walk. Nowadays, the horses are required to remain in pure walking form.

The fox trot is an extremely comfortable gait for the rider, and the horse performs it without fatigue.

The Stepping Pace, or Slow Gait

Familiarity with this gait may be gained by observing five-gaited horses in the show ring. It is sometimes referred to as the "slow rack," though we consider that designation a misnomer. The rule book states that the five-gaited horse must perform "five distinct gaits." If the stepping pace were a slow rack, it could not be called a "distinct gait." It must be admitted, however, that the gait which many horses exhibit is far from a stepping pace in its true form.

The successive order of footfalls in the stepping pace is right rear, right fore, left rear, left fore.

This gait has only a slightly uneven four-beat rhythm. For instance, less time is consumed between the beats of foot number one and number two than between those of number two and number three.

If executed properly, this is one of the most beautifully rhythmic of all gaits. In it and the rack, much weight is carried by the hindquarters. Crouching behind and with extreme animation in front, the animal seems to climb higher and higher with each succeeding step.

Viewed from the side in both the stepping pace and the rack, the horse's body seems to slope downward to the hindquarters. If the extreme upper parts of the front and back legs—that is, the stifle joint and the shoulder—are watched carefully it will be noticed that they start their forward movement almost simultaneously. However, because of the fairly low hind action and extremely high front action, the rear foot necessarily strikes the ground before the front one. With the combination of the crouching form and animated front action, there are moments when both front feet are off the ground at the same time, thereby shifting the entire weight of the horse first to one rear leg and then the other. This displacement of weight causes the hindquarters of the animal to sway ever so slightly from side to side. This feature of the stepping pace is peculiar to it alone, for when the horse speeds into the rack, the weight is not held in suspension for so long a time.

The beauty of the stepping pace lies in its collection and slowness. The rule book states that it shall be no faster than a park trot.

The Rack

The rack is a four-beat gait in which each foot strikes the ground separately in evenly spaced rhythm. This is the reason that it is often called a "single-foot."

It is executed at near racing speed and is by far the fastest of all the "easy gaits." The squatting form and climbing action of the stepping pace are apparent, plus the thrill of tremendous speed. This is one of the best loved spectator gaits, yet it is so strenuous that a horse cannot endure it for long periods. There have been horses that could rack at a speed faster than 2:30 for the mile. The mare Bird Harrison was reputed to be the fastest racker of her day. She showed trials of 2:23 at the pace, and it is said that she could rack faster than she could pace.

The Single-foot

The term "single-foot" is correctly applied to the rack gait. To most people, however, it denotes the easy gait of the Western-type horse. The Western single-foot is a slow-moving gait that is recognized by its shuffling motion. The order of footfalls is almost identical with those of the rack and stepping pace. Its sound is recognizable as four distinct beats.

The speed of the single-foot is comparable to a fox trot or slow running walk. A single-footing horse is capable of performing this gait for long periods without fatigue, and it offers extreme comfort to the rider.

American Saddle Horse

❦ 4 ❦

The American Saddle Horse

"The Peacock of the Horse World" is the phrase aptly used to describe the American Saddle Horse. The long, graceful neck with fine, lofty head and alert ears; the short, straight back and level croup with high-set tail; the powerful, sloping shoulder and depth of chest and heart girth; trim legs that show strength in their well-modeled fineness—these are a few details of Saddle Horse standards.

Everyone who has attended a horse show and seen the animals performing in the fine-harness and the three- and five-gaited classes will agree that the American Saddle Horse breed has attained a pinnacle of fiery elegance among all horses.

Yet the Saddle Horse possesses something that is perhaps more important than his beauty. That is his inherent tendency to do the "easy" gaits. From the explanations in the preceding chapter on gaits we must realize that the

COLONIAL SADDLE HORSES

American Saddle Horse

The American Saddle Horse combines symmetry, power, style, and fineness. Proudness of carriage and perfection of gaits have won this breed acclaim in show-horse circles.

Tapered head is topped with alert, slender ears. Eyes are large and wide-set; muzzle is fine with sensitive nostrils.

Back is extremely short and straight. Barrel is rounded and firmly welded at the flanks. Girth shows considerable depth.

Croup more nearly horizontal than that of any other breed except Arab. Hips rounded; tail set high in the rump.

Best individuals exhibit long, slender, arching necks which rise up loftily from the shoulders. Fineness of the throat is typical.

Legs fine and shapely; tendons clearly modeled. Pasterns long and springy.

Shoulders are well muscled and chest shows sufficient width between forelegs.

Saddle Horse breed stems in part from the early pacers. While Denmark, a Thoroughbred, is listed as the foundation sire of the American Saddle Horse, it is generally agreed that Denmark, being of Oriental extraction, imparted none of the gaiting tendencies to the breed he is credited with founding. Indeed, there were American Saddle Horses standing at the hitching racks of the English colonists long before Imported Hedgeford, the English Thoroughbred, set a hoof on American soil in 1832 and before his illustrious son Denmark was foaled.

From what source, then, did the American colonists secure pacing-gaited stock?

It is a likely possibility that pacing stock existed in Britain even before 55 B.C., the year Julius Caesar conquered the Britons. The fact that from that time on pacing horses were popular is proved by many written records.

The Canterbury monk, William Fitz Stephen, who lived during the reign of Richard the Lionhearted, described in careful detail the pacing gait of horses being brought to the sales field. The Great Seals of the government from the time of King Richard to Queen Elizabeth pictured an armored knight mounted on a pacing horse. In 1509, an official of the Italian Church, one Polydore Virgil, visited England. His writings state that most of the English horses ambled but did not trot.

An Englishman, Blundeville, in the sixteenth century, described at great length the pacing tendencies of the Irish Hobbies and Scotch Galloways. An interesting point in his writings is that when these native mares were crossed with Spanish Jennet stallions, which were of Oriental blood, they produced exceptionally fine saddlers. This observation is particularly interesting here because it was almost this identical cross that centuries later produced the forerunner of the present-day American Saddle Horse through similar crossbreeding of Denmark and the Cockspur mare.

From this and other evidence, it is clear that pacers were English favorites until the early 1600s. Then within a few years, the pacing horse in England almost completely disappeared. The reasons for this decline were several. James I became interested in horses of Oriental blood and influenced horsemen to import Barb and Arab stallions. He himself paid 500 guineas for the Markham Arabian. The English discovered that their once favorite pacers did not compare in beauty with the hot-blooded Orientals. Moreover, the outcross between the Barb stallions and the English mares seemed to produce larger animals than the parent stock.

Perhaps the most important reason for the decline of the pacers was that England was beginning the construction of better roads. Vehicles gradually began to supplant the use of saddle animals. The trotting horse, better suited to pull coaches, rapidly gained favor. The lateral gait fell into disfavor and the diagonal-gaited animals spelled doom for the amblers.

In the new Colonial land, however, there were few roads and they were rough—not much more than forest trails over mountains and through valleys. The subjects of the new land urgently needed a saddle animal adapted to long-distance travel—a horse that was hardy and could carry its rider in sure-footed comfort without fatigue to itself.

The ideal horse for the colonist was the pacer. The horse that had served the English people during the preroad era was the ideal type for the new wilderness trails along the Atlantic frontier. Thus, the amblers were shipped across the Atlantic and were soon found in all parts of the Colonies.

Two areas became especially noted for the excellence of their pacing-gaited stock.

THE NARRAGANSETT HORSES

In the state of Rhode Island there is a bay called Narragansett, so named for a tribe of Indians that formerly dwelt on its banks. Accident, or one of those unaccountable freaks which nature sometimes plays in the animal world, gave rise to a breed of horses which were once well known in America by the name of Narragansetts. They were small, commonly of the color called sorrel in America, and distinguished by their habit of pacing. Horses of this race were, and still are, in much request as saddle horses, on account of their hardiness, and ease of their movements. As they were also sure of foot, the Narragansetts were much sought for by females who were obliged to travel over the roots and holes in new countries.

The above is a quotation from James Fenimore Cooper's *The Last of the Mohicans*. So famous were the little horses inhabiting the area mentioned by Cooper that they were referred to as a breed—the Narragansett Pacer.

A certain mystery as to the origin of this race of horses is hinted at in the quotation. There is also a widely accepted story that Governor Robinson imported a Spanish Jennet stallion which became the ancestor of the Narragansett horses. Some refute this possibility by saying that the Jennets were Oriental and could not have produced pacing colts. However, it is not impossible for the mares to have supplied the pacing gait. As there is also mystery shrouding the extinct Jennet breed, this story seems to me more an attempt to connect two legends.

Another less likely story is that an unknown stallion swam in from the sea to become the founder of the Narragansetts. All these stories seem to point to the fact that the Narragansetts were greatly admired horses, and in view of the lack of evidence, stories pertaining to their origin and ultimate extinction or disappearance were highly imaginative.

An explanation which one historian gives seems logical. He states that the source of this breed was England, as was the case in the other colonies. Rhode Island, however, was settled by liberals from the other New England colonies. In many instances, they were refugees and often just plain fugitives. With many of the inhabitants not as rigidly religious as in some of the other colonies, they were not averse to establishing race tracks and offering prizes to the winners. This led to selective breeding which produced the best and fastest pacers in the British colonies.

In 1721, Dr. James McSparran, an Episcopalian clergyman, visited Rhode Island in the interests of the London Society for the Propagation of the Gospel in Foreign Parts. This gentleman of the cloth seemingly found fault with anything in the New World which differed from its counterpart in his homeland. Hence the sturdy little Narragansett horses bore the brunt of Clergyman McSparran's criticism because they were pacers and not trotters like the horses he knew so well in Britain.

However, in spite of Dr. McSparran's dislike for the Narragansett Pacers, his book *America Dissected,* printed in Dublin in 1753, carries a passage which is a glowing, even if unconscious, tribute to these little horses: "I saw some of them pace a mile in a little more than two minutes, a good deal less than three."

Some analysts interpret this to mean that at least a few of the Rhode Island pacers could travel a mile in approximately 2:15 to 2:20.

Of one thing we can be certain. These astoundingly fast records must have been made on badly constructed tracks and probably with the weight of a rider upon the horse's back. Even with today's light sulkies and fast tracks, horses that travel in harness under 2:05 or even 2:10 are considered close to tops.

From the time of Dr. McSparran's stay in Rhode Island, one century and seventy-six years were to pass before Star Pointer, the first "two-minute horse" in history, would pace his famous mile in 1:59¼ on the twenty-eighth day of August, 1897, on the Readville track near Boston.

It was inevitable that with pre-Revolutionary racing between the country gentlemen of the English colonies, some of the best Narragansett Pacers would be brought into Virginia, Kentucky, and Tennessee.

CANADIAN PACERS

Another area which undoubtedly produced some of the finest stock later to influence the American Saddle Horse was to the north. In the Canadian provinces, a hardy little horse was being developed. He was said to be a cross of French importations with stallions obtained in New England and New York containing a probable mixture of English and Dutch stock. These horses became known as "Canadian Pacers." Early Colonial horsemen bred Canadian mares to Thoroughbred stallions and produced horses highly suited to the needs of the people of those times.

One of the most famous Canadian Pacers was Tom Hal, a blue roan stallion foaled about 1806. He was imported from Canada to Philadelphia and thence to Kentucky. His fastest gait was the pace.

Tom Hal, number 3237 in the *American Saddle Horse Register,* was the founder of the Hal family of Tennessee, the Blue Bull family of Indiana, and the famous Tom Hal Saddlers of Kentucky. As will be noted in later chapters, old Tom Hal's blood influenced two American breeds besides the Saddlers. These were the Standard Breds and the Tennessee Walking Horses.

Many interesting tales are told about the great Tom Hal. His owner, a Dr. Boswell, rode him from Lexington to Louisville, over 80 miles, from sunrise to sunset, and back to Lexington the next day. This feat of endurance was performed at the pace and won for his owner a $100 wager.

Tom Hal was never known to lie down except to roll. During the day or night he could always be found standing or walking. Even when eating, he walked as he masticated his food. This remarkable horse lived to the astonishing age of forty-one years.

These, then, were the contents of the melting pot that went into the making of one of America's great horse breeds—ambling horses from early Britain, the famous Narragansetts, Canadian Pacers, Dutch horses, as well as the beautiful Denmark and his Thoroughbred line with Oriental background.

FURTHER DEVELOPMENT OF THE SADDLER

Today, many people think of the American Saddle Horse as strictly a show animal. Actually, his development in the beginning came about in an entirely different way. Early Saddle Horses were a necessity in an entirely different economic regime. During the early development of the breed and up until the turn of the present century, these horses were used to draw wagons, pull the plow, haul logs, and at other times to transport their owners when horseback travel became necessary.

EARLY ROAD USE

Later, as roads were constructed, the coarser, rougher gaited animals were segregated to perform the heavier duties, while the finer, easier gaited horses were reserved for riding and drawing light vehicles. In these latter animals, owners began to take special pride, and their desire for horses of greater beauty increased.

As the land became more settled, the people began to enjoy an agrarian existence. For instance, early in Kentucky history, county fairs and horse shows became a basic part of their lives, and thus the utility animal became the forerunner of the later show horse. Such meetings encouraged the spirit of competition, and breeders strove to develop quality in their horses. Also, consideration was given to the refinement of the saddle gaits.

EARLY AMERICAN HORSE SHOW

In order to get horses of larger size, with more stamina, fineness, and beauty, breeders began to cross new blood with their saddle-gaited stock. At this point, they turned to horses of Thoroughbred breeding. As we have previously related, Denmark, the Thoroughbred stallion, was bred to the Colonial Saddler known as "the Stevenson mare" of Cockspur breeding, and the product of this union was Gaines' Denmark, foaled in 1851.

As the years rolled on toward the War between the States and past it, great horses were bred and greater colts were foaled.

The four famous sons of Gaines' Denmark—Washington Denmark, Diamond Denmark, Star Denmark and Sumpter Denmark—flashed brilliantly into the horse world. Cabell's Lexington, who traced to famous old Justin

Morgan on his top line and the Tom Hal family on his dam's side, was foaled in 1863. Montrose, the first Saddle Horse to sell for $5,000, was foaled in 1869. Harrison Chief, the founder of the great line of Chief horses, was foaled in 1872. Black Squirrel, sire preeminent, was foaled in 1876. In 1891, Annie C., dam of the famous trio of sons—Montgomery Chief, Bourbon King, and Marvel King—was foaled.

This was a year to note in Saddle Horse history, for it was during that year that such men as General John P. Castleman, Will A. Gaines, W. W. Donnell, E. T. Halsey, Colonel Ion B. Nall, and others, gathered together to form an association to establish and further improve and promote one of the greatest breeds of horses the world has ever known.

These men realized that a great horse breed existed in their midst. They also knew that steps must be taken to protect the Saddle Horse through strict adherence to a recognized type. Better care must be exercised in breeding to encourage rigid selection of both stallions and mares. A register of pedigrees must be set up.

In April, 1891, in the offices of the *Farmers' Home Journal*, the National Saddle Horse Breeders' Association was founded and a Saddle Horse register was provided. Later, in 1899, a resolution was adopted by the stockholders changing the name of the association to American Saddle Horse Breeders' Association.

Soon after establishment of the Association, it was necessary that certain sires be selected to enter as sources of Saddle stock. The list originally selected was as follows:

DENMARK	TEXAS
BRINKER'S DRENNON	PRINCE ALBERT
SAM BOOKER	PETERS' HALCORN
JOHN DILLARD	VARNON'S ROEBUCK
TOM HAL	DAVY CROCKETT (added in 1893)
VAN METER'S WAXY	HARRISON CHIEF (added in 1898)
CABELL'S LEXINGTON	PAT CLEBURNE (added in 1899)
COPPERBOTTOM	COLEMAN'S EUREKA
STUMP THE DEALER	

At the annual meeting of the Association in 1902, the above list was revised and the following stallions were removed and given numbers in the *Register:*

BRINKER'S DRENNON	1600	TEXAS	1604
COPPERBOTTOM	1601	PRINCE ALBERT	1605
VARNON'S ROEBUCK	1602	HARRISON CHIEF	1606
SAM BOOKER	1603		

This reduced the list of foundation sires to ten, as follows:

DENMARK	JOHN DILLARD
TOM HAL	CABELL'S LEXINGTON
COLEMAN'S EUREKA	VAN METER'S WAXY
STUMP THE DEALER	PETERS' HALCORN
DAVY CROCKETT	PAT CLEBURNE

The list remained thus until the Association's annual meeting held in April, 1908, at which time it was decided to recognize the Thoroughbred horse Denmark by Imported Hedgeford alone as foundation sire. The other sires on the list were removed and given numbers in the Noted Deceased Sires List.

Saddle Horse enthusiasts have come to the realization that from the above listed stock two great families stood out. These were the Denmarks and the Chiefs.

The Denmarks are the descendants of Thoroughbred horses whose blood was mixed with others in whom there was a strong pacing tendency. The Denmarks were possessed of extreme fineness and quality, plus the easy-gaited way of traveling, which stemmed from the inherited tendency to pace.

The Chiefs, with equal certainty, are the descendants of Thoroughbred horses whose blood has been mixed with others that were strong in the trotting gait. The Chiefs were more noted than the Denmarks for their loftiness of carriage and extreme action of knee and hock. This speed and brilliancy were undoubtedly inherited from their trotting ancestors.

Harrison Chief, the head of the Chief family, was strictly a trotting-bred horse. He was never trained as a trotter, however, but instead was destined to show in the harness ring, where he was invincible for eight years.

Harrison Chief's sire was Clark Chief 89, by Mambrino Chief 11, by Mambrino Paymaster, by Mambrino, by Imported Messenger (Thoroughbred). It is interesting to note here that though not a trotter himself, Imported Messenger, a Thoroughbred, was the progenitor of the trotting-horse line in America. To add interest to this fact is the significant point that Imported Messenger's sire in England, Mambrino, became the head of the most famous family of British coach horses, which were trotters.

Though Harrison Chief was noted as a sire of Saddle Horses, he was exclusively a harness horse and probably never was saddled in his entire life. It is doubtful that Harrison Chief had within his brain the tendency to pace. However, through his matings, such horses as Montgomery Chief and Bourbon Chief were produced to create the great Chief family of Saddlers. In most Saddlers of top ability at the present time, the qualities of both the Chiefs and the Denmarks have been fused.

The qualities transmitted to the American Saddle Horse by the Thoroughbred line are many, but the qualities of the original Colonial stock should
not be discounted nor dismissed. While the Thoroughbred horse Denmark
was made the sole foundation sire of the American Saddle Horse breed, it is
generally admitted that the real founder of the Denmark family was Denmark's son, Gaines' Denmark 61. The "Stevenson mare," dam of Gaines' Denmark, was a natural ambler. To her must go the credit for the easy saddle
gaits of the Denmark line.

It is interesting to note a few statistics taken from the volumes of the *Saddle
Horse Register*. In the first volume 1,653 entries have direct male trace to
Denmark, F.S., and of these, 1,647 trace through Gaines' Denmark; in the
second volume, out of 2,378 entries tracing to Denmark, F.S., 2,372 are
through Gaines' Denmark. In Volume III, Gaines' Denmark is responsible
for 1,995 of the 1,998 tracing to Denmark, F.S. In Volume IV, out of a total
of 1,282, Gaines' Denmark is responsible for 1,277.

In total figures this indicates that out of 7,311 entries tracing to Denmark,
F.S., 7,291, or all except twenty, traced through Gaines' Denmark. If we are
fair and impartial, this means that we must credit the fine old ambling-gaited
Cockspur mare with 50 per cent of the blood of almost the entire total of
entries.

CONFORMATION OF THE AMERICAN
SADDLE HORSE

Regardless of breed, most good horses can be described in the same terms.
I was once amused at a horseman's description of what constitutes a well-
built horse. He stated that to be well formed a horse must be shaped like a
canoe—the bottom line rounded and full and the top line short.

Another horseman stated the same thing in a different way. A horse, in his
manner of description, should be at the same time both long and short. The
underside must be long to contain a prominent breast, heart girth, abdominal
cavity, and hindquarters. The top line must be short—first, to ensure weight-
carrying ability of back and couplings at the hindquarters, and second, to
cause the proper angle of slope through the shoulders, from withers to breast.

In describing a high-type Saddle Horse we will, of course, find it necessary
to use some of the adjectives and terms that might apply to good horses of
other breeds. However, there are certain characteristics which are more or
less pronounced in the American Saddle Horse. An attempt will be made to
contrast these points with those of other breeds.

The Saddle Horse is usually between 15 and 16 hands in height. Solid colors are most common, frequently with white markings. Chestnuts, bays, blacks, and browns predominate. Incidentally, Saddle Horses are never described as sorrel, that color not being admitted by the *Saddle Horse Register*.

The head is small, with prominent nostrils and large eyes. When viewed from the side, the front of the face is straight, not dished as in the Arabian nor convex as in some draft stock. The ears are pointed and quite slender. They sit well forward and the points "look at each other."

An outstanding characteristic of the model Saddle Horse is his neck, which sweeps upward from the shoulders and arches gracefully at its attachment with the head. This conformation of the neck is one of the reasons for the Saddler's perfection of balance and ability of action. As in other breeds, some individuals become "rooster-necked," usually because the trainer or rider has pulled the head of the horse backward too far without proper flexion at the poll. This, in turn, causes an unsightly bulge of muscles, similar to a goiter, on the underside and an undercurve on the top line. The neck of the Saddle Horse as compared with that of other breeds is usually longer. The neck of the Thoroughbred is possibly as long, but the manner of attachment at the shoulders is different.

The shoulder bone is flat, and if a line were drawn through it from the place of its beginning at the withers to its point at the breast, that line would not be vertical but would be well over 45 degrees from the vertical. This is one of the features that makes this breed a comfort to the rider. The extreme degree of slope cushions the gait as the forefeet strike the ground. Height of front action is also improved because of this feature.

When the barrel, or torso, of the American Saddle Horse is viewed in profile, its bottom line should be full and deep at the front end, curving slightly upward as it merges into the flanks and hindquarters. The top line should come very nearly straight and horizontally back from the withers and merge without pronounced angle into the croup. This lack of angle at the juncture of the back and hips is caused by two characteristics. First, the muscles over the loins and kidney area are powerful, and second, the croup of the Saddle Horse is almost horizontal. The straight croup is similar to the Arabian's and unlike that of the Quarter Horse. The naturally high-set tail also pronounces the straightness of the croup.

When viewed from the top, the barrel is not bulky at the forward part where the rider's legs fit, but the ribs are sprung wider back toward the hips.

The forelegs of the Saddler should be straight, well-muscled in the forearm, and cleanly modeled in the lower leg. By this it is meant that there is a good definition between bones and tendons. The bones of the lower legs, both fore and hind, are "flat." A simple explanation of this is to say that when viewed from the front, the bone appears narrow; when viewed from the side, it is wider. The reason for this is readily understood when we consider the function of the horse's legs. They were meant to carry him forward. The stress of forward movement does not so strenuously affect a bone that has its greatest dimension from front to back.

The pasterns are moderately long and sloping. This feature also adds to the springiness and easy-riding quality of the breed.

The hips of the Saddle Horse are rounded. The peak that is often so pronounced in the Thoroughbred is absent here. Good muscles run well down into the gaskins. The hock is neatly shaped. Observation has led me to believe that the Saddle Horse's leg is more curving as it goes into the hock than is the case in the Thoroughbred, Morgan, and Quarter Horse. Horsemen express this feature in various terms. When it is extreme, the horse is referred to as "dog-legged" or "crooked-legged." Considering the function of the Saddle Horse, this should not be considered faulty unless exaggerated. It adds to the springiness of the animal's gait and, furthermore, I believe, it aids the forward engagement of the hind legs and execution of the gaits and action for which the Saddler is so famous. It can easily be seen that if the leg is slightly curved between the stifle and the hock there is an opportunity for more action and height of lift at the point of the hock when the horse is in motion.

The feet are of moderately good size. When the feet are properly cared for and the animal's diet is correct, the walls of the hoof are straight-grained and tough. Aside from Hackneys and show ponies, no other horse is required to carry a proportionately longer foot and with more weight than the Saddler. If his feet were small, they could not stand up under such requirements.

Now that we have taken the Saddle Horse apart, let us look at him as a whole. There is an absence of angles. The Saddler is closely knit, yet he does not give the appearance of being chunky.

Top Saddlers have a great deal of poise and gracefulness. In action, they are naturally "showy." To strut and show pride is perhaps one of their most admired qualities. In the show ring, this is called "bloom" or "show-horse presence."

THE AMERICAN SADDLE HORSE IN THE SHOW RING

Although show horses are distinctly a minority group, they serve as a measuring stick of quality. Horse shows become proving grounds for the production of better stock. In the show ring, the performing ability of one horse can be tested and compared with another. The champions of the show ring have much to do with improving the qualities of lesser known horses which serve for pleasure and utility.

The *American Horse Shows Association Rule Book* divides the Saddle Horse division into three parts: three-gaited and five-gaited Saddle Horses and fine-harness horses.

THREE-GAITED
SADDLE HORSE

The Three-gaited Horse

Three-gaited Saddle Horses are distinguished by their shaved manes and tails. The qualifying gaits are

1. *The walk:* true, flat-footed, rapid, and elastic.
2. *The trot:* square, collected, balanced, and free from Hackney form.
3. *The canter:* smooth, slow, and straight on both leads.

In championship classes, this type of horse is judged on performance, presence, quality, conformation, and manners. Importance of the listed items is in the order named.

The three-gaited Saddle Horse, or "walk-trot" as he is frequently called, should be extremely fine. He should have a long, slender neck with a fine throttle, or throat latch. The withers should be high and well pronounced.

The bones, tendons, and general structure should carry out the pattern of fineness and quality.

The *walk* is the slowest of the three gaits that the walk-trot is required to perform. The most desirable walk is one in which the horse moves straight forward in a free, fast, flat-footed manner. The gait should be performed in perfect four-beat rhythm, with the knees and hocks working and the hind feet striding well forward. The head and neck should nod in perfect coordination with the movement and rhythm of the legs. A feeling of balance and spirited-ness should pervade the bearing of the animal.

The *trot* should be square and in even one-two cadence. The horse should not appear to be climbing at this gait; neither should the speed be too rapid.

The foot and leg of a walk-trot should travel at an even, consistent speed at all times. As the horse moves past us in profile, the foot should transcribe a circle. This is the meaning of the term "circular trot." The "high-school" trot is undesirable in a three-gaited horse. Some horses are high-schooled in their early training to force them into higher leg action. Such training may cause the animal seemingly to hold the foot for a slight instant when up or to stretch it forward in a pointing, knee-stiffening manner. This, in turn, may cause the foot to "dwell" clumsily on the ground. Jerkiness or mincingness is undesirable, as the foot should flow smoothly and naturally in the circular manner described above.

There is no set rule by which to measure the most desirable height of action. However, if we were to imagine a horizontal line drawn through the forearm at the moment of maximum elevation of the foreleg, the forearm should be horizontal or with the knee slightly above the horizontal line. If a horizontal line were drawn through the point of the elbow of the foreleg at this position and extended back to the hindquarters, the point of the hock would nearly touch it.

The *canter* as performed by this type of animal is not a speed gait; in fact, slowness is one of the prime requisites. The horse should possess at all times a feeling of perfect balance and control. At this gait the horse should rock gently before and behind, with a fair amount of leg action all around. This is the explanation of the "two-ended" canter.

Roxie Highland, foaled in 1924, was considered by many to be the out-standing three-gaited mare of all time. Unquestionably she was the greatest of her day.

Originally called Belle Delight, Roxie Highland won 257 firsts out of 260 times shown. Another astonishing fact is that she earned in cash winnings $65,000 in her eight years of showing. No horse before her time had ever won the McElroy $1,000 Challenge Cup twice in succession. Roxie Highland won this coveted award six times in six successive years.

Three-gaited horses are also shown in a class designated as "road hacks" or sometimes as "park hacks." The road-hack class should show the animal's suitability for roadwork under saddle. The horse is shown in the flat-footed walk at a loose rein, a collected and extended trot, an easy canter, and a hand gallop, with the ability to push on at greater speed if the judge so orders. The road hack must be so easily controlled that he can be changed from any gait to the flat-footed walk with a loose rein.

The three-gaited horse is shown in harness only in a combination class. First the horses are shown to a suitable four-wheeled vehicle at the trot and walk. The driver remains seated in his buggy, after showing in harness, until the judge has inspected all horses in the ring. Then the horse is unhitched and saddled and shown under saddle at the three gaits. In a combination class, the horse is judged 50 per cent for suitability to harness and 50 per cent for suitability as a saddle mount.

The Five-gaited Horse

The five-gaited Saddle Horse differs from the three-gaited in that he carries a natural long mane and a full tail and is decorated with a braid of ribbon in his foretop and another in the first lock of mane behind the bridle notch.

FIVE-GAITED
SADDLE HORSE

The qualifying gaits are

1. *Walk:* same as for three-gaited horses.
2. *Trot:* same as for three-gaited horses.
3. *Canter:* same as for three-gaited horses.
4. *The slow gait:* the stepping pace, no faster than a park trot.
5. *The rack:* an elastic four-beat gait in which each foot strikes the ground in rhythmic sequence, and as fast as the horse is capable of traveling without loss of form, and without inclination to pace.

In general, the five-gaited horse is not considered to be as fine as the three-gaited individual. He must certainly be sturdy and powerful if he is to show two additional gaits; especially the rack, which is strenuous to perform and is executed at racing speed. The Thoroughbred race horse exerts himself at full speed for only one or two minutes at a time. A class for five-gaited horses frequently consumes the better part of an hour.

The walk, trot, and canter of the five-gaited horse should be as nearly perfect as those exhibited by the three-gaited horse. However, all things being equal, it is perhaps the slow gait and rack which the judge considers more strongly in this type of horse.

The Fine-harness Horse

Harness horses of many different types and breeds are shown in horse-show rings—heavy-harness horses, which may or may not be heavy Hackneys; Hack-

FINE-HARNESS
HORSE

ney ponies in different hitches such as tandems, teams, singles, unicorns; harness show ponies. Nearly every show has classes for light-harness horses, usually Standard Bred and called "roadsters. Each harness class is judged in a different way.

The *American Horse Shows Association Rule Book* says, of fine-harness horses:

> The horse must be of American Saddle Horse Breed, must wear long mane and tail and should be shown to a four-wheeled road show wagon without top, or with top down. Light harness with a snaffle bit is required.
> The horse shall be shown at an animated park trot, extreme speed to be penalized. He must stand quietly and back readily, good manners essential.

Championship classes are judged on performance, presence, quality, conformation, and manners.

In order to understand better the role of this horse, let us consider his original use. In the early days, horses of this type were light utility animals. They may have carried the master under saddle on business excursions during the week, and on week ends they would be hitched and driven to church and the social affairs that interested the lady of the household.

Their driving excursions were not generally long, fast trips but short drives on smooth roads. A horse with proud, animated action was admired, and of course good manners were a necessary requirement.

Fine-harness teams were popular in earlier times, both for utility and in the show ring. Indian Chief was considered to be one of the greatest harness horses of all time. It was a pair of Indian Chiefs that the friends of President Garfield bought when they were looking for the finest driving team in America.

Lady DeJarnette (by Indian Chief) was the most brilliant harness mare of her day, winning the highest honors wherever she was shown. Hitched with Harrison Chief, the old founder of the Chief family, she was stiff competition with other teams of good quality.

As in almost all harness classes, fine-harness horses are judged at the trotting gait. The head should be carried high, though it is not essential that the chin be tucked in to the degree that is desirable for a horse under saddle. Every good judge and trainer wishes to see the gait decisive, positive, and bold, without fumbling or mincing. The animal should "step away." There should be no teetering, skipping, hopping, dwelling, or pointing. There should be an indication of grace and tirelessness, and the feet and legs should move forward in a straight line, with no trace of winging or plaiting. Above all, the fine-harness horse must be "airy" and light-going, with excellent all-round carriage.

The ideal harness horse is extremely fine, at the same time filling the harness. As harness training is usually a strict essential in the education of any horse, many that are first shown in fine harness are later trained and prepared for the saddle classes. The clipped mane and tail of the three-gaited horse precludes his use in any harness performance except three-gaited combination ride-and-drive classes, but many gaited horses are shown both in fine-harness and saddle events. Usually, an individual will be superior in one or the other.

Occasionally, there are animals that show equally well in fine-harness and the gaited classes. One noted example was Miss Rex, a steel-gray mare of exquisite beauty, trained and exhibited by Tom Bass. Miss Rex was an outstanding all-round winner.

One of the greatest recent-day harness horses was Vanity 23974, registered as Meadow Vanity, who made her first appearance at the Illinois State Fair in 1938. Many horsemen compare her career to that of the invincible Lady DeJarnette of earlier fame; in her entire seven-year career, though shown in great competition, she was defeated only three times, and these in her four-year-old form. This beautiful bay mare trotted her way up the ladder of fame by receiving 266 firsts, including championships and grand championships. She was honored with the *American Horseman's* title of "Grand Champion of Winners" for her accumulation of brilliant successes during the year 1943.

GREAT SADDLERS OF THE PAST

Many volumes would be required to relate the stories of all the outstanding gaited horses that have flashed brilliantly over the tanbark rings and county tracks of the past. The names of great mares—Lou Chief, Gypsy Queen, Edna May, Hazel Dawn—have been emblazoned on the Saddle Horse records. Montrose, Black Squirrel, Bourbon Chief, Cabell's Lexington are only a few of the great horses—champions whose stories time does not dim.

Rex McDonald was one of the greatest of them all. It is believed that he did more to popularize the American Saddler than any other horse of his breed. Certainly his remarkable prepotency has done much to improve the blood of the Saddle Horse of America.

The interesting chain of circumstances which led up to producing Rex McDonald involved two other famous horses. One was Rex Denmark, his sire, and the other was Black Squirrel, sire of his dam.

Rex Denmark was purchased by the Harrison brothers in Kentucky. The Harrisons showed Rex Denmark successfully at many fairs. Black Squirrel, another great stallion, bred in 1877 by J. C. Graves of Kentucky, and brought to Mexico, Missouri, as a three-year-old by L. B. Morris, was turned over to Joe McDonald for training.

Asked to compare the two stallions, Joe McDonald made his prophetic remark that has lived through the decades wherever Saddle Horse enthusiasts gather: "Rex Denmark is a bulldog. He has plenty of fight, and is not beaten until the last ribbon is tied. But Black Squirrel is the king of them all. To him I am going to breed my Star Davis mare. If she produces a filly colt, I will breed it to Rex Denmark—and if they 'nick' properly, they will produce the greatest show horse we have ever seen."

Mr. McDonald brought his mare to the court of Black Squirrel, as he had promised. From this union was produced a chestnut filly which he named Lucy Mack, in honor of his wife. Lucy Mack was the first step toward his goal of achieving the greatest show horse in the world.

The descriptions relate that Lucy Mack was a large and rangy mare standing 16 hands high and weighing 1,200 pounds or more when mature. One account states that Joe McDonald brought his mare to the Harrison farm, at Auxvasse, to breed to Montrose 106. However, it was out of the question for him to breed Lucy Mack to Montrose, for that stallion's book was full for the season, and the Harrisons persuaded Joe McDonald to breed Lucy Mack to Rex Denmark. Thus, through the advice of others, he carried out his promise of several years previous.

On May 30, 1890, Lucy Mack foaled her first colt by Rex Denmark.

The accounts have it that both Mr. McDonald and the Harrisons were not too pleased with the result. The little black fellow was about as poor a specimen of a colt of fine blood as one ever saw. He had long hair, and it is said that he was a short, punched-up colt both in neck and body. The only good points he seemed to possess were his beautiful head, ears, and eyes.

If Mr. McDonald was disappointed at that point, he was not a month later, for upon inspecting the colt, who had by that time grown beyond the highest expectations, he said:

"Boys, we have made a mistake, for this colt is far the best I have yet seen, and if he develops as I now believe he will, he will be one of the greatest stallions from this time on."

Later in the fall of 1890, Mr. McDonald's health caused him to disperse his stock at auction. When the auctioneer's gavel finally descended, R. T.

Freeman of Mexico, Missouri, for a price of $105, was the new owner of the black colt at Lucy Mack's side.

In due time, Rex McDonald's ripple of fame started and grew ever wider. His first winnings were in his own county. Great horses began to tumble before the young warrior's advance. Each time he entered a show ring, a new star was added to his crown of achievement. At the age of three, at the St. Louis Fair, he defeated his own sire, Rex Denmark. In 1894, he defeated the great Lou Chief at Mexico, Missouri, and again at the St. Louis Fair in the sweepstakes class. Monte Cristo, Jr. fell before his onslaught in the stallion class.

It is sad to relate that Mr. Joe McDonald did not live to see his prediction concerning Rex McDonald come to pass.

Rex's popularity increased with his age. In describing this great Saddle stallion, the late Herbert J. Krum wrote:

No saddle horse has ever lived that has had quite the same place in the minds and hearts of the American people as has Rex McDonald. No other stallion in this country has ever been so well known, and his name is a household word throughout the length and breadth of the land. He is exactly the same thing to the Saddle Horse as is the immortal Dan Patch to the harness horse, and he counts his admirers by thousands all over the country. . . .

He is a horse of beautiful conformation, of that blue-black raven dye of color which shines and shimmers in the sunlight of the open air, or beneath the electric lights. . . .

He has a beautiful tail which he carries in a proud and proper fashion which is the result of nature and not of art, nor of man's appliances. . . . He was a horse that in motion had that stealthy, cat-like, creeping suppleness and grace which is sometimes found in horses and occasionally in human beings. He never made a slow motion nor an awkward one. In walking he steps with an exaggerated action as though he scorned the earth and was ever upon dress parade had he but himself alone for an audience.

In his slow gaits of which he was a master, he portrayed the poetry of motion, and suggested the embodiment of ease for a rider. He cantered in collected form, always maintaining a perfect balance and with a retarded movement which seemed to make him suggest a rocking chair or cradle. At the trot he went with the straightness of an arrow, and the perfect rhythm one-two unison. But it was the rack which was his especial glory. . . . At this gait he had the most remarkable speed and a fairly dazzling brilliancy of motion. It was not necessary with him as it is with so many other saddle horses for the rider to jerk and haul and hold his horse together, lifting his head and keeping up a continual duel with the bit.

Rex would rack as though it was the most natural thing in the world for him to do, and would step at a thirty gait if urged by his rider, though the latter laid the reins upon his neck and folded his arms. It is not possible for the human mind to conceive a form of locomotion that is more completely the embodiment of ease and comfort in movement than to sit upon the back of this horse when performing at this gait.

It is said that Rex McDonald suffered only six defeats in his entire career. Notwithstanding his popularity and the high esteem in which he was held by everyone, because of the caliber of his competition he had to fight harder for his championships than almost any other horse ever exhibited. True, he knew defeat on several occasions, but as Tom Bass, the world-famous and beloved Negro trainer, so beautifully expressed it—and Tom Bass rode horses which defeated Rex—he wished to feel that he defeated the rider and not the immortal Rex.

TRAINING

A sage remark made by an old-time horseman sticks in one's memory: "In order to train a colt," he said solemnly, "you've got to have more time than he has."

Every good horse trainer will tell you that the most important thing about training any horse is first to understand the individual character of the animal with which you are working. The animal should be studied in each phase of his training before putting any leather or hand on him. Once you are convinced that your analysis will produce the desired results, proceed with it until that bit of education is thoroughly understood by the student. Too many colts are confused by being presented with a second phase of training before they have learned the first.

Naturally, an intelligent horse will learn more quickly than one which is dull. Remember, however, that this same intelligent horse will also learn a bad habit more quickly.

Another thing to remember from the beginning is that horses are most frequently taught to do things through association with force. For instance, a show horse is supposed to stand in a posed position, with front and hind legs stretched slightly. Most trainers teach the colt to pose by thumping him on the back of the forelegs with their toe or a whip. When they mount, they jab him in the elbow with their boot, which is unsightly to the spectators and unpleasant to the horse. We must admit that this is a method of force from beginning to end, with no signal with which to associate it.

In my opinion there is a better method which I have used with success on several saddle mounts. Stand at the colt's side, holding his head in place with the left hand on the halter or bridle. See that the hind feet are in the properly aligned position opposite each other. Now place the right hand at his withers, with the thumb on the near side and the fingers on the off side. Bear in mind that this position of the right hand is one that can easily be assumed when sitting in the saddle.

With one of your toes touch the near leg on the tendon just above the fetlock joint and at the same time push the animal slightly away from you with your thumb. This will shift his weight to the right leg and allow him to lift his left foot and set it forward at the suggestion of mild force from your toe. The moment the left foot is solidly on the ground, pull the animal toward you and repeat the performance with his right foot. When he is in the pose you desire, repeat the word "stand" to him.

By this method the student soon learns to associate the pressure on the sides of his withers with the fact that you wish him to extend his forelegs. When you are mounted, depending on which side you press his withers, he will extend either his left or right foot.

Everyone may not wish to teach his horse to pose, but this bit of training procedure is given as an example of the way in which a horse associates a signal, your hand on his withers, with force, your toe on his leg. Bear in mind that the signal must be concise and always the same. The force should not be too severe, lest the colt become fearful and forget the purpose of the lesson.

One precaution might be mentioned. Colts of this breeding have an inherent love of people, and their fearlessness may cause them to allow more intimate fondling. Care should be exercised that they do not become spoiled because of this. It may seem fun to tease the colt into begging for sugar by nuzzling around your pockets, but there may be times when this will be extremely annoying, especially when you are trying to get him to pay attention to a lesson you are teaching him. The feed box is a good place to feed the horse, and he will appreciate it just as much, because he is primarily interested in getting something to eat.

Saddle Horses may be more high-strung than those of some other breeds. Be careful not to abuse their sensitivity by training periods that are too lengthy and, above all, punish them exceedingly little and not harshly. Initial training of the American Saddle colt does not differ from the methods used on the young of other breeds.

After the colt has learned to allow his trainer to handle him and pick up his feet, to be tied and led, to stand and be "long-lined" in a circle, his training may follow different courses, depending upon the use to which he will be put.

I am firmly convinced that almost every type of horse should receive harnesswork as a part of his schooling, and that this should commence when he is eighteen months to two years of age. If a colt's training is delayed until he is large enough to ride, he may also be strong enough to give the trainer trouble and make it necessary to resort to severe methods of control. Harnesswork seems to be more natural to a horse that has not yet felt the weight of a rider. He has been taught to lead and have the halter placed on his head. The bitting harness is only a step removed from the halter, but a weight upon his back is quite a different thing to him. It is best that he know the signals "get up," "whoa," and "back," and the meaning of the reins before he has the added worry of a rider. Many good trainers jog their show horses more often than they ride them, in the belief that harnesswork steadies an animal more effectively than does saddle work.

When working the colt, you should protect his legs with quarter and shin boots. His awkwardness and the excitement of the new phase of training may cause him to do injury to himself if this precaution is not taken.

Briefly, the bitting rig is a simple harness composed of bridle, surcingle, crupper, overcheck, and side checks. Later, this harness can be used for ground driving by removing the side checks and replacing them with lines, which should be long enough to place the trainer a good distance behind the colt's heels. The primary purpose of the bitting rig is to compel the colt to set his head in the proper position; also it familiarizes him with a harness and its discipline.

The stall is a good place in which to introduce the colt to the bitting rig. Some trainers then prefer to turn the harnessed colt at liberty in a small enclosed area so that he may become acquainted with this new form of restriction by himself. Other trainers immediately attach a lunge line to the bridle and, with the aid of an assistant to urge the colt forward from behind, circle the pupil in both directions.

After a number of short daily lessons, the colt will cease to fret at the bit and learn to flex the muscles in his neck. The side checks are removed at this point and replaced with driving lines. For the sake of safety to the colt, two persons may do this phase of the training. An assistant attaches the lunge line to the bridle and stands in the center while the trainer drives the colt around in a circle with the long lines. The assistant can be dispensed with as soon as the animal gains sufficient experience to travel in a straight line. If he is harnessed so that the lines are kept low on either side of his hips, it will eliminate his tendency to turn around and face the driver.

In this phase of training, the colt should never be kept in the checks longer than ten or fifteen minutes without respite, and the daily lesson should not be longer than thirty to forty-five minutes.

It is a good idea to start the foregoing training in the fall, keeping the colt at it for only a few weeks. He may then be roughed out for the winter without further training, except the usual handling, leading, and tying.

Early the following spring, his education may be resumed. He will not have forgotten his earlier training and will go ahead rapidly. After working him again in the bitting rig for a few days to brush him up on the finer points, you may hitch him with harness to a breaking cart.

It may be advisable to use an assistant again with the lunge line attached to the bridle. Often an older horse working loose alongside the colt will give him confidence and aid in teaching him signals and commands. These, we repeat, should be concise and always the same.

If it is planned to show the colt in fine harness, it is well to continue with his training and enter him in late showings for junior horses. He should not be shown more than a few times, and then only with horses of his own class. Remember, he is still a baby, in all probability does not fill his harness like a mature horse, and is certainly not yet strong enough to withstand arduous travel and the excitement of a horse show.

After such fall showings, the colt may again be let down for winter. Early the next spring, his training should be resumed in earnest. Now that he is older he will be able to undergo more strenuous training. He is now ready to start developing for more highly competitive classes. He can be worked for longer periods. Perfection of gaits, consistency of performance, and those points which make a high-type harness horse may be inculcated in him.

If he is to be trained as a saddle animal, this is the proper time to commence such training. Whether the horse is to be used as a three-gaited or five-gaited show horse or pleasure Saddle Horse does not alter the early training. We shall assume that the initial stages of saddling, bridling, mounting, etc., have been done months prior to this time.

If the colt has become accustomed to the saddle and snaffle bridle and has been allowed to walk, trot, and gallop freely, the next step is to add the curb bit and begin to teach him collection at the various gaits.

The terms "collection," "flexion," "suppleness," and "balance" may be confusing to the aspiring trainer, but a horse that is collected presents an entirely different appearance from one which is not.

Note that the collected horse seems more compact—his front and hindquarters are in harmony. His head is up and his face is nearly vertical. His neck is arched. Legs give the appearance of being well under him. His entire physical structure is like a spring, capable of any movement. He is mentally alert, ready for any command. Every nerve and muscle of his body is beautifully poised.

COLLECTED   UNCOLLECTED

Compare this appearance with the picture of the "strung out" horse. He is not ready for any sudden movement. If there were a rider on his back, the horse would be incapable of immediate response to the commands of his master. He is sluggish and awkward in his movements and lacks the spirited brilliance of the balanced horse.

It is an interesting fact that one and the same horse can present both appearances, depending upon how he is ridden. The rider, through training and proper use of hands, legs, and weight, can bring about this change.

The word "supple" means (1) pliant, flexible; (2) yielding, compliant, not obstinate; (3) bending to the humor of others. The curb bit is one of the tools used to aid in suppling a horse. Its tendency is to tuck the chin and thereby cause the horse to place weight on his haunches. It can easily be seen that a horse's head is used for balance. If the nose is thrust forward, more weight is thrown on the forelegs. If the horse can be made to yield, by arching his neck and tucking his chin, he immediately changes his center of balance back toward the hindquarters, his most powerful propelling area.

Almost everyone has heard that a horse must "go into the bit." This does not mean that he must pull hard on the reins, for this would defeat the purpose; it means that the animal must contact the bit with the bars of his mouth sufficiently to feel any movement of the reins. Lightness of this contact is desirable because it is then that he is most sensitive to hand signals.

The same lightness is desired in the rider's leg contact at his sides. The better students of dressage riding have developed this sensitivity of legs and hands to the extent that the casual observer can detect no movement on the part of the rider as his mount is put through the various movements.

If the process of suppling the colt has been successful, it will affect each gait at which he travels. Instead of clopping along in a haphazard manner at the walk, trot, slow gait, rack, and canter, he will make of each of these a beautifully poised action.

The Walk

As we have said, the walk is a four-beat gait. In teaching the horse to perform it properly we must urge him forward so that he does not acquire lazy habits. At the same time, he should not be excited nor pushed to the extent that he jigs. There is nothing more exasperating than to ride a horse that will not walk but instead prances continually. Furthermore, there is no show class that I know of which calls for the jig as one of its gaits, and it is definitely not a pleasure gait.

The Trot

We know that the trot is a diagonal, two-beat gait. If the horse has been driven, he will undoubtedly have developed a fair trot. Most horses will assume this gait when pushed beyond the walk. The trotting gait should be bold, square, and with a fair amount of speed. If we maintain the horse in collection, we will improve his animation and style.

Proper shoeing and weighting will help increase foot and leg action. Through intelligent, corrective shoeing it is often possible to eliminate imperfections of gait due to an unbalanced foot. However, it should be clearly understood that iron alone will not put proper action on a horse.

At early stages of saddle training, the colt should not be asked for extremely long periods of collection. Let him rest occasionally, for he is using muscles that are not yet hardened to this new stress. If this warning is not heeded, he may "lay into the bit" and become a "borer" with a hard mouth, or if your pressure is too insistent he may get behind the bit and become "rooster-necked" or a "skygazer." The contact which is maintained on the reins must at all times be "alive." When the colt yields, the trainer must lessen the pressure, and when the colt extends his nose, the trainer, with slight pulsating pulls, must again set his head properly. At all times the colt should be kept going on a straight line forward. He should never be allowed to break out of his gait until the signal is given to change. He should be started at the different gaits from a flat walk. He should not be changed from one gait to another too often. Let him work long enough in each one to learn something about it.

The Slow Gait and Rack

Up to this point, the training for all saddle colts is much the same. The next steps, however, are determined by his future use. If he is to be a three-gaited or pleasure horse, we proceed with the canter. If he is to be trained in the slow gait and rack, we should commence with these before the canter. We should at all times refrain from skipping around in training the individual gaits. A child does not learn to spell before he recognizes the letters of the alphabet. Neither does he learn to add before he can count. A colt should not be taught to trot until he can walk fairly well under saddle, and certainly no attempt should be made to teach him the slow gait and rack before he has learned to do a square trot.

As we have pointed out, the American Saddle Horse contains within his brain the instinct to do the "easy" gaits. Almost every expert agrees that these gaits stem from the pace.

Different trainers have different methods for awakening this instinctive gait within the colt. Some pull the front shoes and let the feet become tender. Others work the colt down a slight grade. One trainer in whom I have great confidence works the colt with a snaffle bit and a martingale. The colt's head is moved slightly from side to side and held back, while at the same time he is urged to go on with the legs. The rider's body feels the saddle gait and helps with its weight. It is a happy moment when the colt first "hits a lick." With patience, these instances become more numerous, and the colt should be allowed to know through an encouraging voice that he is doing what is expected of him.

After a few lessons, the pupil will be going at a four-beat gait with consistency. At first, it will be awkward and he may wind and twist a great deal. Needless to say, the young animal should not be kept at this gait for long periods. It has always seemed to me that a gait of this nature requires considerable concentration on the part of the performer. He is handling each foot separately with an almost relentless rhythm. This rhythm must become a pattern in his brain that burns deeper and deeper until it controls completely the nervous system to the legs.

As the colt becomes more proficient at the new gait, the trainer should again strive to collect him into proper form and begin to urge him to greater speed. At first, under pressure, he may try to break into a trot, or he may start to hitch behind in an attempt to gallop. Worst of all, he may settle into an outright pace. None of these should be allowed. All are an indication that his mind or body is being pushed beyond ability, and the best policy is to start over again or, better yet, rest him until the next day.

Breaking to a trot or gallop may be fairly simple to correct, but beware that you do not let him fall into the easy habit of pacing. All sorts of remedies are suggested. Some say the animal can be corrected by lessening curb pressure so that he can get his weight forward; others advise the opposite. Crossed hobbles are sometimes resorted to, but they should never be used except by an expert. One trainer's remedy is to raise the horse's head with the snaffle bit. Another believes that a severe curb bit is the answer.

It must be realized that all horses succumb to different methods, and the trainer should analyze carefully which method will work best for him. It always holds good, however, to start with the essentials. Anyone with a trained ear can sense the true four-beat gait. In the colt's first training, deviation from the proper gait should never be allowed. It is much easier to train him properly at first than to correct something that he has learned wrong.

The Canter

In Chapter 3, we described the gallop as an uneven four-beat gait. The canter is actually a slow, collected gallop. We may experience some difficulty in the first stages of training this gait, mainly because the colt recognizes it as the one with which he has heretofore attained speed.

In the pasture there is usually a transition of medium speed at the trot before changing to the gallop. One of the main objectives is to teach the colt that he must commence to canter from either a standstill or a flat walk. There are two reasons for this. First, he must learn that the canter is not a speed gait. There should be no excitement in connection with it. The second reason is that if he is permitted to break from the rack or trot into the canter, he will surely ruin those gaits; he will not learn to attain speed at the rack or trot if he is permitted to change to the gallop while executing them.

It is essential that leg, weight, and hand signals be utilized from the beginning so that he will associate the canter with *them* rather than with the fact that he was rushed into a fast way of traveling.

Making the proper lead is another factor in the canter. If a horse is traveling in a circle to the left, or making turns in that direction, he should lead to the left, and vice versa. His safety is involved with this technique. If the horse is turning to the left and leading with the *right* foreleg, he is apt to trip by crossing in front. All classes in the show ring are judged quite closely on this point.

When a horse begins to canter, he usually lifts himself in front and places his hind feet well forward under his body. It is at this precise moment that he determines with which side he will lead. One or the other of the hind legs will carry weight first. If the right hind foot is placed on the ground first, he will automatically be on the *left* lead.

Most horsemen, of course, look at the forelegs to determine with which leg the horse is leading. If he leads with his left foreleg, that one will rise higher than the other. The rider cannot see the hind legs, and if he cannot sense the lead by feeling, he must look at the front legs. It has been my experience that if the rider sits in a normal position and looks down past the front of the shoulder, he will usually be able to see the knee of the leading foreleg, because of its high action at each stride.

An important point, noted in the chapter on gaits, is that the leading forefoot hits the ground after the opposite forefoot and rises first. In other words, the nonleading leg carries weight for a longer period of time at each stride than the leading leg.

There are two methods for setting the horse at the correct lead. The most common method is called the "lateral aid." Assuming that the left lead is to be taken, the horse is flexed, and the rider leans to the left and slightly forward. The offreins are used as a bearing against the horse's neck, and the near reins are opened away from the neck. Both legs exert pressure, with the right heel or spur further back than the left.

The "diagonal aid" is different from the lateral in that the weight of the rider is placed on the opposite side. Assuming that the left lead is being taken, the rider leans slightly back and to the right. The animal's head is turned slightly to the right with the offrein, and the head is lifted with the near rein. The right spur is pressed behind the girth, and the left is used farther forward. Some trainers touch the left elbow of the horse with the toe.

The theory of the diagonal aid is that the weight is away from the shoulder and side that should remain light. This method has considerable merit because it allows for the fact that the horse leads first with his hind legs. With the rider's weight placed to the right rear, the off hind leg is encouraged to lead first to support this shifting of weight. Once the canter is started, the rider will lean to the left when turning to the left to maintain balance.

With the diagonal aids, the horse is less likely to break into a "false lead," wherein the forelegs are forced to lead correctly but the hind legs lead incorrectly. Referred to as a "cross canter," this occurs frequently when horses are changed from one lead to the other while in suspension or when the horse is in motion. It is extremely uncomfortable, and the rider feels that the horse is twisting under him. In such cases, the animal should be stopped immediately and started again correctly.

In the first cantering lessons, the colt will undoubtedly take a few trotting steps before galloping and will have more speed than is desired in a canter. If he has been worked in collected form at the other gaits, he will be more easily controlled at this point.

In teaching the slow canter and proper leads, many trainers work the pupil in a small circular ring. It is extremely difficult for a horse to lead off improperly if he is being worked in a small circle, and the confining enclosure will also make it impossible for him to generate much speed.

Once the colt has hit a gallop, it is desirable to let him remain at it two or three minutes so that he will know he is doing the right thing. He should be soothed and encouraged by voice while he is moving; when stopped, he should be further rewarded with a few pats on the neck. If the colt performs properly a couple of times at his leads, he should be rested until the next day. It is always wise to discontinue the lesson on a happy note. Even if the colt refuses to take his leads properly at first, he should not be abused or worked too long. This will only confuse him and tend to make·him "sour."

As soon as the colt seems to understand the lead signals and the desirability of slowness at this gait, he should be worked in a larger, oval ring.

Incidentally, horses at liberty in pasture rarely take the improper lead. In my years of observing them I have never seen one make a mistake. Under saddle, most horses seem to be "left-footed," and it is 'next to impossible to force some of them to take the right-hand lead. A few are "right-footed." Working in a small circle may be most beneficial in such cases.

Backing the Colt

Unfortunately, many horses have not been taught to back easily and readily upon command. Every horse should obey this command willingly. Most show classes require it, and even if your riding is altogether for pleasure, it is still essential.

This phase of training should begin with the trainer on the ground. If the colt is in harness, allow him to stand quietly a few moments, then pick up the lines so that he will pay attention to you. At the moment you say "back," exert slight jerks on one line and then the other. Under no circumstances should you drag him backward on his haunches.

If he does not respond after several such attempts, it may be necessary to use an assistant. One procedure is to have the assistant stand directly in front of the colt with a whip in his hand. When the trainer directs the colt from behind, the assistant gives the colt light taps of the whip across the forelegs. Another method is similar except that the assistant approaches the colt's face with the brush end of a broom. He will automatically back away from it.

Every effort should be made to keep the colt in a straight line as he moves backward. At first, two or three steps are sufficient. A short lesson every day will soon teach the pupil to back as much as eight or ten steps at a time. When the colt has backed a few steps, he should immediately be made to take a step or two forward, otherwise he may learn to "lay away" from the bit or, to use another horsemen's expression, "get behind the bit."

In teaching the colt to back under saddle, we again commence from the ground. Stand beside his head, facing toward his hindquarters. Grasp all the reins in the left hand and exert backward pressure, with a slight tremor to the movement. It may be necessary to aid by pressing backward against his chest. While doing this, give the verbal command "back."

In the saddle, assume a relaxed seat and lean slightly back. Flex the colt's head and exert slight interrupted pulls backward, at the same time maintaining a minimum of leg pressure and voicing the command "back." He should step backward, lifting each foot separately. Hold him in a straight line. The word "back" should be dispensed with as soon as possible.

If at this time he refuses to perform the movement, an assistant may be used, as previously explained. Another method is to ride the colt straight to a wall with his face almost against it and then give him the signals to back. Usually he will respond correctly because there is no other place for him to go. Furthermore, he may recognize the logic of backing away from a wall.

These brief instructions on training are not intended to be all-inclusive. They are an attempt only to demonstrate the simple basic rules for developing show and pleasure horses in the ways of good behavior and for your own greater riding enjoyment.

Ring Rules and Etiquette

There are certain written and many unwritten rules that should govern the conduct of riders and exhibitors participating in horse-show events. A code that seems to me to contain the proper spirit underlying the showing of horses is the "Sportsman's Charter," quoted from the opening pages of the *American Horse Shows Association Rule Book:*

That sport is something done for the fun of doing it and that it ceases to be sport when it becomes a business, something done for what there is in it;

That amateurism is something of the heart and spirit—not a matter of exact technical qualifications;

That the good manners of sport are fundamentally important. That the code must be strictly upheld;

That the whole structure of sport is not only preserved from the absurdity of undue importance, but is justified by a kind of romance which animates it, and by the positive virtues of courage, patience, good temper, and unselfishness which are demanded by the code;

That the exploitation of sport for profit kills the spirit and retains only the husk and semblance of the thing;

That the qualities of frankness, courage, and sincerity which mark the good sportsman in private life shall mark all discussions of his interests at a show.

Courtesy in the ring is of first importance. In most classes, the contestants, upon entering the show ring, should go counterclockwise. After showing on the left-hand lead, they are requested to reverse and proceed clockwise. If a class has been lined up and certain contestants are asked to take the track again, they will go to the wall and proceed counterclockwise unless otherwise instructed.

When the steward or ringmaster asks for reversal in a saddle class, there are three common methods for executing this change, as illustrated in drawings *A, B,* and *C.*

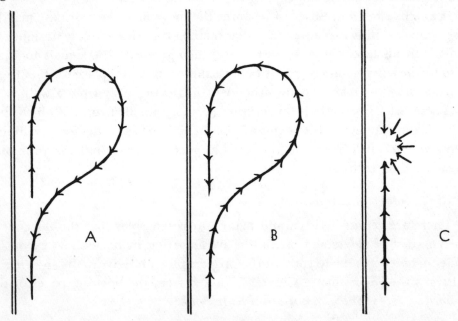

THREE METHODS OF REVERSING
HORSES IN SHOW RING

Of the three, *A* has the least to recommend it. It tends to put the horse in the center of the ring where he is apt to want to stay, especially if ridden by a weak rider. It may also force the horse to cut into others following too closely behind him, causing confusion throughout the class.

B is better, but it also tends to put the horse near the center of the ring. Another drawback is that in its initial stages it may suggest to a nervous horse that a canter is desired, as many riders start that gait by pulling away from the rail and then coming back to it as the canter is commenced.

C is a method favored by many successful showmen. In this movement, the horse is simply stopped and turned on his forehand until he is headed in the opposite direction. It neither points the horse toward the center of the ring nor does it give him the cue to canter. With a horse that is extremely nervous, the complete halt quiets him and at the same time is unobtrusive to riders in front or behind.

To reverse fine-harness horses, the driver pulls his horse away from the wall and, in most instances, goes diagonally across the ring to the opposite wall, taking care not to interfere with other oncoming horses.

Riders should space themselves evenly around the ring. Nothing looks more amateurish to the spectators than a "bunched" class. Furthermore, it is unfair to the judge. If one individual animal travels faster than the others, he should be circled out of line and taken back in where there is more space.

If it is necessary to pass another horse, the rider should take the track near the center of the ring; no effort should be made to crowd between another contestant and the wall. As a matter of courtesy, one horse should not be allowed to remain alongside another, especially when passing the judge. Above all, a rider should not "grandstand" by circling around the judge; he will create a better impression by remaining in line.

It seems needless to say that such unsportsmanlike actions as running horses into corner pockets or interfering in any way with other mounts have no place in the show ring.

The attitude of the contestant to the judge is important. Under no circumstances should a rider speak to the judge unless first spoken to.

If a rider wishes to leave the ring owing to lameness or a thrown shoe, permission should be obtained from the ringmaster or steward.

Abuse and undue punishment of a horse either in or outside the ring is strictly forbidden in horse-show rules.

When asked to line up, the contestants should come to the center of the ring and face in the direction the ringmaster indicates, standing side by side and abreast. In championship classes, where the saddles are removed for conformation judging, the horse should be lined up head to tail in tandem formation.

THE AMERICAN SADDLER AS A PLEASURE HORSE

It may be safely said that pleasure horses outnumber all other kinds of horses in America. For every horse shown in the ring there are dozens in use for pleasure, and their number is increasing rapidly. In many suburban areas, a small barn and paddock are becoming a necessary adjunct to the house.

Parents are learning that, in addition to being a wholesome and invigorating education for their children, horses and horseback riding get the adults out of doors as well and blot out, for a time at least, the press and worry of their affairs.

PLEASURE USE

A pleasure mount should, above all else, be endowed with a kind disposition and trained in the essentials of good manners. Next, he should possess easy-riding qualities and the intelligence to learn quickly and respond to his master's desires. If he has beauty, he will add further to the pleasure of prideful ownership. While there are exceptions, as in all breeds, the average American Saddle Horse will measure up well to all these requirements.

He is a good trail horse and covers the ground rapidly and with sureness

of foot and ease to his rider. These were the purposes for which he was originally bred. He has great style and beauty under a stock or flat English-type
saddle, whichever his owner prefers. He has sufficient size, carriage, and animation to suit the owner who may prefer those qualities.

Throughout the country, there are thousands of riding clubs. The activities of most of these groups include trail rides, group drill rides, and competitive riding contests. The American Saddle Horse is well suited to all
these activities.

Western-type sheriffs' posses are springing up in countless numbers
throughout the East, as well as the West where they originated. More and
more posse members are purchasing American Saddlers for use in this connection. They have found that these horses are responsive and eager to perform
in their complicated drill-team work. As a parade horse, the American Saddler is without equal.

In short, the American Saddle Horse has been bred and is ideal as a pleasure mount of good disposition, beauty, and easy-riding qualities. I recommend him without hesitation as one of the most versatile of American breeds.

Arabian Horse

This oldest of domesticated breeds shows exceeding fineness in all parts of its body. Proud and alert, nevertheless docile, the Arab has been widely adopted by American horsemen.

Line of croup nearly horizontal; hips long and deep. Extreme length from point of hip to hock. Tail set extremely high and carried gaily.

Legs fine with chiseled modeling of bones and tendons. Square knees and hocks proportionately larger than in other breeds. Pasterns springy, large, and strongly constructed.

Upward-sweeping neck not long, but arched and shapely. Outstanding feature is the *Mitbah*.

Jibbah, or forehead, prominently rounded; face profile extremely dished; ears small and sharp, the tips usually held together; jawbone disks wide apart, deep, and circular; soft nostrils capable of great dilation; eyes extremely large and set low.

Withers prominent and set well into back. Back itself is straight and the shortest in any breed.

Shoulder long and extremely sloping; girth markedly deep; chest wide between forelegs.

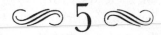

5

The Arabian Horse

The Arab is perhaps the most highly developed of all horse breeds and is unquestionably the oldest living pure strain handed down to modern times. The exact period of history in which it originated is not definitely known, and the details of its earliest domestication and development have been heatedly debated over a long period.

Though the Arab has long been the horse of romantic poets, little is really known about the origin and movements of Near Eastern and North African horses of antiquity. A number of confusing factors have made it difficult for Western people to understand the Arab horse's history and background. The most potent of these is the Eastern philosophy; next is the language and manner of recording pedigrees; and finally, the works of Western authors themselves are confusing and contradict each other with regard to pedigrees, strains, substrains, tribal names, etc. It seems to me that a real and important factor has not been emphasized in these histories: that the Arabs or their forebears in a remote period of history took certain stock and, through selective breeding dictated by the rigid standards of necessity, produced the Arabian horse. The fact that a horse of utmost value has been created indicates that these horses have been in the process of selection and intensification of fixed qualities through countless centuries of trial and hardship.

POSSIBLE ORIGIN

With the hope of clarifying a confusing situation, a few of the possible origins of the Arabian horse will be given here. It should be borne in mind, however, that much of the basis for our beliefs is conjecture and some of it legendary.

Many versions of Arab-horse origin presume that the Arab was an entirely separate and distinct species from other breeds. In the light of knowledge gained from fossil specimens, it is difficult to accept this theory. The belief that there was one main horse species with, of course, many local races or subspecies existent in the prehistoric world, seems to persist, as explained in Chapter 1. Many of the different local groups eventually contributed to domestic horses, but these were so altered by mixture, inbreeding, selection, and so on, that it would be impossible to trace one domestic breed to a certain wild breed or even apportion various percentages of its blood to any particular groups of wild horses.

One argument advanced by those who believe that the Arab is of exclusively wild origin is that the breed has one less vertebra than other breeds in the lumbar region of the backbone and two less vertebrae in the tail, or caudal, region. Actually, the number of vertebrae occasionally varies in different horse breeds, both prehistoric and modern, but this does not mean that when a horse has less than the usual number of vertebrae it is necessarily a result of his relation to an Arab horse or its ancestors. Also, the fact that inbreeding fixed a typical number of vertebrae, as in Arabs, does not necessarily indicate that this number was invariable in any wild species from which these horses sprang. It could, in other words, have been an accident of inbreeding, as could some of the other physical characteristics peculiar to the breed.

A number of years ago, the remains of several Morgan-bred horses were exhumed, and, with the discovery that the skeletons had the same number of vertebrae as Arab horses, an attempt was made to prove the relationship of the Morgan breed to the Arab. I do not doubt that the desert horse supplied this physical structure, but, on the other hand, I do think that it is also quite possible that the unusual formation could have been fixed by selective breeding and then passed on in remote antiquity to other domesticated horses, thus producing horses with short backs and weight-carrying ability.

Other peculiarities, such as horizontal pelvis, diminutive leg callosities (or their complete absence on hind legs), differences in tooth structure, and extreme denseness of bone, are held forth as proof that the Arab is of distinct and separate origin from all other horses. Again, these differences appear to be more the result of centuries of refinement through selective breeding.

Many horsemen believe that a horse possessing a thin skin and hair of fine texture has good breeding in its background. Arabs are noted for this quality and have undoubtedly passed it on to the breeds they have influenced. Yet this quality is not sufficient to set the breed apart as a distinct species.

For centuries Arabs have admired the large brain capacity in certain of their mares, denoted by the *Jibbah,* which may be recognized as a pronounced fullness of the forehead. Not all Arab mares have a pronounced Jibbah, but it is reasonable to believe that, given time—say another few thousand years—the Arabs could produce mares which would all possess a desirable forehead prominence.

One writer indicates a belief that Arab horses were wild in the locality of their domestication in Arabia. It is entirely possible that wild horses were indigenous to the Arabian peninsula in remote prehistoric times; we know that the region was moist and supported trees and rivers necessary to the existence of animal life. The question that cannot be answered, however, is whether horses were continuously native to the area, first in a feral and then in a domesticated state, in unbroken sequence from the days of moistness until the present. Many authorities have concluded that this would have been quite impossible.

Taking leave of the wild-horse theory momentarily, let us consider whether early Arabian horses could have come from nearby ancient civilizations.

The Hittites, Indo-Europeans who made their way into the land around Palestine during the period 2000 B.C., are known to have had horses. They were skilled horse masters and adeptly rode and drove the animals to primitive chariots.

From this period comes a terra-cotta horse head with startlingly Oriental features—the low-placed eye, arched neck, and small tapering nose. This distinct type recurs consistently in Hittite works of art.

Approximately two hundred years before this period, the Amorites settled in what was at first a small upriver town on the Euphrates named Babylon. After a hundred years of warfare, they controlled Mesopotamia, and Hammurabi founded the first Babylonian Empire in 2100 B.C. These people did not possess the domesticated horse. One hundred years of peace and security followed; then nomads from the vast stretches of the unknown East invaded Babylonia and set up their own king. They brought with them the horse and war chariot.

The Hittites to the north of Palestine and the people who conquered the Babylonians along the lower Euphrates both used horses to a great extent and both are presumed to have originated in the East. This is positive indication that the entire upper neck, or entrance, to Arabia was inhabited by horsemen peoples. It does not prove that the Arab tribes availed themselves of horses at that time, but, nevertheless, horses of probable Eastern origin were in the vicinity.

When the Hyksos from around Palestine first began to appear in Egypt about 1900 B.C., they had horses and introduced them to the Egyptians. It is not difficult to imagine that these "Shepherd Kings" filtered down into Arabia as well as Egypt, taking their horses with them.

None of the Bedouin tribes believe that any wild horses have existed in Arabia for a long time. However, Bedouin children to this day play "wild horse," and there may be some legendary basis for the game. One writer believes it to be possible that millenniums ago the Hyksos, Cushites, or Scythians brought horses into Arabia and that some of them escaped, later to be domesticated and improved by the desert tribes. Coinciding with this theory is the legend that Ishmael captured a wild mare, the first stock to be used by his tribes.

A completely opposite theory is that the Hyksos may have obtained their horses originally from Arabian tribes or from wild horses in the region.

In considering all these possibilities, the reader should bear in mind the extremely ancient and sometimes legendary character of this historical background.

The Legends

There are three recognized epochs in the legendary history of Arabian horses. But, since within each epoch there are points which coincide with known historical and archaeological facts, they cannot be considered entirely mythical.

The first epoch covers the time from Ishmael to his fifth-generation direct descendant, Salaman, not to be mistaken for King Solomon who appeared later. Legend relates that Ishmael captured a wild mare about 2000 B.C. From this mare was produced stock which finally gave to the tribe of Ishmael a colt called Benat el Ahwaj, which means the son of the crooked. Story has it that this stallion's dam had become deformed as a result of being carried in a goats'-hair sack on camel back. From this stallion sprang the first strain of pure Arab horses known as *Kuhaylan*.

Fitting into this epoch is the romantic story of *Kuhaylan 'Ajuz*. The common version relates that a certain sheik was being pursued by his enemy. Resting for a short interval, his war mare gave birth to a filly foal. Because he was hard-pressed, the warrior was compelled to remount the mare and travel on. When he halted again, after a hard race across the desert, he was amazed to discover that the young filly had followed the mare and was close at her heels.

The foal was placed in the custody of an old woman who tended her—hence the name "Arabian mare of the old woman."

Lady Wentworth, in her book *The Authentic Arabian Horse,* gives a more logical interpretation of the term. In her translation, *Kuhaylan,* or *Kehilan,* means thoroughbred or, more literally, purebred. She maintains that "old woman" is a mistranslation of *'Ajuz* and that it merely means old. Thus *Kuhaylan 'Ajuz* might more literally mean ancient thoroughbred or old purebred.

An interesting passage from *Gleanings from the Desert of Arabia,* by R. D. Upton, published in London in 1881, is quoted for a better understanding of the meaning of *Kuhaylan:*

> The Arabian horse is of the Kuhl race. Keheilan is the generic name of the Kuhl or Arabian breed of horses. Thus a true Arabian horse is a Keheilan, and a mare a Keheilet—fem.
>
> The blood of the Kuhl race has been preserved in Arabia and handed down by the Badaween in a pure state by "Al-Khamseh" ("The Five"), a family formed by selection from the general or universal race of Kuhl in Arabia, and preserved by the Badaween as the authentic record and register of the Arabian breed of horses. All horses in "Al-Khamseh" are Keheilans, and all mares Keheilets.
>
> Kheilan, the generic name of the true Arabian horse, is derived from the Arabic word Khl, or Kuhl, or Kuhal, signifying "antimony," and was given to the Arabian horse doubtless from the great resemblance which his skin (not only on the face, but all over the body) has to antimony, and not alone from the similar appearance of the eye of the Arabian horse to that of the human female eye when painted with antimony. The skin of the Arabian horse is a bluish black, and often presents a very strong resemblance to skin painted with antimony.

The second epoch in Arabian-horse history covers the period from Salaman to Rabiah al-Faras. Salaman, known as Faras (Horseman), lived at approximately 1635 B.C. This epoch is important from a legendary viewpoint because it was then that the history of *El Khamsa* ("The Five") began. Certain authorities have considered such history or legend to be intimately associated with the Anazah race of people. Though the full meaning of *El Khamsa* is difficult for Western peoples to understand, in simple terms it seems to mean that all Arabian horses of the Kuhaylan designation, including substrains, descended from five select mares. These five are reputed to have been the ones which answered the call of Salaman's trumpeter to come forth from the stream where they were thirstily drinking. Lady Wentworth refers to the legend as a "wearisome myth."

The five legendary mares of *El Khamsa* are said, in another story, to be those blessed by Mohammed and called Rhabda, Noorna, Waya, Sabha, and Hesma. The desert tribesmen do not necessarily accept this version as fact.

From a practical point of view, it seems that *El Khamsa* was a consolidating or selecting of the best horses of the time for the improvement of the breed. Though it may seem an irreverent comparison to the student of Arab horse lore, the selection and intensification of blood contained in *El Khamsa* was similar to the selection of the blood of Rysdyk's Hambletonian in the Standard Bred line of American horses.

DESERT
HORSES

In less colorful words, the romantic versions of *El Khamsa* appear simply to indicate that the tribesmen found in the strains represented a group of horses best suited to perpetuate their requirements.

The third epoch started in the days of Rabiah al-Faras and continues to modern times. Rabiah, surnamed al-Faras, lived about the time of David, father of King Solomon, in biblical history. It is not clear why Nazar, father of Rabiah, selected him, the third or fourth son, to receive through hereditary law the horses descended from *El Khamsa*. Nevertheless, through him to his son Asad and to his grandson Anazah, whose race finally inhabited Khaibar and finally spread over all the pastures of central Arabia (Najd), were passed the purebred Kuhl race of horses.

It is interesting to note that the horses of Arabia are esteemed in the following order:

1. The Kuhaylan of the Anazah.
2. The Kuhaylan of *El Khamsa,* but not Anazah.
3. The remains of the Kuhaylan race of horses outside the confines of *El Khamsa* of Kuhl or Arabian blood, which nevertheless may be pure in some instances. (The latter class is not recognized by the Bedouin.)

The horses in the first class are those of the Anazah Bedouin. Those in the second class are associated with Bedouin tribes other than Anazah, and the third and last group may be represented by Arabian horses that are bred in Iraq or Syria. These are not considered "noble" in the eyes of the Bedouin, nor "chubby" (suitable for breeding).

There are many other legends of the Arab horse, some of them appearing to be different versions of the ones related here, but they do not necessarily add to, or detract from, the general legendary history.

STRAINS, FAMILIES, AND PEDIGREES

We shall not attempt to list here the strains and families of the Arabian breed of horses. *The Horse of the Desert,* by William Robinson Brown (1929), contains a comprehensive list, with notes explaining the meaning of some of the strain names. Reputed to be most complete and authentic, the book lists 189 strain names used by the desert tribes. One hundred and two of these are suffixes of the original Kuhaylan strain.

It is believed that in ancient times the strains were few in number and that where the sire and dam were of the highest type the foal took the strain name of the sire. As strains became more numerous, the mare's strain and pedigree were given so that they showed the manner in which deviation was made from the original strain. The fact that the mare is given preeminence in the pedigree confounds people of the Western world, but in Arabia, the mare is held in high esteem as a source of wealth. It has been said that an edict of the Koran law forbade her sale into other countries.

This does not mean, however, that the sire is not esteemed or that great care is not practiced in his use. To secure proper matings the desert tribesmen go to much trouble, sometimes traveling great distances, to bring about specific pedigrees for their future foals. The stallions are discriminatingly selected, and no unknown horse nor one of doubtful parentage is used. If an undesirable ancestor is known to be represented in his bloodlines, the horse will under no circumstances be used at stud. This almost fanatical abstinence from the use of horses that have the slightest taint of impurity in their bloodlines is explained in the following quotation from Upton:

. . . . In this way do I interpret and understand the following passage in Youatt:—"The most extraordinary care is taken to preserve the purity of the breed. Burckhardt states that the favourite mare of Savud the Wahabee, which he constantly rode in all his expeditions and was known in every part of Arabia, produced a colt of very superior beauty and promise, which grew to be the first stallion of his day. Savud, however, would never permit him to be used for the purpose of breeding, because his mother was not of pure blood; and not knowing what to do with him, as the Bedouin never ride stallions, he sent him as a present to the Sherif." This I understand to mean simply that this mare of the Sawood of that day was either not of "Al-Khamseh," or perhaps the Sawood, as an Anazah, did not consider her of pure blood because she had not come from the Anazah, and not that she was of foreign blood. It is also probable that at the period alluded to, although the Ibn Sawood had commenced to ride other horses than those of their own race, they had not commenced to breed from such. The Sherif to whom it is reported Ibn Sawood sent the horse was, of course, he of Mekka.

Mares are bred within their own strains when possible or to related strains that are known to nick well with the qualities of the mare's bloodlines. The family suffix attached to a name designates the owner of a strain, or a description of peculiarity, or a famous mare from which the branch has descended. After a suffix has grown to great length, the prefix, or original strain, in some cases may be dropped. Thus, names are constantly being reformed and changed. The line of descent through three or four generations, however, is commonly known by most tribesmen.

Among the desert tribes, written pedigrees are nonexistent. Every horse, however, has a pedigree, which is well known by word of mouth. It is said that no Bedouin will ever lie about the pedigree of any of his horses. In the description of the breeding of a horse or mare, he or she is said to be of a certain strain, which is invariably that of the dam. The blood strain of the sire is then stated, which may or may not be the same as that of the dam. The individual parents, grandparents, and so on, of every living horse and mare are known and each has a specific and well-authenticated pedigree.

Particular strains seem to have been fostered by certain tribes, although these tribes may have owned other strains common to their neighbors. Owing to the increased scarcity of horses in the desert, the practice of specialized-strain breeding was sacrificed to a certain extent. Nowadays, it is less common to find horses that are pure line-bred; nevertheless, in spite of the blood admixtures of other strains similar in characteristics, horses do show a preponderance of one strain. This does not mean that such horses are inferior, for they still carry none but the purest of blood represented by the original strains of *El Khamsa*.

The Anazah tribes have been tenaciously resolute in keeping their special selection of strains pure in blood. This is more or less proved by their refusal to acknowledge or to return to the use of any strain which has departed from their hands into foreign parts.

Vague information has created the erroneous idea that there are three breeds of Arab horses—*attechi, kadischi,* and *kochlani*. An explanation of these three categories will clarify the matter.

Attechi is a class of horses considered of little value, at least in the eyes of the Bedouin, with no pretense to pure blood. In some instances, they may carry the blood of Arabian horses in their ancestry. Foreign breeds would be listed in this category by the Arab.

In the *kadischi* group may be found horses carrying considerable blood of the Arab, but not absolutely pure. The word *kadish* is Syrian and means, literally, a gelding, such horses being for traveling or carrying baggage and used as hacks by townsmen and merchants. Certain tribes may have many *kadischi* horses, but they would not be used for breeding in the *kochlani* class. If a pure Arab mare is bred to an *attechi* or *kadischi* stallion, she and her subsequent get lose caste, even though she may be bred later to a pure Arab stallion of *kochlani* class.

The designation *kochlani* simply means pure, uncontaminated Arab horses, naturally encompassed by *El Khamsa*. Such horses are said to be few in number and exist mainly in the tribes of the Anazah. They are of perfect pedigree and known as *asil* (pure).

An interesting custom indicates the strength of the tradition among the Bedouins for maintaining pure breeding of their stock. Should one tribe lose horses to another during a battle, the conquering tribe is allowed to send an agent, without harm, into the midst of the conquered tribe to obtain pedigrees of the horses taken. Thus the record of pedigrees is kept complete in the event the horses or their offspring are returned to the original tribe in subsequent wars.

CONFORMATION, TEMPERAMENT, GAITS, AND CHARACTERISTICS

Having explored briefly the origin and traditions of the Arab horse, let us look at the physical characteristics of the animal which, through centuries of selection and improvement, has served the tribes of Arabia so well.

The structure of the head is probably more distinctive than any other part of the Arab horse. It is relatively small and extremely tapering toward the muzzle. The disks of the jawbone are deep and circular in appearance. The forehead is broad, and the low-set eyes are large, with prominent bony framework. In the structure of the head there are three points which the Arab considers to be of utmost importance.

1. The frontal and parietal bones which form the Jibbah, or forehead, can scarcely be too prominent to please the owner of an Arab horse. In the master's eyes, the Jibbah denotes extreme intelligence and gives an expression of nobility. In the ideal mare, this feature is rounder and more pronounced than in the stallion and descends gracefully in a concave curve to the lower nasal bones, forming the characteristic dish shape of the Arab profile.

2. The attitude and shape of the ears are extremely important, for these features denote alertness and responsive intelligence. To be perfect, the ears should be placed so that the tips almost touch as they point inward. This is particularly true of the stallion. Also, they should be thin of texture, hollowed, and molded delicately and sharply. Usually the ears of the mare will be longer and more open than those of the stallion.

3. *Mitbah* is the term used to describe the manner of excellence in which the head joins the neck. It embodies the graceful curve formed by the windpipe as it enters the point between the wide-set jawbones; hence the curve on the top line of the neck. Its importance lies in the ease of head carriage and the freedom it permits to air passages from head to body. The life of a Bedouin depends upon horses of good wind and endurance. In the words of Sheik Abd-el-Kader, "The highest virtue in a horse, in the mind of the Arab, is endurance, to which, in order to constitute a perfect animal, must be joined great strength and good wind. . . ."

One of the most striking characteristics in the head of the Arab horse is the position of the eyes, the center of which more nearly divides into equal parts the upper and lower portions of the head than in any other breed. Above the eyes the head is large and below them it is extremely small, sensitive, and delicate. The lips are firm, thin, and long, with the lower lip frequently protruding slightly. The nostrils are long, curved, and thin in texture, possessing the ability of extreme expansion when the animal is in action or under stress of excitement.

While the neck is of moderate length, it should curve gracefully from the "gamecock" Mitbah to the withers. It is neither too fine nor too masculine but gives an appearance of being graceful and refined, yet strong. The stallion naturally will possess a larger crest than the mare.

The withers are high, although not so pronounced as in the typical Thoroughbred, and run well into the back, which is extremely short. The loins are powerful, with good depth downward through the flanks, assuring weight-carrying ability. The croup is high and the top line of the hips is level, which brings us to another of the distinctive points of the Arab—his high-set tail, which is elevated gaily when the animal is in motion.

The hindquarters have been described as both long and deep. The gaskins are sufficiently full without being heavy; neither are they cut-hammed. While the cannons, both fore and hind, are extremely fine and well modeled, with prominent tendons and ligaments, the hocks and square-shaped knees are large, well formed, and, by comparison with other breeds, near the ground.

The shoulder of the ideal Arab is long, leanly powerful, and of course is greatly sloped in degree of angle from the vertical. The forearms should be long, lean, and muscular.

The pastern joints, in harmony with the knees and hocks, are large and strongly constructed. While the pasterns themselves are long, sloping, and elastic, they are at the same time large and powerful. The fetlock joints are noticeably free of feather or long hairs as contrasted with most other breeds. The feet are of fair size and remarkably round in the shape of their track, with considerable width in the heel.

The chest is broad, rounded, and muscular, and the girth is markedly deep. The ribs are well sprung to form a barrel-type body.

When the Arab is in motion, we are struck at once by his proud and fiery attitude. His natural carriage of head and tail is lofty. It is now that we are particularly cognizant of the three chiefly admired points—the beautiful head, the graceful arch of neck, and the high tail carriage. As lights dart and dance on the shimmering body, we are aware of the silky fineness of body coat, mane, and tail, and the thin texture of skin as evidenced by prominent veins.

At this point I cannot resist passing on to the reader an eyewitness description made by Major Upton when he was on the desert many years ago. The mare he describes seems to sum up the beauty, fire, and nobility of the breed as seen in its native habitat:

> Another Abayeh Sherrackieh, a chestnut mare, can only be described by the word magnificent. She was fourteen hands two inches in height; of great length, size, and substance; of good bone, and wonderfully handsome. Her head might be said to be of exaggerated beauty, and we both exclaimed, "Had such a head and so fine a muzzle been depicted truthfully on canvas, it would have been pronounced to be most unnatural." Her ears were good, and of the mare type; the Jibbah developed to excess; the eye fine and prominent, but

that part visible through the lids not particularly large (the orbits of the eyes were large and particularly prominent); the jaws deep, and the muzzle excessively fine. She had a splendid neck, with great development of the splenius muscle; her chest was deep and very capacious. She had a fine barrel; she had large and powerful shoulders, fine quarters, a grand haunch, and the sacral bones so high that the setting on the tail appeared to be almost the highest part of her body. Her withers were elevated; her arms were long, very large, and muscular; knees large, square, and deep; good thighs and hocks; short legs, clean, hard, and of good bone. She was very slightly stag-kneed, but the hock sinews were not inclined forward, but perfectly upright; her pasterns of a moderate length; her feet were large and strong, and rather higher than is usual among desert horses. She stood over a great deal of ground; she had a free, grand, long stepping walk. Her formation indicated very high speed, and she had great substance and a powerful frame. She had a very full tail, which she carried when moving high to a degree. I have seen her when she was galloping, with her loins and quarters covered and hidden by her widely spread and high carried tail. She was a mare of the highest courage, easily excited and full of fire. This mare's dam, of course, an Abayeh Sherrackieh; her sire Keheilan 'Ajuz.

Gaits

It has been said that Arabia is a hard school and is no breeding ground for weaklings. The heat, scarcity of food and water, long, tortuous treks across the hot desert to distant battlegrounds, the forays themselves—all have tempered muscles into steel and developed a capacity of endurance beyond imagination.

The movements of the true Arab reflect the rigid requirements of such standards of performance. The animals in their natural habitat show strength, grace, litheness, and a catlike quickness when in motion. Primarily, the Arab is three-gaited, and all his gaits are executed with great stride, the purpose being to cover ground rapidly and effortlessly.

While the Arab is capable, under training, of developing a trot which measures up to saddle standards, it is not at this gait that he excels. He has too much stride for the trot to be a pleasant riding gait. His stride is in harmony with his other two gaits. If his trotting stride were changed, no doubt the other two gaits would suffer as a result. It has been said that the trot is far more labor for the Arab than is the gallop. The mounted Arab's dislike for the trot may be accounted for by different explanations. He may consider the gallop to be safer when traversing rough ground. Furthermore, any trot becomes tiresome if endured for long periods without the aid of stirrups. There may also be an inherent prejudice among Arabian tribesmen against the trotting gait—a carry-over from ancient times when oxen, asses, and horses were less free and were used to draw cumbersome chariots and crude carts. Arabs have been known to discourage the trotting gait by attaching pacing hobbles to the legs. One of the ideal achievements in Arab training is reached when the animal goes easily from a walk to a gallop without resorting to a transitional trot.

The Arab is essentially a galloper by nature. At this gait he is in his full glory; his exhilarating freedom and buoyancy are a joy to behold. Because of the length of his hindquarters, this gait is performed more easily at rapid speed. Remarkable freedom of shoulder movement adds to the flowing stride and ground-covering ability—they are truly "drinkers of the wind." Claims have been made that desert Arabs are capable of galloping great distances without rest. One such account relates that an Arab mare galloped 12 miles before the rider pulled her up.

Through centuries of use the Arab horse has developed a long-striding, free walk. Another quotation from Major Upton's work describes a colt that had an excellent walking gait:

> They all have a free, long, striding walk, the hind foot, I may say, invariably overstepping the place whence the fore foot on the same side had just been raised many inches, from twelve to eighteen inches being quite a common distance, and in some cases to an extent of two or even three feet, and at times, I think, more. The longest stepping horse we saw was a two-year-old colt— Seklawi-Jedran ibn Nedēri. Watching him walking hour after hour in the desert, we estimated the distance he overstepped to be considerably beyond three feet.

Temperament

Spiritedness in horses is frequently mistaken for viciousness. Animals that frisk and play through the joy of living should not be considered malicious when compared with duller individuals. Actually, the environment of companionship with human beings, extending through centuries, has inculcated the true Arab with affection. It has been observed that any breed closely associated with people over a long period of time acquires a quality of natural docility.

In their native habitat, Arab horses exhibit the utmost intelligence and docility. Companionship of a kind difficult for Western people to understand is common between the Arab horse and his master. Authoritative accounts tell of animals that have neighed in the night to warn the master of approaching strangers or other danger—much as a watchdog does—or that have been known to stay peacefully in the tent beside him. During the flush of battle, the Arab frequently defends the master furiously, and if the rider is wounded, the war mare stands faithfully on guard over him.

Size and Color

Arabs are small when compared with most other light breeds. Sizes frequently depend upon conditions of feeding and the bloodlines from which they sprang. The *Saqlawi* individuals may measure in height from 14 to 15 hands, whereas the tallest *Mu'niqi* may attain a height of 15 hands 3 inches. Lofty heads and high tail carriage usually create an illusion of greater size.

The weight of this breed averages from 800 to 1,000 pounds.

Many erroneous ideas have arisen regarding the color of Arab horses. The storybook usually places the Arab sheik on a pure-white horse. It is true that a few pure Arab horses are white, but many of these are aged grays, which color is prevalent in varying shades in certain areas and among individual strains.

At least two authorities place bay as the predominant single color, particularly among those of the Anazah tribes. Lady Wentworth, however, deflates the idea that bays are more speedy than horses of other colors. She claims that this idea may have originated through the Prophet's partiality for the color. The impression that Arabs are partial to a horse of clear color seems to persist. It has been said that the Bedouin is skeptical about very light chestnuts with light manes and tails. Pure blacks are extremely scarce and usually are limited to horses of the *Jilfan* strain. While white markings on face and legs are common and quite acceptable, piebalds, duns, palominos, or yellows are believed to show evidence of impure breeding.

Upton noted a curious fact obtaining among certain Arabian horses:

> I was struck too with another feature—I am not, however, prepared to say it is absolutely a distinctive one to be seen in every Arabian, but it was noticed in so many instances that it looks something like it—a line somewhat darker than the general colour of the animal, to be seen in *colt* foals, running in continuation of the mane along the spine, and to be traced for some way even among the long hair of the tail. I never saw it in a filly; it seemed peculiar to the male sex; it is not obliterated with age; it can be traced in old horses and in those of a very dark colour. It is totally different to the markings of the zebra, quagga, or of any of the hybrids, or to the dark band to be seen down the back

of certain dun-coloured horses, often accompanied by asinine stripes or markings; it appears rather as the first or primitive colour of the animal, which tones away by almost imperceptible degrees from the back to the belly: it may be seen in lines on the males of other wild animals. At certain seasons and as the horse ages, and dependent also in some degree on his condition, the dark colour spreads over the shoulders and upper part of the body, giving on the shoulders and the junction of the neck at the withers, and on the upper part of the body and quarters, an appearance as if shaded with black which is most noticeable in horses of bay colour.

An Arab anecdote concerning color, related by Daumas, is quoted here more for its amusing interest than any fact which might underlie it:

A renowned chief of the desert, happening one day to be pursued by Saad-el-Zenaly, Sheik of the Oulad Yagoub, turned to his son and asked: "What horses are in front of the enemy?" "White horses," replied his son. "It is well; let us make for the sunny side, and they will melt away like butter." Some time afterwards Ben Dyab again turned to his son and said, "What horses are in front of the enemy?" "Black horses," cried his son. "It is well; let us make for stony ground and we shall have nothing to fear—they are negroes of the Soudan, who cannot walk with bare feet upon the flints." He changed his course, and the black horses were speedily distanced. A third time Ben Dyab asked: "And now, what horses are in front of the enemy?" "Dark chestnuts and dark bays." "In that case," exclaimed Ben Dyab, "strike out, my children, strike out, and give your horses the heel, for these might perchance overtake us had we not given barley to ours all summer."

EARLY SPREAD OF THE ARAB HORSE

Undoubtedly the Arab horse of antiquity influenced horse breeding in nearby lands. The countries now known as Turkey, Iraq, and Iran, the southern parts of Russia, Egypt, and the lands of North Africa improved their stock with Arab stallions. As a result of the Oriental practice of exchanging gifts, many horses of noble blood found their way into stables of royalty throughout most of the then known world.

The first large spread of influence occurred several centuries after the beginning of the Christian era. In A.D. 647, the Arab migration and the spread of Mohammedanism started. Egypt was the first to fall, and then, within a few years, Libya and Algeria were taken, and at last Morocco. During the half century following A.D. 647, their power grew and they seemed destined to control much of the world.

In the year A.D. 710, they extended their power north by pushing into Spain in what is known as the "Moslem Invasion." Being superior in the number of war horses at their command, they easily ruled the country. When the Moslems spread north again in an attempt to conquer Gaul, they were repulsed near Poitiers in A.D. 732. Since they had not settled the country, but rather had spoiled it as they advanced, the Moslems were forced to retreat into Spain, where they remained until they were driven back into Granada. They finally lost their Spanish foothold in the year 1492.

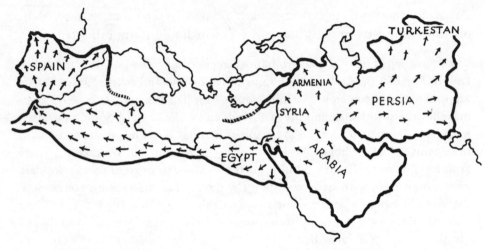

The Extent of the Moslem Empire, A.D. 750, and Spread of Arabian Horses

It was during the Arabs' stay in Spain that the Arab horse took hold in that country and became highly prized for his beauty. Probably because the Arabs were hated so intensely by the Spaniards, the horses were not called "Arabians" but "Spanish Barbs," perhaps because they had been imported in great numbers from the Barbary Coast of Africa. Many students believe that the so-called "Barbs" at first were of pure Arabian strains, particularly those of Morocco.

The Arab also contributed to other foreign breeds—the Russian Orloff, the French Percheron, the English Hackney, the South American Criollo— to name only a few. In fact, there are few domestic light-horse breeds in the world that have not at some period in their development felt the touch of Arabian influence. The blood of the Arab horse has been referred to as "the yeast which perpetuates qualities of greatness" in all equines. Many students of the Arabian horse sincerely believe that its reinfusion into other breeds will be necessary in the future to forestall decadence of quality.

THE ARAB'S INFLUENCE ON AMERICAN BREEDS

If a division can be made, it would appear that Arab blood was introduced into early American horses in two general ways. The first we shall refer to as the "Conquistador transmittals" and the second as "English importations." Because the early Americans needed to produce horses of outstanding qualities, these two sources were fused early in the country's history.

The first horses to place foot on American soil since prehistoric times were those brought here by Spanish conquerors. These horses were of Arabian origin, stemming from the Mohammedan conquest of Spain, mentioned earlier. Two of these types were widely known as "Spanish Barbs" and "Spanish Jennets."

After Columbus's discovery of the New World, the Spaniards established a base on Santo Domingo, from which point later expeditions set out for Cuba, Mexico, Yucatán, South America, and Florida. A few horses were brought to the islands on each sailing of provision ships. Gradually the accumulation of stock became sizable enough to permit impressive mounted expeditions.

Bernal Diaz del Castillo, who wrote the account of Cortez's conquest of Mexico, gave a minute description of the original sixteen horses in the expedition. While it is understood that this handful of stock did not necessarily populate the western plains of America with wild mustangs, the descriptions may be indicative of the type of animals which later influenced the original Western American stock. One characteristic quality mentioned in del Castillo's description is that the animals were good racers, which would indicate the presence of Oriental blood.

In 1800, Colonel Ironside wrote in the *General Stud Book* (English) that Barbs were the offspring of Arab horses and African mares, and that Jennets were by Barb stallions out of Spanish Andalusian mares. Little is known about the Jennet breed, but that they possessed fine quality is evidenced by favorable comments about them down through the years. The early English writer Thomas Blundeville had this to say about the breed: "The pace of the Jennet of Spain is neither trot nor amble, but a comely kind of going like the Turk."

It is reasonable to assume that the gait he referred to was one of the "easy" gaits, a single-foot or running walk. If he had meant a canter, as suggested by some writers, Blundeville would undoubtedly have described it as such, for he was well aware of the primary gaits of horses and would have recognized any variation of the gallop. His comparison with the Turkish horse may strengthen the argument that the Jennet performed a variation of the "easy" gaits.

One cannot help wondering if it was the Jennet that the Canterbury monk, William Fitz Stephen, described in diary form during the twelfth century, when he wrote: "It is pleasant to see the nags with their sleek and shining coats smoothly ambling along. . . ."

Colonel Ironside may have been correct concerning the broad origin of Jennets. Lady Wentworth, in *The Authentic Arabian Horse,* states that the word "Jennet" did not signify a blood horse but meant a small ambler, although many other accounts establish it as a breed. From a study of known facts, the Jennet seems to have been an animal of varying appearances and gaits, depending upon greater or lesser amounts of Arab blood.

Andalusian horses are considered to be an ancient breed. It is known that the Celtiberians possessed horses before the Romans came to conquer. Polybius recorded that the soldiers would ride near to the battlefield, then dismount and fight on foot. The horses were tethered some distance from the action, which is an indication that the animals were valued for their speed rather than as instruments of war. It is believed that the Andalusian horses contained much of the Gothic blood of northern types and later were crossed on horses brought into the country by the Romans, among which were horses of Numidia and other countries under Roman influence. Later, no doubt, following the Moslem invasion, the Andalusian breed was influenced to a great extent by Arab blood.

It is said that the twenty horses that belonged to lancers of Granada and that accompanied Columbus on his first voyage to the New World were Andalusians, which indicates that they were considered trustworthy and valuable in the face of unknown adventure.

All these, then, formed the background of the first horses to land on American soil since the prehistoric times when the horse had trekked out of North America and across Bering Straits. The new arrivals at first served the Spanish conquerors and settlers; later, through raids and battles, many were taken by the Indians, while others escaped to roam the rugged country of western United States.

The wave of Arab influence, which started in England and then reached American shores, occurred during the seventeenth century. Prior to the reign of King James I, which began in 1603, horses of Oriental extraction were gaining attention, at least in small and isolated instances, in Britain. The Romans introduced Eastern racing horses to Britain during their occupation. There is a record of an Arabian horse having been imported to England as early as the twelfth century. Historian Blundeville, in 1580, mentions the presence of many horses of apparent Arabian origin.

However, it was not until James I began the breeding of race horses that the insatiable desire for Eastern-bred horses welled up with overwhelming force in the British. This great movement, starting with James I's purchase of the Markham Arabian, was later to see the importation of the three eminent Oriental sires, the Byerly Turk, the Darley Arabian, and the Godolphin Barb (or Arabian), which were destined to mark strongly with their qualities the subsequent English Thoroughbred breed.

The American cousins of the English fell into the vogue of the times and imported from England some of the stock that was so popular there. Though the importations were to be known as "Thoroughbreds," they were but little removed from pure Arabians, and old paintings and prints show that they resembled the Arab horse more nearly than present-day Thoroughbreds. The settlers of the New World were quick to recognize the value of these horses as breeding stock. Stamina and endurance were a necessity, and the fineness of the imported animals kindled the desire for more beauty and quality in their native stock.

Justin Morgan was one of the first great sires to be produced in America. One eminent authority claims that Justin Morgan received five-eighths of his blood from grade Arabian sources. Besides establishing the breed which was named after him, Justin Morgan influenced almost every other recognized American breed. Unquestionably, the noble blood of the Arabian was indirectly responsible for creating the outstanding horses which trace to Justin Morgan.

The American Saddle Horse is another breed which carries in large part the blood of the Oriental horse. The founders of this breed paid great homage to the Thoroughbred breed, and subsequently to the Arab horse, by establishing Denmark by Imported Hedgeford as the sole foundation sire of American Saddlers. The later Chief family of Saddlers also traces to the Arabian through Imported Messenger, by the English race horse Mambrino.

The background of the Standard Bred Horse of America contains much Arab blood. Imported Messenger has been called the "granddaddy" of trotters in this country. The Standard Bred also drew much of its ability from old Justin Morgan.

The Quarter Horse has been influenced by the Arab as much as, or more than, any of the other American breeds, for almost all the families within this breed trace to Imported Janus, who was by Old Janus, he, in turn, being by the Godolphin Barb (or Arabian). In addition, the stock upon which Imported Janus was crossed included many mares descending from earlier importations by the Spaniards. Thus, the Quarter Horse has received a "double dose" of Arab blood.

THE ARABIAN HORSE CLUB OF AMERICA

Prior to 1908, there was no official register for Arab horses imported directly to, or raised in, the United States. The founding of the Arabian Horse Club of America came about as the result of a disappointment.

To understand the background of this situation we must go back a great many years. In 1791, the *General Stud Book of England* (for Thoroughbreds) was begun. In the beginning, Arab horses were accepted as founding stock. Later, as the Thoroughbred breed became more fixed, a special Arab division was formed for the purpose of registering authentic Arab importations to England. The horses registered in this manner and imported to America were acceptable for registration in the American Jockey Club.

When Homer Davenport, famous American cartoonist, imported twenty-seven head of Arabs direct from Arabia, he applied to the Jockey Club for registration of the horses. His request was denied on the grounds that his horses were not registered in the *General Stud Book of England*. The embarrassment of this incident awakened Mr. Davenport to the need in this country for an official register for pure Arabian horses. He reasoned that such a register should be kept solely for Arabian horses and not be shared with Thoroughbreds, which are now considered to be an entirely separate breed.

Finally, in 1908, the club was established, with Peter B. Bradley serving as its first president, F. L. Ames, vice-president, and H. K. Bush-Brown, secretary-treasurer. As with most horse groups, the Arabian Horse Club of America went through stormy intervals but has maintained a register since its inception.

In 1918, a similar organization was founded in England for the purpose of maintaining a register for pure Arabian horses. Animals so registered are automatically acceptable in the American society.

The above circumstances have resulted in at least a few horses being registered in four registers—the *General Stud Book,* that of the American Jockey Club, the Arab Horse Society of England, and the Arabian Horse Club of America.

At the present time, there are more than four thousand purebred Arabians in the United States. Compared with other breeds, this is not a large number.

Contained within this figure, however, is startling testimony of the growing popularity of Arab horses: Within the past six years, the entire number of purebreds was doubled!

USES OF THE ARAB HORSE

Since the days when returning Crusaders told remarkable tales of the fleet and enduring horses of the East, the Arab has been used for a variety of purposes. Marengo, the cream-white charger of Napoleon; Vonolel, the personal mount of Lord Roberts; the Arab charger which served Colonel Kent in the Crimean War; and the Duke of Wellington's Arab Copenhagen—these are but a few of the famous Arabs which proved the worth of their breed for purposes of war. Now, with mechanized equipment displacing almost all horses on the battlefields, no longer can it be said that he "paweth in the valley, and rejoiceth in his strength" or "goeth on to meet the armed men."

The racecourses for centuries have resounded to the impact of the Arab's flying hoofs. The Thoroughbred race horse, which sprang largely from the Arab, has replaced him in the short races over smooth courses which have become popular in Western countries in comparatively recent years.

Though he is banished from the battlefields by mechanical monsters, and the last echoes of his hoofbeats have died away from the racing stretches, the Arab horse, nevertheless, may be found serving man in many other ways. Those who have experienced the pleasure of visiting the Kellogg Arab Stables at Pomona, California, will readily admit the versatility of the Arab horse, for there he is exhibited in light harness, over the jumps, working under a flat saddle, or performing the difficult movements of a Western stock horse. Most of us have observed him serving as a pleasure horse. He is skillful when trained in the glamorous field of dressage, and more and more often is he found successfully invading the show ring in competition with more specialized animals, as well as performing brilliantly in classes exclusively for his own breed.

It is not claimed that the Arab is an expert in fields of specialized standards. Perhaps it is this fact that makes him unique. Enthusiasts point out that the Arabian possesses a symmetry of natural form unmarred by man, that no part of his physical make-up has been weakened by man's attempt to change him. He has not lost his weight-carrying ability through man's desire to develop him as a harness horse; he has not become light-boned, wasp-waisted, nor long-legged through man's attempt to create a speed machine of him; his ability to traverse rough terrain has not been sacrificed through constant development in tanbark arenas; nor has he attained artificiality of movement.

As a Pleasure Horse

For the reasons mentioned above, the Arab is considered to be a perfect all-round saddle animal. His strong, closely coupled back gives him unusual power for turning and stopping quickly. His substantial, durable hocks serve him in strenuous movements. His intelligence makes him responsive to his master's wishes.

Aside from use as breeding stock, the larger percentage of Arabs is used as pleasure mounts. For those whose riding habits require a cross-country horse, this breed is highly desirable. For general trailwork the Arab's willingness, smoothness, and endurance make him ideal. His maneuverability makes him excellent for drill-team and riding-academy work. Many horsemen of my acquaintance own and ride Arabs in sheriffs' posses and proclaim them to be superior to other horses for such work because of their handy responsiveness.

Private owners who buy feed for their horses do not overlook the "easy-keeping" qualities of the breed. Statistics based on endurance rides conducted in this country show that the Arab bows to no other breed in low food consumption for amount of energy expended.

Owing to its spirited and energetic qualities, this breed is most highly recommended for accomplished horsemen. The Arab cannot be recommended, however, as a pleasure mount for inexperienced riders, in spite of his kindly disposition. A docile nature and spiritedness, when under the saddle, have nothing in common, and most horsemen will agree that the rider of an Arab has considerable horse under him. Accomplished equestrians, however, find the Arab easy to control.

Although the total number of Arab horses is comparatively small, Arab breeders could do much to promote the breed by making more of them available to pleasure-horse owners. Satisfied owners, of course, constitute one of the most powerful advertising forces for any breed. Arab breeders are often reluctant to geld horse colts, thereby creating an unnecessary number of stallions and causing a scarcity of geldings which could be sold at reasonable prices for pleasure-horse use. Furthermore, there are always many horse colts which fall below the standards desirable for breeding stock. Wilfrid Blunt calculated that, regardless of purity in breeding stock, only about one in fifty horse colts will deserve the future position of sire. It was his belief that such animals, though not so perfect as some, were highly suitable for ordinary purposes. While Arab tribesmen do not believe in altering a horse colt (on the grounds that it is inhumane), at the same time they use only the choicest and most perfect stallions for breeding purposes.

As an Endurance Horse

If there is one quality that stands above others in the Arabian breed of horses, it is stamina. Arabs have proved their substance and bottom by winning first place in a large percentage of the long-distance races held in this country, and in every case have given a good account of themselves, carrying weights equal to those carried by horses of greater size. This would appear to refute the idea of many American horsemen that Arabs are too small to be of practical value.

Crabbet, purebred Arabian gelding, owned by Mr. W. R. Brown, gained fame a number of years ago as an endurance racer. This 15½-hand gelding, weighing approximately 925 pounds, won a 96-mile race in 1918 and another of 100 miles in the same year. Perhaps he had his greatest triumph when he won first place in the third of a series of endurance rides for the United States Mounted Service Cup. Held October 10–14, 1921, the event was an especially grueling contest over 310 miles of macadam and concrete-paved roads. It is claimed that the 1921 contest was the most severe to be held before or since that time. Carrying a weight of 245 pounds, accompanied by his stablemate Rustem Bey, a half Arab, half Standard Bred, Crabbet finished a full twenty minutes ahead of the rest of the field with a total traveling time of forty-nine hours four minutes for the five consecutive days of the race. Of the seventeen horses entered, only seven were able to finish, and when the tests for condition were conducted the following morning, the indomitable Crabbet was adjudged to be in nearly perfect condition and was one of the few horses able to gallop freely with no signs of lameness acquired from the ordeal.

Those who have studied the Arab horse in his native habitat are not astonished at such records of stamina. Horses of the Bedouins have always been esteemed for their ability to travel great distances rapidly without suffering fatigue. Indeed, that is the standard for which they have been bred through the centuries. It is not uncommon for horses of the desert to travel across the burning sands without food or water for forty-eight hours at a stretch.

There is a record dated July 27, 1840, which credits an Arab with traveling 400 miles in four consecutive days. Frazer stated in his *Tartar Journeys* that an Arabian horse went 1,560 miles in thirty days, of which eighteen were used in traveling.

Arabs as Jumpers

In America, the Arab has not been considered seriously as a contender in the jumping field. The W. K. Kellogg Institute, however, has demonstrated with its purebred stallion Ralet the natural jumping ability of the Arabian breed.

Lady Wentworth, who is thoroughly versed in the capabilities of Arabs under all conditions, states that they are excellent jumpers and will easily clear obstacles up to 4 feet in the hunting field. As hunters, they may be restive before the chase commences but they steady as soon as the run is under way and are particularly handy in rough going.

The exploits of the late Hon. Ethelred Dillon demonstrated the Arab's ability as a jumper. She used them three days a week in strenuous hunting and drove them in harness at reckless speed the balance of the time. This Irish lady also removed brood mares with foals from the pasture and entered them in competition with top Irish jumpers.

One of these mares, Raschida, at the age of fifteen, with a foal by her side and carrying foal, cleared 5-foot 6-inch jumps while her baby foal excitedly streaked after her around the arena. She placed second at Dublin in 1898 in the high-wall jumping competition. It is said that the aged mare cleared the huge fences at a canter, losing first place only because she knocked off a small pebble.

RASCHIDA AND FOAL

Raschida often cleared 6 feet in practice, as did her stablemate, the Crabbet mare Mejliss, who was evidently capable of going much higher; however, because of a twisting action over the jumps, her riders were unable to stay with her.

The 15½-hand stallion Jeruan, a stylish goer bred by Mr. Powdrill, won many jumping competitions in England. One of the most famous jumping Arabs on record was Maidān, brought to England by Lord Airlie and owned by Ethelred Dillon. This remarkable stallion won three steeplechase races, competing with Thoroughbreds when twenty years of age, and at the astonishing age of twenty-five he won a 3-mile steeplechase against stiff competition!

As a Dressage Performer

Dressage is considered by the best of horsemen as the highest test of ability of the schooled horse. Those who understand this type of schooling agree that such work taxes the mental and physical energies more than any other type of work that horses are required to perform. The dressage horse changes gaits, airs, and paces by almost invisible movements of the rider's weight, legs, and hands.

Many dressage trainers of my acquaintance have expressed a preference for the Arabian horse in this type of work. French and German horsemen who are expert in the higher schooling of horses have indicated their preference for animals of predominantly Arabian blood.

Thousands of showgoers on the Pacific coast and in Canada have thrilled to the brilliant and smooth performance of Sharik, a purebred Arabian stallion owned and trained exclusively by Mr. Ward W. Wells of Portland, Oregon. This beautiful chestnut, registered number 1784 in the Arabian Horse Club, is by Ralet, by Racine, by Skowronek. His dam was Bint Narma 1094. In Sharik's veins flows the blood of the ancient Kohaylan, Saqlawi, and Mu'niqi strains.

DRESSAGE HORSE

Mr. Wells has trained many capable horses of other breeds, but it is his conviction that Arab horses possess qualities which enable them to excel in the difficult dressage movements. In the light of his experience, he feels that the intelligence of the Arab allows faster schooling. From the time he was first saddled at the age of two and a half, Sharik progressed rapidly. Under immediate training he was capable of small circles and figures at the walk, trot, and canter. During the first month, he performed pirouettes on the fore-hand, and soon he was taught to two-track and side-step. After about a year of work on the gymnastic exercises embodied in secondary dressage, Sharik graduated to the movements of superior dressage. He readily learned the passage and was then slowed down to the piaffer, after which he was taught the changes of leads at any given number of steps down to every other one. The dressage schedule of Sharik is varied and entertaining. Each movement from the extended passage to the canter in place is executed with precision, gracefulness, and springy action.

Sharik has proved the Arab's durability under such strenuous routine. In his more than six years of arduous travel and service, he has never suffered a single blemish or unsoundness from the strain. His powerful hocks and short loins, his sturdy pasterns and dense bone, typical of Arab conforma-tion, have undoubtedly helped him withstand the strenuous labor asked of him. Unquestionably these qualities have aided him in his balletlike grace-fulness and balance, thrilling the many audiences which have commanded him.

Arab Stock Horses

Of particular interest to Americans is the role of the Arab as a working stock horse. One of the best qualified authorities on this subject is Mr. Lynn W. Van Vleet, owner of the Lazy VV Ranch high in the rugged Colorado Rockies. Starting with a herd of about thirty head, the Van Vleet Arabian stud has developed into the largest private venture in the country devoted to the Arab horse.

ARAB STOCK HORSE

Though one of Mr. Van Vleet's main purposes was to prove that the Arabian horse could adjust himself to any climate or topographical condition without injurious effect, he soon realized that the purebred Arab was capable of development as a superior working stock horse.

The foundation stallions used at Van Vleet's Lazy VV Ranch are Zarife, A.H.C. 885, gray, foaled in 1928, bred by Prince Mohamed Aly of Cairo, Egypt, imported to the United States in 1932; Kabar, A.H.C. 748, gray, foaled in 1930, sired by Koaba, by Skowronek; Rifage, A.H.C. 1286, gray, foaled in 1936, sired by Mirage, by Skowronek; Kahar, A.H.C. 1159, bay, foaled in 1935, sired by Katar.

The hands at the Lazy VV will tell you that many of their Arab stallions are capable of performing twice the work of native stock horses without fatigue or the unsoundness which often accompanies hard usage. At the venerable age of twenty-one, head stallion Zarife still actively participates in the long cattle drives as well as holding a major position in the Stud's extensive breeding program.

An interesting story is told about the stallion Kahar which attests to the Arab's "cow savvy" as well as to his love for his master. One day, while gathering cattle for calf branding, Kahar was trailing a wayward cow in a belly-deep, ice-cold stream. A willow growth lurking beneath the surface of the water tangled one of the legs of the bay stallion. In his anxiety to stay with the escaping cow, Kahar tried to break the willow's grip on his leg, and in the ensuing struggle he lost his footing as well as his rider. The swift water carried him downstream a considerable distance before he could get on his feet and climb to the bank. Did Kahar run away? Just the opposite. He walked back to the original place of fording and waited for his water-soaked rider to emerge from the stream and mount him so that they could resume the chase of the errant cow.

Though the Arabs at the Lazy VV are not pampered with glass-barred stalls, heated stables, or tasseled trainers, kindness and human affection are lavished upon the horses from early colthood. Everyone is encouraged to play with and strike up a friendship with the youngsters in the belief that such treatment brings out the innate affection of this breed which has been associated with human beings through millenniums of history. In fact, the trainers say that it is simple to halterbreak a colt because he is so used to arms encircling his neck.

Arab colts at the Lazy VV are halterbroken when yearlings. At the age of two, they are trained on the lunge line and some of them are driven. At three, their saddle training commences. Because of their superior intelligence, the

Arab pupils are never "broken"; instead, they are "trained," and they learn quickly and respond willingly. The men at the ranch are sincere when they say that the Arab neck reins more gracefully than most Western horses and is as fast as a Quarter Horse. In fact, Kabar is as fast as a panther; in quick turns he whirls on his hind feet—a trick that not one horse in a thousand learns. It is invaluable in the serious business of driving and cutting cattle.

Bob Pack, foreman of the cattle crews, takes pride in Barek, an Arab stallion which he personally trained for roping. Barek does his job as well as any cow horse—perhaps a little bit better, according to Foreman Pack.

One of the toughest jobs asked of any horse is mountain-trail work, and the purebred Arabians in the Van Vleet "cavvy" excel at it, even though trails are rough, unbelievably steep, and at energy-sapping altitudes. The diminutive classic-type stallion Rifage, standing only 14 hands 1 inch and weighing slightly over 800 pounds, is capable of carrying tirelessly a weight equal to one-third his own for ten hours at a stretch. This is accomplished without his showing any evidence of fatigue or lameness the next day.

Boss Van Vleet believes that his experiment of more than ten years has proved an important point—perhaps it only reiterates an old one—that Arabian horses are tough, courageous, intelligent, and highly adaptable to any kind of work for which man may choose to enlist them.

❧ 6 ❧

Quarter Horses

"He's a sleepy little hoss that can unwind like lightnin'!" That is the Texan's laconic description of the Quarter Horse. Tremendous speed and even temperament are the factors that make this little animal valuable to those who need a "using" horse. From the standpoint of utility, no horse can lay greater claim to his right of being.

The Quarter Horse has always been found at the outermost fringe of the frontiers of America because he could be counted upon when the jobs were difficult.

For those who think that the Quarter-type horse is a "Johnny-come-lately," let us leave the great cow country of the Southwest and go back about three hundred years to the time of the early English colonists in Virginia and the Carolinas.

As early as 1611, Sir Thomas Dale brought seventeen horses from England. Other stock was undoubtedly brought into the English colonies from the Indian and Spanish settlements to the south, and even before there was sufficient timber cut from the land to form an oval race track, "short" horses were burning up the forest paths with their bursts of terrific speed. By 1656, quarter-mile races were popular, and in 1690, short races with substantial purses were offered for Colonial quarter-of-a-mile race horses.

It is interesting to picture the difficult living conditions of those times. It had been only eighty-four years since King James I had given to the Virginia Company, under the royal charter of 1606, a map of the territory which included a 75- to 100-mile strip extending along the Atlantic seaboard from what is now the southern boundary of South Carolina to the Canadian border.

Quarter Horse

Generally outstanding for extreme musculature, short lines and sturdy frame. Noted for speed at short distance.

Neck is medium short and lacks much arch.

Back is of medium length and well coupled at juncture of hips. Withers are not pronounced. Barrel is rounded, with depth through the girth.

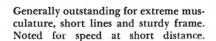

Ears are short; jaw disks are round and muscular; muzzle is extremely short.

Croup is sloped and tail is set low. Quarters and gaskins are extremely muscular.

Cannon bones and pasterns are short and sturdy.

Chest and forearms are well developed.

So wild and impenetrable was this strip that it was believed the great Western ocean lay to its west. The task of hewing a livelihood out of such country was laborious and dangerous. The horses which served the colonist had to be of tough fiber and able to perform the most difficult equine tasks. It would be another eighty-five years before Daniel Boone would be able to thrust open the old Wilderness Trail in Kentucky.

Perhaps many of the racecourses over which Colonial Quarter Horses ran were the old war trails of the Indians who, in the tragic year 1622, had massacred at least one-third of the English settlers in Virginia. It is easy to imagine the reckless abandon with which the early Cavaliers grasped at, in fleeting moments, such sportive equine diversion.

"Where did these horses get their stamina," we may ask, "and where did they originally come from?"

The origin of the early horses along the Atlantic seaboard has never been fully established, but parts of the puzzle can be put together. There is much evidence to support the contention of Quarter Horse breeders and enthusiasts that this little horse is the oldest fixed type in America today. Let us consider some of the possible sources in the century before the English colonists started racing their Quarter Horses.

There is little doubt that the first horses to place a hoof on American soil in any number were the sixteen landed by Cortez in preparation for his conquests in Mexico. These horses—eleven stallions and five mares—were put ashore in the year 1519. They were of Spanish variety, two of them being of the famous Jennet breed. It is possible, but highly improbable, that of the horses that strayed and multiplied, some could have migrated to the eastern part of the continent in the one-hundred-year period before the landing of the first English colonists.

On August 1, 1539, De Soto and his party started northward from Florida with 200 horses. On this expedition he spent considerable time in the land of the Chickasaw Indians. When he was ready to depart from this section, he demanded native male carriers and women. This the Chickasaws considered an insult and they fell upon the Spaniards at dawn. By the time those in the town were aware of what was happening, half the houses were in flames. The confusion that followed left the soldiers no time to arm or saddle their mounts. The terrorized horses snapped their halters and stampeded, a few being lost in the fire. This encounter would have been a complete victory for the Chickasaws and would have put an end to the expedition if the Indians had not mistakenly believed the sound of running horses to mean that the cavalry had managed to mount and pursue them.

EARLY AMERICAN
QUARTER HORSES

It is possible to believe that some of the horses that stampeded that March morning, remained at liberty until the Chickasaws later captured them. Perhaps these were the horses which the Chickasaw Indians are reported to have obtained from the Spanish settlers. Chickasaw horses were raced at quarter-mile distances, but aside from their more glamorous holiday-sports use, the animals were good at plain labor and for purposes of transportation. Writers of those times referred to the Chickasaw as a breed, and their descriptions give an excellent picture of the horse. He was small from the standpoint of height, averaging around 13 hands 2 inches; he was closely coupled and well muscled. At short distances, he showed great speed but was not noted for endurance in long races. It was conceded that the Chickasaw horse was the best all-round utility horse in Colonial America.

After De Soto's death, the survivors of his expedition, headed by Luis de Moscoso, slaughtered for food all the remaining horses, except twenty-two of the best, before starting their river trip back to the sea.

In 1565, Pedro Mendenez de Aviles sailed from Cadiz and dropped anchor, August 28, in a harbor at the mouth of a river and named it Saint Augustine. Before his return to Spain in May, 1567, Mendenez established three permanent settlements on the Atlantic coast—Saint Augustine and San Mateo in Florida, and Santa Elena in South Carolina. He garrisoned forts at Guale in northern Georgia, at Tampa and Charlotte Bays, and at Biscayne Bay and St. Lucie River on the East coast. These settlements were supported by the crown, which undoubtedly furnished horses in good quantity. The Spanish missions and settlements in Florida, Georgia, and South Carolina, from 1570 to 1573, suffered from Indian raids and hunger, and many settlers left the country. Indian raids must have run many horses off the settlements to be later used by them. An account of later years states that raids of English and Indians spread Spanish livestock far to the north.

Other horses, of course, came from England between 1600 and 1630. At that time, the horse in vogue in the British Isles was of pacing-gaited stock.

EARLY IMPROVEMENT

Horsedom in England was undergoing a change. English noblemen who had visited the Continent were learning about the great endurance and bottom of the Oriental horse and were experimenting to improve their horses by crossing Arab and Barb stallions with their native mares.

This was the beginning of what was later to be known as the "Thoroughbred running horse." The vogue for distance racing was being born. It was in 1689 that the Byerly Turk, one of the three Orientals to found the great Thoroughbred breed, was brought to England.

Naturally, American visitors to England succumbed to the "improve-the-horseflesh" movement and brought the idea back to the Colonies. A few horses of Oriental extraction were imported. One of these was Imported Diomede who traces directly to Flying Childers by the Darley Arabian. There was a time in the early days of horse history when nearly every American horse breeder claimed that his horses were from Oriental strains. This fact alone has done much to tangle the records of the true breeding of horses in this country.

At first, the importations were relatively few and the imported line-bred stallions were crossed on Chickasaw mares and other fast Quarter-type mares. These experiments were initially an earnest effort to improve the using stock of the colonists, but as oval tracks were built as a testing ground for the betterment of the horses, a craze for pure distance racing took over.

Some of the get of these crosses produced horses that the "gentlemen breeders" thought suitable. Because of the shortage of imported stallions, the more desirable offspring were used as breeding stock. If, after testing on the track, the young horses were found to lack the staying powers desired, the mares were put into nursery service and the colts were sold down the river to back-country buyers.

A great many of the common colonists did not adhere to the theory of the racing gentlemen that good race horses were necessarily good using horses. As long-distance heat racing was popularized in the older, more established sections of the Colonies, Quarter-racing contests were pushed westward with the new frontiers.

Occasionally these so-called "brush horses" would produce an endurance runner, and he would be brought out of exile to the more esteemed oval racing tracks of civilization.

On analyzing the Quarter Horse, one can find many things which point to the probability that he was largely of Oriental origin even before the "improve-the-horse" movement of the Cavaliers. He has always had a compactness and muscularity. He is given to a speedy way of traveling. He does not show much inclination to the easier saddle gaits, seldom having a good running walk or single-foot gait. While his head is not so fine as an Arab's, he does have the disk-shaped jaw, with width between the jawbones, and a small muzzle. His bones are dense and well shaped and he has clean, strong tendons. He has great width in the region through the heart. Also, there is a striking resemblance between American Quarter Horses and the South American Criollo which comes from Spanish stock. It is interesting to note, in this connection, that the horses of Cortez, De Soto, and the later Spanish settlers were Oriental-bred or, in some cases, what would be referred to today as "grade Arabian."

BLOODLINES

The three Oriental horses which founded the English Thoroughbred were the Byerly Turk, imported to England in 1689, the Darley Arabian in 1712, and the Godolphin Barb in 1732.

These British importations were in line with the general English movement which favored the introduction of the blood of Orientals. The Thoroughbred breed, however, was not established until later. The American cousins of the British started their importations of line-bred Orientals before the English Thoroughbred had been established. The first edition of Weatherby's *General English Stud Book* was published in 1791 and officially opened in 1794, but it was 1827 before the English Thoroughbred was established and purebreds alone were registered.

The reason for establishing the above dates is to show that Imported Janus, conceded to have had more influence on the American Quarter Horse than any other sire, was brought to America in 1752, thirty-nine years before the first edition of Weatherby's *Stud Book* appeared and 116 years before the first volume of the *American* (Thoroughbred) *Stud Book* was published by Col. Sanders D. Bruce.

Imported Janus, by Old Janus, by the Godolphin Barb, was called a "freak horse" because his conformation was that of a Quarter Horse. Although he possessed the same bloodlines that later would establish the English Thoroughbred, he was denied the privilege of being listed in the *English Stud Book.*

Imported Janus lived from 1746 to 1780, and his remarkable prepotency to pass his qualities on to his descendants influenced nine of the eleven important early Quarter Horse strains. The lines that carried such a strong infusion of Imported Janus blood were as follows:

JANUS, 1752	BACCHUS, 1778	PRINTER, 1804
PEACOCK, 1764	CELER, 1780	WHIP, 1809
BABRAM, 1770	TWIGG, 1782	TIGER, 1816

The two families which were not influenced by Janus were Mark Anthony, 1767, established by Lee's Mark Anthony, 1763–1778, and Brimmer, 1787, established by Goode's Brimmer, 1766–1786.

Few, if any, of the modern Quarter Horse families are independent and separate strains; they are branch families of the earlier strains and have practically absorbed them. Thirteen present-day families deserve recognition; quoting from the *American Quarter Horse Official Stud Book and Registry,* Volume I, Number 2, published in 1943, they are as follows:

COPPERBOTTOM, 1832
  Established by Copperbottom, 1828–1860; by Sir Archy, T.B.—mare by
  *Buzzard, T.B. (On his dam's side he traces to Janus.)
SHILOH, 1848
  Established by Shiloh, 1844–1869; by Union—Shiloa.
STEELDUST, 1849
  Established by Steel Dust, 1845–1874; by Harry Bluff—cold-blooded mare.
BILLY, 1866
  Established by Old Billy, 1860–1886; by Shiloh—Ram Cat, Steel Dust.
COLD DECK, 1876
  Established by Old Cold Deck, 1868–1890; by Old Billy—Maudy (Missouri
  mare).
ROAN DICK, 1883
  Established Roan Dick, 1879–1901; by Black Nick—mare by Greenstreet's
  Boanerges.
RONDO, 1884
  Established by Old Rondo (Lock's Rondo), 1880–1897; by Whalebone—
  Mittie Stephens, Shiloh, Jr.
TRAVELER, 1889
  Established by Traveler, 1885–1910. Pedigree untraced. Said to have been
  bred in Kentucky, but may have been by Traveler by Steel Dust.

SYKES, 1891
   Established by Sykes Rondo, 1887–1907; by McCoy Billy—Grasshopper.
FRED, 1897
   Established by Old Fred, 1893–1915, by Black Ball—Mare by John Crowder.
PETER MCCUE, 1899
   Established by Peter McCue, 1895–1923; by Dan Tucker—Nor M., Voltigeur, T.B.
BLAKE, 1900
   Established on Steeldust, Shiloh and Brimmer lines. (Developed by Coke S. Blake, Pryor, Oklahoma.)
JOE BAILEY, 1911
   Established by Old Joe Bailey, 1907–1934; by Eureka—Susie McQuirter, Little Ben.

The names of Quarter Horses are intriguing, for they seem to be reminiscent of the Americans who raised and loved them. Frequently a name seems to be an indication of the character and quality of the horse.

Steel Dust is a magic name in Quarter Horse legend. Many stories are told about old Steel Dust, some true, some not, but they attest to the fact that he was a good horse in the eyes of those who knew him. Steel Dust was a dark, or a blood, bay standing around 14 hands 2 inches. He was originally called Steele and was foaled at Kain, Illinois, in Greene County, around 1845 or 1846. One account says that he was brought to Lancaster, Texas, in 1849 by Mid Perry. Mr. O. G. Murry, grandson of Jones Greene, claims that Steel Dust was brought to Texas about 1846 by a Greene boy and sold to Jones Greene and Middleton Perry for $300.

Steel Dust was by Harry Bluff out of a cold-blooded mare. Harry Bluff was by Short's Whip and out of Big Nance, by Timolian T.B., by Sir Archy. The Steel Dust family traces to the earlier Janus family through the Celer and Whip strains.

The Shiloh family was established in 1848 by Shiloh, 1844–1869, by Union out of Shiloa. Union was by Van Tromp, by Thomas Big Solomon, by Sir Solomon, by Sir Archy.

Shiloh was bred in Tennessee and, like Steel Dust, moved to Texas, being brought there in 1849 by Jack Batchler.

The Shiloh family contributed to, and has been practically absorbed by, the Billy, Cold Deck, Rondo, Fred, Traveler, Sykes, Peter McCue, Blake, and Joe Bailey strains.

It is interesting to note the states to which the thirteen present-day founders of the Quarter Horse gravitated. Nine wound up in Texas, two in Colorado, and one in Oklahoma. Only one, Roan Dick, stayed out of the Southwest. The

Quarter Horses that were handy around the cow pens of the colonists were found to be equally good at handling cattle on the open range country in the Southwest. Here again, they furnished holiday sport with their match races, running for a plug of chewing tobacco or higher stakes.

Whether his name be Little Fred, Shue Fly, Wimpy, Bob Wade or Little Joe, Jr., you may be sure that the chunky little horse traces back, through many years of hardship, to the famous Colonial quarter-of-a-mile race horse.

CONFORMATION

Horses of different breeds are distinguished by their body form. The American Saddle Horse, for example, is one whose conformation is based on pleasing curves and fineness that make of him a veritable peacock in the world of horses. The Hackney is stylish in his smart compactness and weight.

The Quarter Horse, like these, is readily recognized by his body form and characteristics of utility.

Muscular Development

The most outstanding feature of a Quarter Horse is his extreme musculature. Built low to the ground, the ideal height is about 14 hands 3½ inches, the weight approximately 1,175 pounds. Bulging muscles adorn the Quarter Horse on almost every part of his body. The hindquarters carry much muscle, outside as well as inside. The space between forelegs is ample to permit a wide, well-developed chest. The muscular characteristic is notable in the jaws of the breed. The forearms carry more muscle than is found on most horses, as do the shoulders; the coupling over the loins is well supplied with muscle sheaths. These are features which have suggested the term "bulldog type."

Shortness of Frame

While not as fine as those found on some other light-type horses, the bones of a Quarter Horse are trim, dense, and well modeled. This sturdiness seems necessary, however, to support such a strong top line. The neck is not long, and the back is relatively short and closely coupled to the hips and hindquarters. The ribs are well sprung. The cannon bones are short, as are the pasterns, which are strong and do not have as much slope as many saddle horses. The feeling of shortness is also pronounced in the head, the muzzle giving a chopped-off appearance, and is topped by small "fox-type" ears, which lie peculiarly forward when the animal's attention is ahead.

In contrast with that of other breeds, the stance of the Quarter Horse is peculiar to himself. As seen in profile, he stands with his legs well under his body. The head is carried moderately low. The forelegs seem set back from the powerful chest. The neck gives the appearance of coming straight from the point of attachment at the withers and shoulders. If an arch in the neck is present, it is only slight.

The withers are not prominent, although Quarter Horse men insist that a good specimen should not have mutton withers. Another point which they deny is that a well-built Quarter Horse is lower in front than behind, although it must be admitted that many of them give that appearance. A wry remark is frequently heard that any horse that looks as if he were going downhill makes a good Quarter Horse. This, of course, is not true. I believe that part of this illusion is caused by the decided slope to the croup, plus the absence of high withers and high head carriage. The depth of chest may add to the illusion, for there is not much daylight under the front of a good Quarter Horse. Certainly a slightly sloping rump, which throws the balance of the hind feet well under the body, and the comparatively low head carriage are physical factors which add to the success and utility of this breed as a using horse.

Some enthusiasts point out that a low-carried head with no arch in the neck is necessary, as the working rider does not want a high head in his way as he twirls and throws his rope. Certainly it is easier for a horse to follow a fast-weaving critter if he points his nose toward it.

Some individuals may not look upon a sloped-croup horse as their ideal of equine beauty, but a horse with his hind legs balanced well under him is better equipped to come to a full stop in one motion, without bouncing in front, and it is easier for him to turn quickly without raising his front end high off the ground.

Color and Markings

Quarter Horses are found in a variety of colors. A check of 1,700 registered horses showed sorrel to be the slightly predominating color with 413 registered; bay followed closely with 397; and chestnut was next with 316. Other colors followed in order of their numerical importance: 176 duns, 165 browns, 83 blacks, 69 grays, 42 roans, 22 creams, 14 grullos, and 3 whites. No pintos, appaloosas, albinos, or multicolored horses are knowingly accepted by the American Quarter Horse Association for registration. I do not understand the reason for this rule, as I have seen a few paint horses that were, in my opinion, good specimens of the Quarter Horse type. A check into the bloodlines of such individuals may be the cause of a change of mind. Markings on the feet, legs, and face, of course, are permissible.

Temperament

Aside from the physical characteristics of a Quarter Horse, there are other qualities for which he is noted. Paramount among these is his disposition. Most horses would find it difficult to perform as successfully and yet remain as unruffled as a Quarter Horse after a day's work of fast starts, quick stops, standing still, starting again, and rapid turns, all of which are the necessary routine of a using stock horse. Moreover, a horse that excites himself into a nervous sweat after a flurry of action puts his health in jeopardy. Quarter Horses do not require cooling out after chasing a critter.

The Quarter Horse performs admirably under these conditions. Furthermore, he seems to have an inbred instinct to work cattle. One rancher stated it thus: "If I were to saddle that gelding standing there in the barn and get on him, he would see those cows lying down over there about a quarter of a mile and start toward them. This is because Quarter Horses have been bred to have cow savvy."

The intelligence of this breed of horses shows in their honest, wide-set eyes; it is proved by their adaptability to training.

JUDGING

Judging of any type of horse should be done with intelligence and a thorough knowledge of, and interest in, the breed being judged. It naturally follows that the working use for which the animal is intended should be the paramount consideration. For instance, a Hunter is built along lines of conformation which enable him to perform certain tasks which are never asked of a Standard Bred trotter. In other words, *performance* is the essential basis of value when any type of horse is being judged.

Breeders have learned through years of experience that certain general outward characteristics go hand in hand with ability to perform. A sloping shoulder is associated with good riding qualities; well-sprung ribs and depth of body, with endurance; well-developed muscles, with strength; a short back, with weight-carrying ability.

Horse shows and judging should be a fair proving ground, a place where breeders can bring their product for testing and future guidance.

Most judging falls into two divisions.

1. *Breed Classes:* These classes are open to stallions and mares and are usually divided into age groups. The purpose is to judge the animals on their suitability as breeding stock. It is in these classes that pure structure should be considered.

One of the best systems I have seen worked out by a judge was a standardized sheet, pocket-notebook size, in the form shown below.

CLASS _____

Entry No. _____   Date _____

Condition _____   Age _____

CONFORMATION

Head and Neck:

Head _____   Eyes _____

Ears _____   Neck _____

Forequarters:

Shoulders _____   Cannons _____

Arms _____   Pasterns _____

Forearm _____   Feet _____

Knees _____   Legs _____

Body:

Withers _____   Back _____

Chest _____   Loin _____

Ribs _____   Flank _____

Hindquarters:

Hips _____   Gaskins _____

Croup _____   Hocks _____

Tail _____   Cannons _____

Quarters _____   Pasterns _____

Stifle _____   Feet _____

Thighs _____   Legs _____

ACTION

Walk _____   Gallop, or run _____

Trot _____

REMARKS _____
_____

FORM FOR JUDGING BREED CLASSES

Beside each of these many points he scored the horse with "average," "plus," or "minus." The final score decided the excellence of the horse. At the top of each sheet was a place for the number of the contesting animal. After the judging, if the breeder wished to know why his animal did not receive a higher rating, the judge was able to give him his opinion of the horse by looking at the chart.

Horses in breed classes are worked in hand, being walked, trotted, and galloped before the judge. This is to demonstrate quality of action and reveals to some extent the animal's inner feelings and alertness.

2. *Performance Classes:* Such classes offer opportunity for the Quarter Horse to prove his outstanding ability. In view of the fact that most stock-horse classes are not closed to breeds, the subject will be explored more fully in Chapter 11, pertaining to Western Horses as a whole. Performance classes which are devoted exclusively to Quarter Horses are not greatly different from those discussed in the chapter mentioned.

FOUNDING THE STUD

At the present time there are, to my knowledge, two associations which foster and maintain a register for Quarter Horses. The associations differ mainly in registration requirements.

The American Quarter Horse Association, Eagle Pass, Texas, was the first to be formed, in 1940, for the purpose of preserving and promoting the Quarter Horse. The requirements of the A.Q.H.A. are high in that it has set up a threefold standard of conformation, bloodlines, and performance. A horse, upon being admitted under this standard, is entered in the "tentative" registry. Final admission to the "permanent" registry is achieved only after the candidate has proved his (or her) ability to reproduce desirable type characteristics. This, of course, requires a highly intensified program of selective breeding.

The National Quarter Horse Breeders' Association, Hockley, Texas, was formed in 1945 by breeders who did not concur with the practices of the A.Q.H.A. These founders were of the opinion that too much importance was being placed on conformation and not enough on performance, and also that bloodlines were too closely restricted to certain family strains. Furthermore, they felt that a "beefy" build of horse was being developed and that this type did not necessarily represent the old Celebrated American Quarter Horse. In variance with A.Q.H.A., the National Quarter Horse Breeders' Association permits registration on a permanent basis, taking into consideration blood alone, with outstanding performance on the quarter track indicating what is to be deemed Quarter blood. It can be readily seen that such requirements are less rigid than those enforced by the A.Q.H.A. and are not likely to establish a distinctly recognizable type. In support of their principles, however, the N.Q.H.B.A. points out that, in its opinion, the Celebrated American Quarter Horse of the past developed solely as a result of performance and can contribute to the blood of future horses only if purity of blood is not over-emphasized.

Almost fifty years ago, the earliest thoughts for founding a stud book for the American Quarter Horse were in the mind of William Anson, an Englishman by birth who had found his background in west Texas cow country. In William Anson there existed a deep conviction of the economic worth of the Quarter Horse, and thus it was in this animal that he found his equine ideal.

The fact that Billy Anson was a scholar as well as a great horseman made it possible for him to trace the purity of strains back to Quarter Horses of Colonial times. While his efforts to start a registry did not bear immediate fruit, his efforts and research are given much credit in the later establishment of the *American Quarter Horse Stud Book.*

There were others who championed the Quarter Horse. Among these was Dan Casement of Manhattan, Kansas, whose rich store of knowledge lay dormant until his son, Jack Casement, brought it to public attention through his writings. Robert H. Denhardt is another who is tireless in his efforts to credit the Quarter Horse.

Until comparatively recent times there was little public knowledge of this breed. The Quarter Horse was always on the move, following frontiers where his use was most logical. The men who owned him were not versed in the ways of publicity. Also, many an old-timer had the feeling that if a steer couldn't be headed with a horse, a registration paper wouldn't help. The deeds of good horses were advertised merely by word of mouth. If a man owned a stallion who was a proved sire, mares would be brought to him. But many owners of stallions were not always filled to the brim with truth in the claims they made. This has been true of all breeds. In a system where horse husbandry has become a science, such methods cannot long be tolerated. The progress of any breed is based on the accomplishments of its foundation stock and the improvement by study of the future stock. This is made possible by honestly and impartially recording the animals involved and by observing, without bias, their accomplishments.

Those were the facts which led up to the founding of the American Quarter Horse Association, which was the first group to form a stud book and accept for registration Quarter-type horses. This association was officially formed on March 15, 1940, and, as a result, the first stud book and registry appeared the following year. The American Quarter Horse Association claims that 90 per cent of the horses registered are of proved Quarter Horse blood.

The Quarter Horse is rightly becoming recognized as a distinct horse breed. The American Stallions Registration Board has recognized the Quarter Horse as an established light breed, and it is listed by the U.S. Department of Agriculture as one of the modern breeds of livestock. Quarter Horse stallions may be serviced in any state in the Union without being advertised as scrubs. The Quarter Horse is now carried on the prize lists of many state fairs, and it is recognized as a breed by the Horse and Mule Association of America, Inc.

RANCH AND RODEO WORK

The present-day Quarter Horse is not a "Jack-of-all-trades," but he is a master of some. I like to think of this little horse primarily as a work animal, for it is on the ranches where he is perhaps most appreciated. As a stock horse he is unsurpassed. His tremendous short speed and maneuverability are great assets and his tranquillity and intelligence make of him a good pupil in learning the ways of ranching. Not of least importance to ranch owners is his easy-keeping quality. It is possible for him to sustain himself on range grass while he works day after day. There are few breeds better qualified to adapt themselves to extremes of heat and cold found in ranch conditions of work, stabling, and pasturing.

Rodeo is reputed to be the second most important spectator sport in the United States, bowing only to the great American game of baseball. It would be difficult to attend a rodeo these days without seeing many Quarter Horses during the course of the show.

OUTSTANDING FOR RODEO WORK

During the years that have popularized rodeo, competition has become intense. Split seconds count. Without the aid of a good horse working as a team with his rider, it would be impossible for the cowboy to win his day money. If the pony does not put the dogger at the right spot alongside the steer, the purse is lost. The ability of the Quarter Horse to stand quietly one instant and to run at top speed the next makes him a bread-and-butter necessity to the top ropers and pickup men.

There have been many good rodeo horses that were not from the ranks of the Quarter Horse, but the records will prove that the vast majority were "short" horses.

QUARTER-MILE RACING

There is a saying that a Quarter Horse can run as long as he can hold his breath. Whether or not this is true, it is certain that the audience will hold its breath when these equine buzz saws run the quarter.

Quarter-of-a-mile racing on a straightaway between two matched horses from a standing start has been popular in America for three hundred years. My prophecy is that it will continue as long as two men own horses.

In past years, particularly, the outstanding feature of this type of race was its informality. The match races of early Colonial times were the setting for celebration and an opportunity for merrymaking. The gathering was usually a mixture of humanity, made up of Cavalier gentlemen with their slaves, coonskin-capped wilderness hunters, and Indians in paint and feathers. Some of the match races of today are not much different. Frequently, the occasion calls for a barbecue and an all-day *fiesta*. Ranchers, city folk, cowboys, and Mexicans are all present. A fast horse will always attract crowds, and when that horse is one that has the capacity to work one day and race the next, he will continue to capture public fancy.

"The poor man's race horse" is the term frequently applied to the Quarter Horse. Expensive equipment is not required, and costly trainers are not necessary in preparing these horses for a race. Even the ground over which the horses run does not require lavish preparation.

In the past, there were abuses of fair play at such meetings. The only rules were those made by the contestants before the match. Trickery, foul riding, and unfair practices were not uncommon, and it was necessary in many instances to employ the court to decide the result.

With the advent of the A.Q.H.A. and the subsequent N.Q.H.B.A., old abuses are being obliterated and quarter racing is coming into its own.

It would be difficult to foretell the tremendous popularity which this sport will create. A potent modern factor in the standardization of racing practices is the recently formed American Quarter Racing Association. Founded in 1944, this group stands for honesty in the management of Quarter racing and fair play and good sportsmanship on the track.

The A.Q.R.A. has done much to set up uniform standards of competition and it has adopted a code of rules and regulations. Its function does not interfere with the operation of the Quarter Horse associations, but it makes available descriptions, through markings and brands, ownership, pedigree, color, sex, etc., thereby eliminating unfair practices such as running "ringers" or "sleepers." Race records of all recognized tracks are accurately filed and indexed, thus furnishing exact data which improves and promotes close competition. Perfection of the starting gate and rigid adherence to standardized rules are assisting in promoting the sport of Quarter racing.

It is interesting to note the names and records of some of the great Quarter Horse racers. A horse that can run the quarter from a standing start in twenty-three seconds is good, to say the least. There have been some who were able to clip time off that. Following is a list showing the marks of some of the famous horses who ran between 1880 and 1902:

			Time, Sec.
APRIL FOOL	Fresno, Calif.	Oct. 2, 1891	21¾
BELLE	Galveston, Tex.	Jul. 3, 1880	21¾
BOB WADE	Butte, Mont.	Aug. 20, 1890	21¼
JIM MILLER	Deer Lodge, Mont.	Aug. 16, 1888	21½
JUDGE THOMAS	Butte, Mont.	Aug. 15, 1902	21¾
LARK	Butte, Mont.	Aug. 15, 1896	21½
NETTIE S.	Helena, Mont.	Aug. 23, 1890	21¾
QUEEN T.	Butte, Mont.	Aug. 9, 1902	21½
SILVER DICK	Butte, Mont.	Aug. 7, 1902	21½
SLEEPY DICK	Kiowa, Kan.	Nov. 24, 1888	21½

From the years 1900 to 1940, there was a great decline during which few Quarter races were run. In the recent period following 1940, three Quarter Horses stand out with time of 22⅕ seconds:

CLABBER	Eagle Pass, Tex.	1941
GINGER ROGERS	Junction, Tex.	1939
SHUE FLY	Eagle Pass, Tex.	1942

Of recent nationwide interest was the race between Barbra B, registered Quarter mare, and Fair Truckle, registered Thoroughbred Horse, at the Hollywood Park Track, August 4, 1947. Following is a quotation, in part, of the official report of the American Quarter Racing Association:

Inglewood, California, August 4, 1947—Quarter Racing earned the right to be recognized as a major equestrian sport this afternoon. Roy Gill's four year old bay Quarter mare Barbra B ran a special matched race at the Hollywood Park Track against C. S. Howard's four year old brown Thoroughbred Horse "Fair Truckle" and won decisively by two lengths in time that was just about as fast as horses run.

The race was started from a four stall schooling gate. Barbra B, having drawn the rail, was loaded in No. 1 gate and Fair Truckle in No. 4 in order to avoid any chance of bumping when they came out. The start was good—if anything the Thoroughbred broke a little ahead of the mare but she quickly moved into the lead and when the horse, as was expected, bore over towards the rail, he crossed behind her without interference. Barbra B seemed to flounder at first under too much drive but her rider quickly steadied her and when he again went to his bat at the eighth pole she responded and was able to meet Fair Truckle's challenge and maintain her two length lead to the wire. Fair Truckle was ridden by Johnnie Longden and Barbra B by Tony Licata. Both boys weighed in at 110 pounds.

This race was publicized in advance as a contest between a Quarter Horse and a Thoroughbred and there will be those who will claim that it settles that argument. However, one of the present co-holders of the World's Record for one quarter of a mile, from a standing start, is the registered Thoroughbred mare Woven Web, better known as Miss Princess down in Texas, so the rivalry between the breeds will continue to make interesting copy for some years to come.

In addition to ranch and rodeo work and short racing, Quarter Horses have been successful on the polo field. I have seen Quarter Horses which made excellent trick and liberty horses in circuses. Their even temperament, intelligence, and sturdiness served them well in this work. There may be other fields in which this placid little horse will eventually find himself.

Many of the horsemen who love the Quarter Horse most do not recommend him as an all-round pleasure mount. They say that his gaits are not usually comfortable for long periods of riding. On the other hand, some enthusiasts claim that he is becoming more and more popular as a pleasure horse. Such owners have found that he is an ideal family horse, owing to his quiet disposition. They claim that he can be used all summer, turned out in the fall and winter, and does not require a breaking-out period when he is caught up again in the spring.

For those who require a horse that is an easy keeper, plucky and tough, and have a job to do which requires a level head, rapid breaking speed, and extreme handiness, I unwaveringly recommend the Quarter Horse.

7

Morgan Horses

Justin Morgan—or Figure, as he was first named—came into the world unheralded and without ceremony over a century and a half ago. Considered in retrospect, Justin Morgan was perhaps the most important single horse ever to be foaled on the North American continent, for he founded the first distinctively American breed, and his blood has influenced every other American breed that exists today.

Geneticists agree that Justin Morgan was a mutant, or sport—that is, a sudden variation of type, rather than one in which new characteristics became fully developed only after many generations. A true mutant is a genetic species variation which breeds true to its new likeness. Prior to the time of Justin Morgan there had never been a horse quite like him.

As with all great characters, many stories and legends have sprung up about this immortal stallion, and it has been difficult to extricate truth from myth. In fact, there has been so much controversy over his ancestry and bloodlines that it seems best to present several of the stories and let the reader draw his own conclusions. In considering these stories, it must be remembered that none of them lessens the greatness of Justin Morgan, for during his life he proved his merit through strength and courage. His blood, through subsequent generations, immortalized him.

The first of the stories is a quotation from *Famous Saddle Horses* by Susanne:

The real facts about him are . . . few in number. . . . It has been determined, however, that there was living in Springfield, Mass., a school teacher named Justin Morgan. He was the owner of a mare of medium size, said to belong to the "Wildair" breed. This mare was bred to a son of Imp. Morton's

137

Morgan Horse

Trim power and style are notable features of the Morgan. This powerhouse among light horses has served America admirably in a variety of saddle and harness uses.

The crested neck is medium short and heavily muscled. Nevertheless it rises upward to present a lofty head carriage.

Back medium short and powerfully coupled to hips. Shoulders built up to withers, minimizing any prominence of bone there. Barrel rounded. No wasp waists.

Ears short; profile of face ordinarily straight; wide-set eyes intelligent in appearance. Jaws powerful.

Slightly sloping croup tops rounded thighs and muscular gaskins. Tail set low but carried well in action.

Legs straight, with considerable bone. Great length from elbow to knee and from stifle to hock; extremely short cannon bones. Fetlock joints heavily feathered in comparison to those of other light breeds.

More width of chest than most other breeds. Shoulders covered with powerful muscles.

Traveler, Thoroughbred. This son went by the two names of True Briton and Beautiful Bay. It was from this mating that Justin Morgan was born.

From the same book we take another quotation:

The mare, according to another story . . . was by his stock horse, Diamond. He mated her with a horse John Morgan, of West Springfield, Mass., had in his possession named True Briton, owned by Lilah Norton, of East Hartford, Conn. True Briton is said to have been bred by General DeLancy, commander of the Loyalist refugees on Long Island during the Revolutionary War, and this horse was stolen from him by a man named Smith, who took him to The American Army at White Plains, where he sold him to Joseph Ward, of East Hartford, Conn., for $300. Mr. Ward rode and drove True Briton for four years and then sold him to Mr. Norton who rented him to John Morgan. From the mating with True Briton, the Diamond mare produced the colt, Justin Morgan, in 1789, which was named Figure, a name which he bore until after Mr. Morgan's death, when he was named Justin Morgan in honor of his breeder. Mr. Morgan disposed of his horses in 1792 and moved to Randolph, Vt., and later returned to collect some money and is said to have taken Figure or Justin Morgan and another young horse in on the debt. Mr. Morgan made three seasons with him in 1793, 1794, and 1795, advertising him under the name of Figure.

In his book *The Horse of America*, Mr. Wallace refutes these versions and gives the benefit of his own research:

Mr. Justin Morgan, the central figure in this investigation, was born in West Springfield, 1747, where he married and lived till 1788, when he removed to Randolph, Vt., where he died, March, 1798. He was a reputable citizen, fairly well educated for his time, and taught school for a living. He owned a wayside house of entertainment, and during the early summer he usually had a stallion to keep on the shares. In the spring of 1785 he had charge of the horse True Briton, or Beautiful Bay, and I will here add that three years later, John Morgan, Jr., had charge of the same horse at Springfield, for the seasons of 1788 and 1789. This John Morgan, Jr., removed to Lima, N.Y., late in 1790 or early in 1791. Justin had sold his place in West Springfield to Abner Morgan, on long payments, and in the summer of 1795 he came back to West Springfield to collect some money that was due him, presumably on the price of his former home, but he failed to get money and took two colts instead. One was a three-year-old gelding and the other was a two-year-old bay colt, entire. He led the three-year-old with a halter and the two-year-old followed. The date of this visit to the old home is fixed by Justin Morgan, Jr., then a lad of the right age to remember such things, and by Solomon Steele and Judge Griswold, who fixed the date in the late summer of 1795. The horse was sold and resold and sold again, as a foal of 1793, and that date never left him till he died in 1821. I look upon this date as perfectly immovable, and every attempt that had been made to overthrow it had not been based on any reasonable evidence. . . . After a lapse of fifty years an attempt was made to fix up a pedigree for the "Original Morgan Horse," claiming that he was got by True Briton or Beautiful Bay—represented to be a great race horse, stolen from the great race horse man, Colonel De Lancey, in the Revolutionary War. I must, therefore, consider, briefly, this part of the fiction.

First. As a starting point in the pedigree it is assumed that the race horse in question was stolen, during the War of the Revolution, from James De Lancey, perhaps the largest and most widely known of all the colonial horsemen of that day. . . . He was very rich, in politics a Tory, and on the eve of hostilities he sold out every horse he owned . . . went back to England and never returned. This disposes of the false assumption that the sire of the original Morgan was stolen from him.

Second. There was another James De Lancey, cousin to the preceding . . . colonel of a body of Tory cavalry operating in Westchester County from 1777 to 1782. . . . His name is not to be found anywhere in connection with horses. He bore, in full, the same name as the distinguished horseman, and was mistaken for him, although he was on the other side of the ocean.

Third. It is claimed that "one Smith" stole the horse in question from Colonel De Lancey. . . . Who was this "one Smith" and where did he belong? Where is the evidence that this "one Smith" stole a horse from Colonel De Lancey?

Fourth. In the New York Packet, then published at Fishkill, under date of October 19, 1780, we find the following: "Last week Lieutenant Wright Carpenter and two others went down to Colonel James De Lancey's quarters and lay in wait for his appearance. He accordingly came and having tied his horse at the door, went into the house; upon which Carpenter seized the horse and mounted. When De Lancey discovered him, he immediately alarmed his men, who pursued him to White Plains, but in vain," etc. This Lieutenant Carpenter . . . is the man that stole the horse, this is the contemporaneous evidence of it, and "one Smith" had nothing to do with it.

In these four points we have what may be considered the first chapter of this investigation. . . . We must, therefore, look further on for the time when, and the person by whom, this pedigree was manufactured.

In 1784 this horse was advertised at Lanesboro, Mass., under the name of Beautiful Bay, and no attempt was made to give a pedigree or origin of the horse.

In 1785 he was at West Springfield, Mass., in charge of Justin Morgan, still called Beautiful Bay, and still no pedigree.

In 1788 and 1789 he was in charge of John Morgan, Jr., of Springfield, Mass., and here, for the first time, he is designated as the "famous full-blooded English horse, called True Briton or Beautiful Bay," but no pedigree is given.

In 1791 he was advertised at East Hartford, Conn., by his owner, Selah Norton, and his pedigree is here given for the first time as follows: "True Briton, or Beautiful Bay, got by Imp. Traveler, dam De Lancey's racer." After advertising him for seven years without a pedigree, at last Mr. Selah Norton manufactures one and gives it over his own signature.

In 1793 he is again called Beautiful Bay, but no pedigree, at South Hadley, Mass.

In 1794 and 1795 he was kept at Ashfield, Mass., by Mr. Norton himself, and called Traveler, and his pedigree is again given in amended form as follows: "Sired by the famous old Traveler, imported from Ireland, dam Colonel De Lancey's imported racer."

This is the last trace we have of the horse Beautiful Bay. . . . From first to last Selah Norton seems to have been his owner. If he had received the pedigree, and the romantic story of his theft, from "one Smith," as claimed, is it conceivable that he would have concealed that story from the public when it would have added so much to the patronage of his horse? . . . In 1794 and 1795 we find him at Ashfield, Mass. . . . For some reason that can be better imagined than explained, the names Beautiful Bay and True Briton are there dropped and he is re-christened as Traveler. To this change of name the old pedigree is attached, with a very important change in that also as follows: "Sired by famous old Traveler, imported from Ireland, dam Colonel De Lancey's imported racer." These three words, "imported from Ireland," are very important in two particulars, for they not only throw out the "Feather-heads" who have always maintained that the important Traveler meant Lloyd's Traveler of New Jersey, son of Morton's Traveler, that was imported from Yorkshire into Virginia about 1750, but it convicts Selah Norton of inventing this pedigree, for there was no such horse brought from Ireland. I will here end the second chapter of this investigation. . . .

The only serious attempt that has been made to controvert the date of 1793 as the date of the foaling of Justin Morgan was that made in the name of John Morgan, of Lima, N.Y., in 1842, he being then eighty years old, in the Albany "Cultivator." Unfortunately the editor fails to publish the letter he professed to have received from John Morgan and only gives his construction of it. . . . The editor represents him to say "that the two-year-old stud which he (Justin) took with him to Vermont was sired by a horse owned by Selah Norton, of East Hartford, Conn., called True Briton or Beautiful Bay." Justin Morgan removed to Randolph, Vt., in the spring of 1788, and this John Morgan removed to Lima, N.Y., about February, 1790. They were not brothers, but distant relatives. If John means to say that Justin "took with him," when he removed to Vermont, a two-year-old son of Beautiful Bay, that colt must have been foaled in 1786, which would make him twelve years old instead of five when he was sold upon the death of his owner, and thirty-six years old instead of twenty-nine when he died from a kick. Now, if we concede that Justin did take with him a two-year-old son of Beautiful Bay, the dates render it impossible that he should have been the founder of the Morgan horse family and we have no trace of him whatever. . . .

There are several incidents connected with the life of the colt of 1793 that fixed his identity and age upon the recollections of the neighbors and friends of Justin Morgan. Solomon Steele, Evans, Rice, and others who knew the colts well, all agree that the colt followed his companion and playmate from West Springfield to Randolph in the autumn of 1795, and that he was not then halter broken. . . . They all agree that Justin Morgan died in March, 1798, and that the colt was then sold as a five-year-old. The death was an immovable date fixer around which everything in connection with these events must be determined. And when the horse died in 1821 nobody had ever doubted that he was foaled in 1793.

Justin Morgan, Jr., was in his tenth year when the colt was brought home, and he was twelve years old when his father died. In 1842, Justin Morgan, Jr., in a communication to the Albany "Cultivator" says: "The said two-year-old colt was the same that has since been known all over New England by the name of the Morgan horse. I know that my father always, while he lived, called him a Dutch horse. I have a perfect recollection of the horse when my father owned him and afterward, and well remember that my father always spoke of him as of the best blood."

When he made these clean-cut and emphatic declarations Justin Morgan, Jr., was fifty-six years old, and it has been suggested that he was too young, at the time, to have remembered about the colt. This is a grave mistake, for farmers' boys remember a thousand things better then than they ever do afterwards. . . .

Did Justin Morgan know what he was saying when he "always, while he lived, called him a Dutch horse"? And did he understand the historical meaning of his words when "he always spoke of him as of the best blood"? To answer these questions we must make some reference to history. The Dutch horses were a breed wholly distinct from the horses of the other colonies. The colony of New Netherlands (New York) received its supply from Utrecht, in Holland, commencing in 1624 and a few years following. In forty years they had so increased that the colony was well supplied. These horses were about fourteen hands and one inch high, which was about one hand higher than the horses supplied to the English colonies. They were not only higher, but they had more bone and muscle, and I think, more shapely necks. In every respect they were better except that they were not so good for the saddle, for the reason, I think, that they were not pacers. The standard that determined their superiority was the higher prices at which they were bought and sold, over the New England horses, as shown by the official reports of the colony. When the colony passed under British rule, the first governor immediately established a

race course in Hempstead Plains, Long Island, and there in 1665 the first organized race in this country took place. This was long before the English race
horse had reached the character of a breed, and a round hundred years before
the first representative of that breed reached New York. The horses that ran
at Hempstead Plains were undoubtedly Dutch horses, for the inhabitants of
New York and Long Island attended these annual meetings in great numbers,
and as they were nearly all Dutch they would not have gone a stone's throw to
see an English horse run. These annual race meetings were kept up a great
many years by the successive governors.

In 1635 two shiploads of Dutch horses, from the same quarter, chiefly mares,
reached Salem, Mass., and were sold at prices enormously high as compared
with the prices of those sent from England to the same colony. These two shiploads added materially to the average size of the horses of the colony of Massachusetts Bay, as shown by statistics, as well as the other colonies getting their
foundation stock from that source. We may safely conclude, I think, that some
of the descendants of these shiploads were taken to the valley of the Connecticut when Hartford was planted, for we not infrequently meet with the term
"Dutch horse" in the old prints of that valley. Besides this source the valley of
the Hudson was full of them. They retained their distinctive appellation till
about the beginning of this century.

Mr. O. W. Cook, of Springfield, Mass., did a great deal of fundamental investigation on the origin of this family. . . . Among other important things
he unearths an advertisement of Young Bulrock that was advertised to stand
at Springfield, 1792, as follows: "Young Bulrock is a horse of the Dutch breed,
of a large size, and a bright bay color, etc." In speaking of his pedigree, Mr.
Cook most pithily remarks: "In view of the threefold concurrence of time and
place and breed, it fits into the vacuum in the Morgan's lineage as a fragment
of pottery fits into its complement." There was another horse advertised in
Springfield that year, but he had neither name nor breed, and in color he was
gray. The advertisement of Young Bulrock fits in time, fits in color, and fits
in breed; and thus removes all reasonable doubt that he was the sire of the
original Morgan horse. This is the reason why Justin Morgan "always, while
he lived, called him a Dutch horse"; and the little scrap of history given above
will show why he always spoke of him as "of the best blood." He was right in
the former and he was right in the latter declaration. It is not possible, at this
day, to prove, technically, these matters of a hundred years ago, but after considering all the facts in the case, we must conclude that they are satisfying to
the human understanding, and that Justin Morgan told the truth. . . .

Thus Historian Wallace ends his lengthy but interesting remarks concerning the bloodlines of Justin Morgan. As we have noted, he builds up a case
which asserts that the Dutch stallion Young Bulrock was the sire instead of
True Briton or Beautiful Bay.

A great number of other historians have delved into the background and lineage of Justin Morgan. Though they may disagree concerning his origin and ancestry, all agree that as an individual he was a remarkable animal and that as a sire he ranks with the noblest stallions of all time. Nature seemed to have mysteriously blessed him with the prepotency to transmit his special characteristics to his descendants and thus establish the distinctive horse breed that has been known by his name ever since.

The qualities of old Justin Morgan transcend the importance of ancestry. The short back, the long, sloping shoulder, the deep chest and powerful muscles, and the cleanly shaped legs that mark his offspring denote the strength and stamina which so well served the people of this nation. The willing spirit of the Morgan breed has been admired by aristocracy as well as by those who used his descendants at many menial tasks in the building of America. Indeed, his fiber seems to have been a vital part of this nation's structure, his sinews, through countless offspring, lending strength to the people of the land in times when the horse was an absolute necessity.

Though many may not agree that he was a descendant of such great horses as Godolphin's Arabian, none can deny that he stands in posterity with the Godolphins, the Matchems, the Messengers, or the horses of any other great line.

Phil Stong's book *Horses and Americans* deals interestingly with noted sires of questionable ancestry. We quote as follows:

The whole story of the founding stock—for one can only consider the official list of "Foundation Sires" as arbitrary, abbreviated, and nouvelle élite—is necessarily incoherent, and tentative as to authority. The business is complicated by crossbreedings of gaited horses. Denmark was a great ancestor of runners, and Messenger was a great ancestor of trotters, and Denmark was a great ancestor of trotters, and Messenger was a great ancestor of runners. The subject would hardly be worth exploring for the small residue of verifiable fact and it would not be important if it were not a phenomenon of the most absolute democracy—if one can speak of an absolute democracy—in nature; the democracy of biogenesis.

For where are the nobles of the blood royal? Serving very notably on plows and mowing machines; filling out the stables of the Army Remount; pulling ice wagons; running races; filling soldiers' bellies during the World War; winning blue ribbons in Kansas City and Madison Square Garden at the great horse shows; trotting the gizzards out of vacationists in Vermont and Montana. More than one derivative of Godolphin's Arabian has pulled a plow, just as the gets of the Hanovers, Hohenzollerns and Bourbons may not all be at resplendent occupations. As far as that is concerned, very little was known about a tanner's daughter, the dam of William the Conqueror.

"Davy Crockett," parents unknown, died at the age of five. He is a Foundation Sire. Denmark's son, Rob Roy, was a Foundation Sire, and he also died at the age of five but left some excellent soldiers for the Civil War. The dates of the births or deaths, or both, of ten of the twenty-three are not known. What horses they may have bred before they were knighted is equally unknown; even what horses they may have bred through the long years.

While even in early times the finest studs might stand at fifty guineas or more, they had plenty of sons who would serve for a guinea and plenty of their descendants are certainly standing out in Iowa, Minnesota, Illinois and Missouri for twenty, ten or five dollars—on a dull day in the stable for whatever can be obtained. Selection and gelding save the country from an overflow of horse Bourbons but the occasional appearance of some obscure, unheralded and unpedigreed prodigy usually marks an atavism—a belated reference back to very gentle blood.

The horse who left the greatest name was a little bay stallion. He dragged logs for a farmer who was cutting off one of the spotty clearings in the difficult State of Vermont. He was Justin Morgan, named for one of his owners, who would have rested unknown for this century and a half, had he not attached his own name to a two-year-old stud colt which he acquired with a three-year-old gelding in West Springfield, Mass., in 1791 most probably.

It might have made a difference in American history if the colt had been the gelding. Forrester, in 1857, refers with the implied irony of italics to the attempt to set up the little bay not only as the head of a line but as the great ancestor of a whole family of horses, on a titular par with Arabs, Percherons, Thoroughbreds, Belgians, Suffolks, Shires, Hackneys and Saddle Horses today.

Eighty-odd years later we can see that the attempt was successful. The Morgan breed is the only one that derives its breed name from an individual horse. There are types and there are families, but Morgan started a family that was and still is a type—the Morgan horse. Rose Wilder Lane's novel of the 1880's, *Free Land,* remarks the covetousness of Dakota settlers for a horse of old Morgan's blood; the United States Army and the United States Department of Agriculture still prize and maintain the offspring of the little bay who was born from God knows what about 1793. Today his breed has declined in usefulness and numbers, but every horseman knows his name.

He has plowed fields and pulled stumps and fought wars for the people of America for a great deal more than a century, through his descendants, by some unbelievable succession of genes which evidently go back to the old patriarch. With no ancestry, harnessed continually at his daily work, a nameless, ordinary, smallish stallion who came from nowhere and died in 1821 of a kick that was not properly attended, made himself his own royal name, Tudor, Stuart, Hohenzollern, Romanov, or Son of the Sun, in the world of horses. Messenger and Denmark have left what seem to be immortal names in horse history, but there is no Messenger breed and no Denmark breed. There are twenty common breeds or so now but only one of them is named for a single horse—Morgan.

There is a magnificence in this circumstance that dazzles everyone who attempts to write on the history of horses. Several men have spent years of their mature lives in working out biographies and histories of Justin Morgan; most particularly, his pedigree. A Mr. D. C. Linsley published a book about 1860 in which the dates of the correspondence prove that he spent at least six years and very probably much more principally in gathering data on Justin Morgan. Battell's history and registry fills four volumes. The amount of writing that has been done to show that Justin Morgan was the son of a "Thoroughbred"— Beautiful Bay—would fill out forty-one detective novels and an application for membership in the Liars' Club. Quite possibly he came from Beautiful Bay and quite possibly he didn't. No one knows; no one has ever known; no one will ever know. If Beautiful Bay had been properly registered or even noted someone would have produced proper evidence, in nearly a century and a half, that he was the father of the great sire.

Dr. C. D. Parks of Honesdale, Pennsylvania, is recognized as one of the country's best authorities on the Morgan breed. On May 10, 1947, at the Hotel Kenmore in Boston, Dr. Parks talked before a gathering of the New England Morgan Horse breeders on "The Morgan of Distinction." This speech later appeared as an article in the *Western Horseman* from which we quote the part pertaining to the bloodlines of Justin Morgan:

The horse, Justin Morgan, came into the world unannounced, about 1790. His pedigree is given as being sired by True Briton and out of a Wild Air mare. A close examination of this pedigree of Justin Morgan, given in the front of Vol. I of *The Morgan Horse and Register,* will show that True Briton was predominantly Arabian and Barb. The Wild Air mare was sired by Diamond by Church's Wild Air of the same blood as True Briton. Diamond's dam and the second dam of Justin Morgan were of unknown breeding.

The horses native to the Connecticut valley at the time of Justin Morgan's birth were of this breeding plus the Dutch horse brought to what is now New York by the Dutch settlers. Little is known about the Dutch horses other than that they were a light draft horse, short legged, heavy bodied with heavy mane and tail and considerable hair about the fetlocks.

The description of the dam of Justin Morgan given on page 95 of Vol. I of the *Register* is as follows: "The dam of the Morgan horse was of the Wild Air or Wildair breed; she was of middling size, her color was a light bay, mane and tail not dark, hair on legs rather long; she was a smooth handsome traveler. Her sire was the Diamond, a thick heavy horse of middle size; he had a thick bushy mane and tail; a smooth traveler."

It is, therefore, reasonable to believe that the dam of Justin Morgan was three-quarters Dutch and one-quarter grade Arabian; his sire grade Arabian. Justin Morgan would, then, be five-eighths grade Arabian and three-eighths Dutch. He had the bay color, heavy black mane and tail and long hair about the fetlocks, which belonged to the Dutch horse.

The horses, so far as we can determine, native to the section of Vermont where Justin Morgan produced most of his offspring, were essentially the same as those credited with producing *him*.

The *Morgan Horse Register,* as stated by Dr. Parks, has accepted True Briton as the sire of Justin Morgan and the Wild Air mare as his dam. Undoubtedly they have used the research of D. C. Linsley as their source.

Summarizing all the known research and findings, we are confronted with a complex matter. Was Justin Morgan sired by the Dutch horse Young Bulrock? If we accept the date of his birth as 1793, it is possible, for Young Bulrock stood in Springfield, the place where Justin Morgan was foaled, in 1792. If the Morgan horse was foaled in 1789 or 1790, it is more likely that he was sired by True Briton because the Dutch horse Young Bulrock had not yet arrived and there is a record that True Briton or Beautiful Bay stood at Springfield during the years 1788 and 1789. Even if the birth date of Morgan had been in any one of the years from 1785 to 1795, he could have been sired by True Briton because that horse was in the nearby vicinity during those years.

There is also a question as to the year in which Mr. Morgan acquired the bay colt and took him to Randolph, Vermont. Was he taken there when the family moved in 1788, or are we to believe the more romantic story that Justin Morgan was the result of an unpaid bill and followed the older playmate which was led back to Vermont by Mr. Morgan late in the summer of 1795?

Then there is the question of bloodlines in the ancestry of Beautiful Bay, alias True Briton, alias Traveler. Was he truthfully from the racing stock of the Colonial horseman James De Lancey, or was he instead the horse that was stolen from the other Colonel James De Lancey of the Tory cavalry operating in Westchester County?

If each of the accounts is examined closely, possible errors in dates and facts may be detected; also, in some of them, there seems to be misjudgment in the appraisal of human behavior. It has been said that men otherwise known to be of the stanchest integrity seem to lose all sense of the equity of things when it comes to breeding, selling, or swapping horses, a fact which has clouded to a certain extent true knowledge of nearly every American breed that exists.

While it would be interesting to clear up the tantalizing 150-year-old mystery that has plagued the origin and breeding of Justin Morgan, it has always seemed to me that the blood of the little stallion who was "worth his weight in silver cartwheels" has erased completely the need for further investigations.

I am reminded of a time when I was younger and looked searchingly into the sky, wondering where space ended. An older, more experienced friend instructed me to look upward into the blue distance as far as I could possibly see. Thinking that I might discover the answer to my question, I hopefully strained my eyes. My friend asked, "Are you now looking as far as you can see?" I answered, "Yes," and while I did not then fully realize the meaning of his words I do now. He replied, "Then you are looking at the end of space in so far as it affects you."

Perhaps this is the way in which we should consider the question of Justin Morgan's ancestry. We know that he alone was the fountainhead for a great and useful breed. The fact that his own peculiarly superb qualities and his ability to transmit them were the true basis of his worth seem sufficient to me. Seventeen-ninety or 1793—True Briton or Young Bulrock—Arabian, Barb, or Dutch blood—what does it matter. They will in no way detract from the true meaning of Justin Morgan, for he was, is, and always will be just plain American!

GLIMPSES OF OLD JUSTIN MORGAN

Let us step back into American history about a hundred and fifty years to view the original Morgan horse. First of all, we are struck by his small size. He stands about 14 hands high and weighs approximately nine hundred and fifty pounds. Our attention, however, is immediately attracted to the extreme musculature of a horse so small. The breast is broad, and the powerful shoulders are sloping. The rib cage is round, with great depth. If at first glance we think the body is long, we soon realize that it only seems so by comparison with the short, sturdy legs. The top line is broad, with muscular loin, and there is a strong coupling of the back with the hindquarters. He is a veritable power machine mounted on four straight legs.

We notice that his fine, glossy coat is a dark bay and that he has black legs, mane, and tail. We are intrigued by the lofty manner in which he carries his heavily crested neck and finely modeled head. The sparkling eyes and large nostrils give him an intelligent and spirited countenance.

And then, as he travels off in proud animation, we understand why he is in such great demand as a parade mount by the military gentlemen of the day. The action of his legs is square, quick, and high, suggesting sure-footed speed, comfort to his rider, and power, if necessary, for drawing heavy loads.

This was the stylish little horse that Mr. Morgan leased to Robert Evans for $15 a year so that he might clear 15 acres of Vermont timberland for a Mr. Fish. Figure, he was called then.

There are many stories and legends about Justin Morgan, the equine Paul Bunyan, and one of the most interesting was reputed to have happened when he was in the charge of Robert Evans. Months in the woods with the little horse had proved to the man that explosive power lay in the muscles that rippled beneath the sleek bay coat.

The story commences at dusk one day after many hours of labor in the woods. Evans rode up to the village tavern, presumably to wet his dry throat with a glass before supper. According to Nathan Nye, an eyewitness, Evans was told about a certain pine log, lying 10 rods' distance from the mill on the nearby branch of the White River, which other teamsters had been unable to move. In fact, some of the horses that had been hitched to it weighed 1,200 pounds but none of them could move the timber as much as its own length.

After surveying the situation, Robert Evans hurried back to the tavern and challenged the mill-company authorities to bet a gallon of rum that his horse could not pull the log onto the logway in three starts. After a prompt acceptance and another round of drinks, the Vermonters all went jovially to the spot where the contest was to be held.

It is not known whether Evans had become addleheaded by the few drinks he had just imbibed at the tavern. In any case, he boasted that he was ashamed

EQUINE
POWERHOUSE

to hitch his horse to such a small log and wondered if three of the assembled gentlemen would make the contest more worth while by seating themselves upon it, adding that he would forfeit the rum if Figure could not draw the entire load. Naturally, three of the most befuddled ones were happy to make a good thing better and entered into the spirit of the banter by taking their positions astride the log.

At a word of command, the little bay released the tension on the tugs very slightly; then squatting behind and arching his beautiful neck, he pulled to the side. The chains rumbled in protest, then the log broke reluctantly from the earth's firm grasp and started to move, slowly at first, then faster as the Morgan horse's legs began to work with the speed of pistons. At a point more than halfway to the mill saw, Evans stopped the horse for a short breather. Then bending to it again, the horse removed the log to the spot agreed upon, and Evans had won his wager, to the astonishment of all.

From that time on, it is said, the little bay Figure was in great demand as a breeding stallion. The hardy Vermonters needed using horses that had bone and muscle and courage to do the rough labor necessary in developing a mountainous countryside. The colts that the Morgan horse got were this kind.

Not only did Justin Morgan prove himself superior as a draft animal, but it is said that he could outwalk, outtrot, and outrun all competitors in his vicinity. It has been told of him that he could walk at the rate of 6 miles an hour. He was a fast runner for short distances, and the best horses of his own state were no match for him. On occasion, horses from more distant points were brought in to challenge him.

There is record of one such case in which he was matched against two fine horses from outside the Green Mountain State. These matches were held in Brookfield, Vermont, June 26, 1796, one against a horse called Sweepstakes, from Long Island, the other against Silver Trail, from St. Lawrence County, New York. The distance was 80 rods and the Morgan horse beat both contestants handily. Justin Morgan's owner gave the owner of Silver Trail two opportunities to retrieve part of his losses by matching the horses first in a walking race and then in a trotting race, but the man evidently knew when he was beaten, for he declined to enter into any further contests.

Justin Morgan knew many owners and much hard toil during his long lifetime. Following Evans's lease, Figure was taken in on a debt by a Mr. Rice and was removed from Randolph to Woodstock. There he was sold in 1796 to Jonathan Shepherd, of Montpelier, who used him to breed mares. Later he was disposed of in a trade to James Hawkins. Robert Evans, the former lessee of Figure, bought him from Hawkins about 1801. Under this ownership the little bay horse toiled strenuously until Evans was sued for debt. Colonel John Goss took the horse as security against his bail and finally became the legal owner by paying Evans's debt. Colonel Goss turned the animal over to his brother, David Goss, for keeping. During the year that this man kept the horse, he became extremely fond of him and made arrangements to become his legal owner. The Morgan Horse worked in the service of Goss for a number of years. In 1811, he passed into the ownership of Jacob Sanderson and then to William Langmaid.

By this time Justin Morgan had reached an age of approximately twenty years, which is old for a horse. In spite of this, Langmaid is reported to have used the horse severely, working him in a six-horse hitch hauling freight between Windsor and Chelsea. As a result of these hardships, he became worn and poor. He was sold to a man in Chelsea for a trifling sum and again to Joel Goss of Claremont, New Hampshire, who, in turn, sold him to Samuel Stone. Under this ownership, he returned again to his old home ground at Randolph, Vermont. He remained there until 1819, when he was sold to a Levi Bean. His end came at the astonishing age, considering his hard usage, of over thirty years. It is a sad note on human compassion that he died from lack of proper care. While in a corral with other horses, he received a kick in the flank. As a result of the lack of shelter in the cold wintry weather, infection set in and he died.

In later years, Justin Morgan was honored by the presentation by the Morgan Horse Club to the government of a beautiful bronze statue, in the likeness of the "big little horse" that could not be forgotten. Monumentally Justin Morgan stands at Middlebury, Vermont, alert and lofty to view the Green Mountains as he did in real life.

Massachusetts, too, lays claim upon this great stallion, for on Brush Hill Farm at West Springfield lies a tablet, marking his birthplace, which reads:

> From this farm came the stallion
> JUSTIN MORGAN
> progenitor of that useful breed known as
> Morgan Horses

THE SONS OF JUSTIN

Justin Morgan's blood was perpetuated principally by three sons whose names were Sherman (5), Bulrush (6), and Woodbury (7).

For information concerning their dams as well as their offspring, let us quote again from Dr. Parks's speech and article:

The dam of Sherman given on page 132 of Vol. I of the *Register* is as follows: "She was a chestnut, of good size, high spirited and an elegant animal. We called her of Spanish breed." This would indicate that she was a grade Arabian. The dam of Bulrush described on page 149 of Vol. I of the *Register* is as follows: "She was a dark bay, with black legs, and heavy black mane and tail; she was low and compact, had heavy limbs, with large joints, neck rather long, a good head, but did not carry it up well; she was a sharp trotter, but was not a very spirited driver; she was said to be and had the appearance of being part French." The dam of Woodbury #7 given on page 142 of the *Register* is as follows: "She was large, being over fifteen hands high, and weighed about eleven hundred pounds; she was a deep bay color with black legs, mane and tail, a small white spot on the forehead and no other marks. She was not very compactly made, and was rather flat ribbed; but she had an excellent chest, fine shoulders and hips, and excellent limbs. Her head was very fine, ears good and mane and tail beautiful. She carried her head high, and was a very free, spirited driver, and was called fast at that time. She both paced and trotted, generally starting in at the former gait, and after going a short distance changing it for a trot. When trotting she made a fine appearance, and going fast attracted much attention. She was a very fast walker." The description would indicate Thoroughbred, Dutch, and possibly Narragansett pacing blood.

From these descriptions of the dams of these three most noted progenitors of Justin Morgan blood, it is very evident that they were not at all alike, but probably possessed a common blood to some degree, namely: Thoroughbred, which may just as well be called grade Arabian plus Dutch blood.

These three sons of Justin Morgan were remarkably similar and of Justin Morgan's pattern, possessing his distinguishing characteristics, according to the best authorities who have left records concerning the early Morgans. The next two or three generations making three or four from Justin Morgan were produced, with few exceptions, by the same blood with the same result. This brings us to the year 1850 or a little before. Justin Morgan had come into the world fifty years before, unannounced, and his ability to produce a breed had not been anticipated. The consistent reproduction of the distinctive qualities of Justin Morgan by his immediate offspring during these fifty years, impressed those familiar with them. . . .

One of the most vivid word pictures of what to me is a true Morgan of distinguished characteristics appears on page 26 of Vol. I of the *Register*. I quote:

"James D. Ladd, in an article in *Wallace's Monthly*, 1882, says: 'When I was a young man, on a visit to Saratoga Springs, I sat one evening on the verandah of Congress Hall. The time was the week preceding the New York State Agriculture fair, which was to be there that year. Silas Hale rode Green Mountain Morgan through the street of the then village of Saratoga. The moment I saw him I was upon my feet, and with a great crowd was hurrying to get a closer view of that horse and to find out what family he was of, and where he came from. If Jumbo was today driven through that now much more populous street, I question if he would attract more attention than the Green Mountain Morgan then did. And why? Not because of his reputation for speed; he had not trotted very fast, or run very fast, or done anything to greatly distinguish him from hundreds of other horses that were daily seen on that street. It was nothing more or less than his consummate get-up; it was his style, his manner of action.

"Next morning I went to see him in his stable. In the same barn I found Fred Wier, with old Gifford Morgan, then said to be 32 years old, shrunken with extreme age, but lively and active. His counterpart, Gen. Gifford, stood in the same box, and the old horse would follow him into the show ring without bit or strap of any kind, and at Wier's command he would walk or trot, promptly and cheerfully as a colt. Near by was David Hill with Black Hawk and his daughter, the Belle of Saratoga, and old Lady Suffolk.

"I had been with these horses since childhood. I was familiar with the best horses of Virginia, Maryland, Pennsylvania, and Ohio; but in these, the two Giffords, Black Hawk and Green Mountain Morgan, I saw what impressed me as the most horse to the inches I had ever seen, and from that day to this I have known a Morgan horse wherever I have met them. I cannot say so of any other family of horses; not only when I have seen him, but wherever I have used him I have found the same form, the same constitution, the same disposition, the same general character. I see horses every day with perhaps a thirty-second part of the blood of Justin Morgan, but there it is still predominating; there is the Morgan still so plainly seen that he who runs may read. Every close observer, every discerning judge of horses I meet, be he an admirer or a despiser of the Morgan, always admits this wonderful tendency of his blood."

JUSTIN MORGAN'S INFLUENCE ON OTHER AMERICAN BREEDS

The American Saddle Horse

The American Saddle Horse has derived his greatness from various sources. His fineness comes in great part from the Thoroughbred line, his ability to do the "easy" gaits from the early pacing stock of Colonial times. From the Morgan strain, it can be stated with assurance, has come the Saddler's ability for brilliant, animated action. Substance and bottom are additional qualities deriving from the same source.

American horsemen of early times selected and bred horses because of their individual merit. The Morgans had intelligence, good looks, and a bold, spirited appearance, combined with a gentle disposition. Their high, trappy style of traveling and their grit and determination to complete a journey at a steady and rapid gait made them popular and in great demand.

Naturally, when the Saddle Horse Breeders' Association was formed, many stallions of Morgan descent were selected as founders of the breed. Among early sires we find such famous horses as Cabell's Lexington, Blood's Black Hawk, Blood Chief, Indian Chief, and Telegraph. Undoubtedly these horses with Morgan blood in their veins did much toward supplying indispensable portions of quality through their conformation, finish, animation, and action.

It is interesting to note that of the 11,997 horses registered in the first four volumes of the *Saddle Horse Register,* there are 714 entries with direct male trace to old Justin Morgan. It is known that Morgan dams also were strong in their support.

One of the greatest horses of Morgan blood in the *American Saddle Horse Register* is Benjamin's Whirlwind (119), foaled in 1877, died in 1908. This stallion is of unusual significance because he was an inbred Morgan. His sire was Whirlwind (2359), by Indian Chief (1718), by Blood's Black Hawk, by Vermont Morgan (5), by Sherman Morgan, by Justin Morgan. His dam was Arabian Maid, by Vermont Morgan; second dam, daughter of Imported Zilcadi; third dam, daughter of Imported Barefoot. It will be noted that Benjamin's Whirlwind had none of the blood of any of the old foundation sires of the *American Saddle Horse Register*.

There is no record that this stallion was ever entered in the show ring, but as his colts showed more and more brilliance on the tanbark, he came to be in extremely great demand as a sire par excellence. A striking 16-hand horse of mahogany-bay coloring, he was continually sought after by leading breeders. This is important when we realize that through his entire career he was in competition with such great Saddle Horse sires as old Montrose and Le Grand. Whirlwind colts were so superior for their finish, airiness, and presence that they were bought up at very young ages. Many of the greatest colts of Grand McDonald and Rex McDonald were out of Benjamin's Whirlwind mares.

The invincible harness stallion Indian Chief carried much Morgan blood. He was by Blood's Black Hawk, by Vermont Black Hawk (5), by Sherman Morgan, by Justin Morgan. Indian Chief's dam was Lou Berry, by Ned For-

rest, by Young Bashaw. The dam of Ned Forrest is claimed to be by Salt-
peter and out of a full-blooded Morgan mare. Indian Chief, a beautifully
formed bay horse standing 15 hands 3 inches, with left hind coronet white,
was foaled in 1857 and died in 1879. In his day, he was almost an uncon-
querable champion, winning in fine-harness and roadster classes. To him
must go the credit for siring the famous Lady DeJarnette who, many believe,
has never been equaled by any mare in harness even to the present day. Indian Chief has the distinction of being one of the few horses to be registered
in the *American Saddle Horse Register*, the *Trotting Register*, and the *Morgan
Register*.

The name Rex Peavine is supreme among Saddle Horse enthusiasts, and for
at least a part of his preeminence we must credit old Justin Morgan. This
great sire's ancestry traced to Morgan through his dam, which was by Peavine
(85), by Rattler, by Stockbridge Chief, by Black Hawk, by Sherman Morgan,
by Justin Morgan. Though a good show horse with a successful career, Rex
Peavine was not as outstanding in the show ring as he was esteemed a sire.
Mares from every Saddle Horse–producing state in the nation visited his
court. As a Saddle Horse sire he has been paralleled with Peter the Great of
the trotters.

Edna May, pronounced by some horsemen to be the greatest saddle type
ever seen in America, is especially interesting because she carried four
crosses to Morgan. She was by Rex Peavine and was out of a Peavine mare.
Undoubtedly she owed much of her greatness to the Morgan strain. This
strikingly handsome mare was noted for her bold, flashy way of traveling.
Seldom defeated, her career was a long string of hard-fought victories, considering the great horses against whom she showed. Edna May's greatness
did not end with her own performances. In 1918, she foaled Edna May's
King, by Bourbon King, who, in 1924, made history by winning the $10,000
stake at the Kentucky State Fair, and again in 1930 when sold by his owner,
Revel Lindsay English, for the record-breaking price of $40,000.

Bourbon King (1788), in whom the great Chief family of Saddle Horses
culminated, had as his dam Annie C., sired by Richelieu King who is shown
in the *Morgan Register*.

Of course, there are many other great American Saddle Horses whose
ancestry traces to Justin Morgan. The influence of Morgan blood on the
American Saddle line can be appreciated more greatly when we realize that
every winner of the $10,000 championship stake at Louisville, Kentucky,
from 1917 through 1931 drew, in part, its champion qualities from that great
old horse—Justin Morgan.

The American Standard Bred Horse

Another great American breed which has been influenced by Morgan blood is the Standard Bred Horse. As will be described in a later chapter, the trotting and pacing races of today originated as amateur matches up and down village streets or on the open road. It is natural that horses of such great driving utility as the Morgans should be used extensively as light-harness animals. Their intelligence, docility, and tractability fitted them well for such tasks. Owners were proud of the beautiful carriage and animation displayed by horses of Morgan breeding, and power and endurance were necessary requirements. A city businessman, a country doctor, or milady journeying in the interests of charity or social duties—all found the Morgan an ideal harness horse.

UNEXCELLED AS ROADSTER

In writing of the Morgan breed, W. H. Gocher, historian of the *American Trotter and Pacer,* said:

> It established a type which in time became the trademark of the first great American family of horses, and it is so different from all others that when an Australian or Englishman refers to a horse as a "Vermont Morgan," an idea of his general appearance is conveyed as lucidly to the resident of Australia or England as it would be if addressed to a New Englander. The words carry with them the memory of the ideal form of Ethan Allen as well as the pure trotting gait, nervy, stylish way of going and perfect manners which made that son of Vermont Black Hawk a favorite with the patrons of the track and the road in his day.

As to the early period of road-horse development, let us turn again to the remarks made by Dr. Parks in his Boston speech:

> The Morgan in his true form was bred and used as a general utility horse; that is, farm work and road work up to the advent of the automobile. With the advent of the automobile, the numbers of these true Morgans decreased.

Fortunately a few breeders preserved the type and there are a few available at the present time.

Going back to about 1850, when the intensification of the blood began, a horse with speed was a very valuable animal. The horse was the only means of transportation; roads were improved and harness racing was a favorite sport. The Morgan up to this time and for a few more years was the fastest available harness horse. Black Hawk #20, a grandson of Justin Morgan, and Ethan Allen #50, a great grandson, were the champion trotting stallions of their day.

Hambletonian 10 was foaled in 1849 and produced, during his twenty-six years of life, 1,321 offspring. The offspring of this horse mixed with the fast Morgans of the next few years produced the Standardbred, which was faster and more popular as a harness horse than the true Morgan. Several families of Morgans were absorbed in this way and forgotten. The Morrill family is a good example of this.

The horse Ethan Allen, which has been mentioned so frequently up to this point, perhaps represented the pinnacle of road-horse perfection in true Morgan form. Probably no horse ever received more public attention in his day than this son of Black Hawk, he by Sherman Morgan, the son of the original Justin Morgan.

Ethan Allen, though a small horse, was admired for his handsome form and stylish fashion of traveling. The eyes of the nation were attracted to him at the Burlington Fair of 1856. Later, when hitched with a pole-horse running mate, he put an end to the career of the famous trotting mare Flora Temple. In a wonderful race of mile heats, three in five, over the Fashion Course on Long Island, on June 21, 1867, Ethan Allen and mate bested Dexter with the time of 2:15, 2:16, and 2:19.

Of this stallion John Wallace wrote: "Others have gone faster singly, but no one has done it in greater perfection of motion. In his great flights of speed he was not bounding in the air but down close to the ground with a gliding motion that steals rapidly from quarter-pole to quarter-pole with inconceivable rapidity."

George Wilkes, alias Robert Fillingham, well-known sire in the *Standard Bred Register,* was by Hambletonian. This little brown stallion was the cornerstone for a great line of trotters in Kentucky and has been referred to as a "second Hambletonian." From the viewpoint of this chapter, it is significant, however, that George Wilkes's dam was Dolly Spanker, a mare which was credited as Morgan and whose description fits the Morgan just as George Wilkes himself showed strong characteristics of this breed.

The research and findings of Joseph Battell place in the *Morgan Register* Seely's American Star and the old pacer Pilot. It has been said that without the brood-mare lines springing from such sires, much greatness would be lost from the trotting-horse families generically termed "Hambletonian" through the custom of continuing the name of the male line. In considering such recognition of direct trace to Justin Morgan, we must admit the distinct Morgan influence in the great present-day trotting families of Peter the Great and Axworthy. It cannot be denied that Morgan blood should be credited for much of the beauty of finish and purity of gait of such record-making horses as Uhlan, Lee Axworthy, The Harvester, and Hamburg Belle.

The use of Morgans in the early days spread in all directions. The migration of this breed into Canada undoubtedly gave that Dominion its original harness race horses. It is interesting to note that when the great Canadian pacer Gratton Bars was retired unbeaten a few years ago, inquiry was made as to his pedigree, and it was disclosed that he had a Morgan background.

The Tennessee Walking Horse

Prior to 1850, Tennessee breeders found the Morgan well adapted to producing saddle horses of quality. As the years rolled on, these horsemen developed a race of powerful, handsome, easy-riding horses of unique character and great merit, and containing admixtures of Morgan blood. The breed is known as the "Tennessee Walking Horse."

In tracing pedigrees of this breed, we discover that it is compounded from the strains of Copperbottoms, Hals, Pilots, Slashers, Brooks, Allens, and many others.

Perhaps the most notable of this breed is the number-one foundation sire Allan F–1. Allan was a black horse foaled in 1886. In establishing this stallion as the technical sole fountainhead of the strain he founded, it was demonstrated that no other horse was worthy to stand by his side as a recognized deceased sire.

Allan F–1 was sired by Allandorf, by Onward, by George Wilkes. Allan's dam was Maggie Marshall, by Bradford's Telegraph, by Black Hawk, by Sherman Morgan, by Justin Morgan. Thus, it will be noticed that on the top line of his pedigree, Allan traces to Morgan through the dam of Georges Wilkes, Dolly Spanker, who, we have already noted, was of Morgan blood. Maggie Marshall, the dam of Allan, goes directly to Morgan through the top line of her pedigree.

Two horses appear frequently in the extended pedigrees of Tennessee Walking Horses—old Imported Copperbottom (Canadian) and old Tom

Hal (Canadian). Both of them appear as foundation sires in the *American Saddle Horse Registry* and both carry the notation "No record of pedigree." Morgan enthusiasts claim that both these horses trace to the original Morgan Horse as a result of migrations of Vermont horses into Canada. If horses of Canadian birth trekked as far south as Kentucky and Tennessee, it is reasonable to assume that they could have traveled the shorter distance from the state of Vermont to Canada, just across the border.

Both Tom Hal and Copperbottom were multiple-gaited horses. I have always felt, however, that there was no pacing tendency within the brain of Justin Morgan, although his get could have gained this quality through some of their dams. It has already been noted that the dam of Woodbury (7) was a pacer and possibly contained some Narragansett blood. The Canadians had long been interested in "easy"-gaited saddle horses and pacers. The influx of Morgan stock could easily have been mixed with already popular Narragansett horses. There seems to be no stumbling block here about the fact that Morgans could have sired such pacing horses as Tom Hal and Copperbottom.

Old Tom Hal was registered number 31 in the *Morgan Register* as a pacer bred in Canada by Justin Morgan or a son of Justin Morgan. There is some question about the foaling date of old Copperbottom, who is registered number 66 in the *Morgan Register*. One claim has been made that he was a son of Justin Morgan, bred by David Blount of Vermont, foaled in 1809, and brought to Kentucky in 1816. Other historians put strong faith in the belief that he was a Canadian Morgan, foaled about 1809, and taken to Kentucky by way of Detroit between 1812 and 1816. None of the above dates rules out the possibility that Copperbottom or Tom Hal could have been closely related to Justin Morgan, though both of them were pacers. Copperbottom was a very common name in the early nineteenth century. Many Morgans were registered in Volume III of the *Register* under that name. The Copperbottom strain of Morgans has died out, but undoubtedly it did much to influence every other American breed.

If the two old-time sires Tom Hal and Copperbottom could be positively traced to Justin Morgan, it would indeed add even greater glory to the Morgan breed as a progenitor of great horses.

In checking through the list of foundation stock in the *Tennessee Walking Horse Register,* it is extremely difficult to find pedigrees that are not sprinkled profusely with Morgan, through the Black Hawk strain, or the Copperbottoms or the Tom Hals.

Other Horses Influenced by Justin Morgan

Many Western horses were undoubtedly influenced by the blood of Justin Morgan as civilization trekked westward, taking its good stock with it. Americans have long been proud to claim Morgan blood in their horses. While the eyes of the nation were on such horses as Ethan Allen, others less publicized were improving the blood of horses used at menial tasks on early frontiers. It has been said that the Morgan is more than a breed. To those who understand his true value, he has been a symbol of vibrant, tireless force in American pioneering. In early days, he was found to fill the needs of a hard-working, hard-driving people, and his blood was sought by every state and for every purpose for which a horse could be used.

One of the sons of Ethan Allen, Headlight Morgan (4863), influenced the Morgan stock of the southwest United States. Sold to Mrs. Margaret C. Parks of Englewood, Kansas, in 1893, by the Morgan Horse Company, Carpentersville, Illinois, this horse was the major influence on the horses bred by Mr. Sellman at Rochelle, Texas, and subsequently influenced many of the Morgan Horses in California.

Since 1920, a great number of stallions from the United States Morgan Horse Farm have been sold in the West and they have been one of the greatest factors in developing the present-day Morgan all over the country.   ·

It has been said by some that the Northern Army would have lost the War between the States had it not been for Morgan-blooded horses. One of the greatest of these war horses was General Sheridan's charger Rienzi, as he was first called, foaled near Grand Rapids, Michigan, of Black Hawk stock. Brought into the Union Army by an officer of the Second Michigan Cavalry, he was presented to Sheridan, the colonel of the regiment, by the officers in the spring of 1862, while the regiment was stationed at Rienzi, Mississippi. The horse was three years old at the time, over 17 hands in height, powerfully built, with a deep chest, strong shoulders, a broad forehead, and clear eye, and of great intelligence. In his prime, he was one of the strongest horses Sheridan ever knew, very active and one of the fastest walkers in the Union Army. Rienzi always held his head high and by the quickness of his movements created the impression that he was exceedingly impetuous, but Sheridan was always able to control him by a firm hand and a few words. He was as cool and quiet under fire as any veteran trooper in the cavalry corps.

At the Battle of Cedar Creek, October 19, 1864, the name of the horse was changed from Rienzi to Winchester, a name derived from the town made famous by Sheridan's ride to save his army in the Shenandoah Valley.

Though this book is devoted to light horses, the chapter on Morgans would be incomplete if Morgan draft horses were not mentioned. Morgan stallions crossed on Percheron, Belgian, or Suffolk mares have produced extremely valuable draft animals. Most Morgan drafters seem to be endowed with strong legs, short backs, and collar-filling shoulders. They are good-tempered, handsome, easy to raise and train, durable, and long-lived. It is claimed that their abundant energy and stamina, as well as their ability to stand more heat than larger animals, have made them extremely useful to the dirt farmer.

The Morgan Register

The Morgan breed owes much to the late Colonel Joseph Battell of Middlebury, Vermont, who devoted a major part of his long life to service in the interest of the Morgan Horse and who founded the *Morgan Horse Register*.

In the 1870s, Colonel Battell began gathering information from every available source pertaining to the descendants of Justin Morgan. A great deal of information came from D. C. Linsley's research, which had been published in 1850. In 1894, Colonel Battell privately published Volume I of the *Morgan Horse and Register,* and it was entered, in accordance with an act of Congress, in the Library of Congress at Washington, D.C.

Volume II, published in 1905, contained much supplementary data to Volume I and included later animals. Colonel Battell had Volume III almost ready for publication when he died January 23, 1915, thus bringing to a close his years of personal devotion to the Morgan breed. He was a man of considerable means and the whole of his residuary estate was bequeathed to Middlebury College. The *Morgan Horse and Register,* as a part of the estate, also went to the college.

This institution carried on Colonel Battell's work by publishing the nearly completed Volume III. No numbers had been assigned to the animals appearing in Volumes I and II. In Volume III, they were enumerated and many more were added. At that time, numbers were assigned to all stallions; the mares were shown without numbers.

Shortly after Colonel Battell's death, Mr. C. Chauncey Stillman of New York, a breeder of Morgans and secretary of the Morgan Horse Club, at that time an informal organization, personally purchased from Middlebury College the *Morgan Horse and Register* and all rights thereto. He then set up the *American Morgan Horse Register, Inc.,* and considered Volumes I, II, and III of the *Morgan Horse and Register* to be Volumes I, II, and III of the *American Morgan Horse Register* and the basis for the later expansion of the *Register.* Mr. Stillman opened an office for the *Register* in New York and encouraged breeders of Morgan horses to register their animals. In 1921, he published Volume IV, including registrations made from about 1914 or 1915 up to 1921. In Volume IV, he listed the mares that had appeared in the first three volumes and assigned numbers to them.

Mr. Stillman died suddenly in the autumn of 1926, at a time when the breeding of Morgans had fallen to its lowest point and the club had only thirty or forty members. Many of the breeders who had been active earlier had passed on, but among the older breeders was Mr. Charles A. Stone, chairman of the engineering firm of Stone and Webster. He had bred Morgans, as well as other horses, in New England for a great many years. It was to this man that ·Mr. Stillman's brother appealed for help in disposing of the *Register.* After conferring with some of the other members of the club, Mr. Stone offered to carry on until the club could make other arrangements. The Stillman heirs offered to give the *Register* to the club. In order to make this possible, the Morgan Horse Club was incorporated under the laws of New York in 1927. Immediately thereafter, the assets of the *American Morgan Horse Register, Inc.,* were turned over to the Morgan Horse Club, Inc. Carrying on the *Register* then became the principal responsibility of the Morgan Horse Club.

All documents and paraphernalia of the *Register* were sent to Mr. Stone's offices in New York, where it fell to the lot of Mr. F. B. Hills, who was versed in registration procedure, to take over as secretary and registrar. In this capacity, Mr. Hills has acted capably through the years to the present time.

In 1939, the club published Volume V of the *Register,* which included all registrations and transfers from about 1921 to 1937, inclusive. At the time of this writing, Volume VI is in the process of preparation and printing. It will include registrations and transfers from 1938 to 1947, inclusive.

The number of animals registered annually began to increase during 1931 and 1932. From a low of about seventy-five registrations a year, the number climbed until, in 1947, about seven hundred animals were registered.

Until Mr. Charles A. Stone's death, in 1941, he aided generously in providing facilities for carrying on the *Register.* Since then, his son Whitney Stone, who is active in horse matters, has continued to help the Morgan Horse Club and *Register.* Directors of the club hope to be able, in the near future, to open a breed office, preferably in some Vermont town, with the necessary personnel to carry on the work of registering and perpetuating the descendants of old Justin Morgan.

THE UNITED STATES MORGAN HORSE FARM

The original tract for the United States Morgan Horse Farm at Middlebury, Vermont, was donated to the government in 1907 by Colonel Battell. It is here that the bronze statue of Justin Morgan, by the famous sculptor Frederick G. Roth, stands. Subsequent purchases of land were added to the original Battell tract until now the farm consists of about a thousand acres. The government farm at Middlebury is unique, for it is the only institution in the United States founded for the sole purpose of perpetuating a breed of horses. It should be understood, of course, that the government farm is a substation of the Bureau of Animal Husbandry, Department of Agriculture, and that a part of its activity is devoted to experimentation.

The stallion General Gates was selected by the farm to serve as its foundation sire. This stallion was by the Morgan Horse Denning Allen (74) and out of a Thoroughbred mare. Bennington by General Gates was the next sire used. He was out of Mrs. Culvers, a registered American Saddlebred mare. Mansfield, by Bennington out of Artemesia (02731), a very well-bred Morgan mare by Ethan Allen 3d, was used as a leading sire at the farm.

At least a few Morgan enthusiasts believe that this stock has been inbred and line-bred so extensively that it has lost the distinctive Morgan characteristics and that these have been replaced by those of the American Saddle, Standard Bred, and Thoroughbred. Others are quick to point out that the farm has produced many superior individuals.

For over thirty years, breeding stock from this farm has been distributed throughout the United States and its possessions and to many foreign countries. It is interesting to note that most Indian agencies of the country own Morgans, thereby improving their stock of horses.

In a letter from the Morgan Horse Club, I am informed that the state of California boasts almost one-third of the total number of breeders of Morgan Horses. A list of breeders indicates that the mother state of Vermont contains the next largest number, and there is a great interest in the states of Illinois, Iowa, Kansas, Nebraska, South Dakota, and Wyoming, although nearly every state in the Union is represented as well.

THE MODERN MORGAN

The breeding of true-type Morgans reached a point of intensification about the time of Ethan Allen, almost one hundred years ago. Because race horses of greater trotting speed were being developed on other family lines, the Morgan Horse, as such, was abandoned.

The Morgan, however, carried on as a premier road horse until the coming of the automobile, when the need for a general-utility horse diminished rapidly and this once-popular and highly useful type was threatened with extinction.

However, when the automobile became entrenched as a means of transportation, breeders foresaw the increasing demand for saddle horses in sport and pleasure. It was at this point that the breeding policy reached a fork in the road. Supposedly to produce Morgans better suited to the new uses, certain breeders introduced the blood of the American Saddle Horse into the Morgan by outcrossing. Such breeders took the view that many of the Morgans which were left from the active-harness era were not too successful for saddle purposes. They sought to improve certain features, mainly the shoulders and pasterns.

Taking the other view, more conservative breeders felt that the results of such outcrossing were neither good Saddlers nor good Morgans. These breeders adhered to the true type of the original Morgan horse, feeling that their breeding represented the only true Morgan Horses. In a way, they were attempting to combat the invasion of outcrosses much the same as D. C. Linsley had done as early as 1856 when he advocated the value of breeding Morgans of true type. He advised against selecting for speed in these words:

> The general business qualities of the Morgan are what gave him his great value. His admirable traveling gait, stoutness, courage and endurance. . . . Many persons can be found who will pick up some long-legged, rangy trotting mare, which might trot a mile in 2:30 and think by breeding her to a Morgan stallion something very fine may be expected. In most cases it will end in loss and disappointment.

In recent years, outcrossing was stopped when the *Register* was closed to all applicants whose sires and dams did not appear as Morgan-registered animals. However, a few present-day breeders believe that much damage has been done through the use of outcrossed animals which were registered before the new rule went into effect. They advocate the use of the best available Morgan mares, especially those showing strong Morgan characteristics, and stallions of the same qualities which, in addition, have not contained any outside blood for at least five generations.

Others state that there has been a definite gain in uniformity within the breed during the past few years. Furthermore, they believe that within a few years the effects of outcrossing will largely have disappeared, that the breed will again become stabilized, and that it will not have lost its good qualities.

THE TYPICAL MORGAN

Old Justin Morgan himself represents the ideal type, the only exception being that present-day Morgans may be slightly larger. At the present time, most people prefer the Morgan from 14 hands 3 inches to 15 hands 1 inch, but the general range is from 14–2 to 15–2.

In color, bays and chestnuts appear more frequently, with an occasional black. White markings occur in some families. Spotted horses or palominos do not occur without the admixture of other blood.

In viewing the ideal type, we are impressed most by its stocky appearance, almost the extreme opposite of the rangier Thoroughbred. The head is rather short and broad, with heavy jaw, and exceedingly short ears set well apart. The eyes and nostrils are prominent, and the bones of the head are well modeled, giving an appearance of alert intelligence.

The neck is relatively shorter than that of most other breeds, and we become aware of its decided crest and heavy muscles. It is deep from the withers to the breast at its point of attachment to the shoulders. The throat latch is not as slender as in the Thoroughbred or American Saddle Horse. The neck rises up, giving a lofty carriage to the head.

The shoulders are powerful, with a considerable degree of slope. Naturally, the withers do not appear as bony and prominently defined as in some rangier breeds.

The back is short and broad, owing to the well-sprung ribs which round out into the deep, broad chest and body. The coupling of the hindquarters and the body at the point of the loins is short and strong. Moreover, there is no indication of a drawn-in, or "waspish," waist at the flanks. These points are important when considering the Morgan's superior weight-carrying ability and easy-keeping quality.

We notice that the croup, or top line, of the muscular hips is not as sloping as in the Quarter Horse; nor is it as level as in the typical American Saddler. The outline of the croup is rounding. The thighs and gaskins are well developed muscularly to harmonize with the rest of the powerful body.

As we survey the Morgan's legs, we are particularly attracted by their long dimension from elbow to knee in front and from stifle to hock behind, and their extremely short dimension in the cannons, or lower leg bones. Here again we note another typical characteristic of the Morgan breed. The hair on the fetlocks shows considerably more "feather" than in other light breeds. The pasterns are not long, neither are they upright, which would give us a jarring ride.

In temperament, the Morgan is docile and at the same time spirited, with an apparent abundance of nervous energy. He will serve willingly but will not tolerate unnecessary abuse. A good Morgan possesses a "never-say-die" perseverance and will never quit on any job.

Watching the Morgan in action, we soon become aware of his distinctive traveling gaits. Every movement gives the impression of pent-up energy. He raises his feet quickly and places them firmly on the ground. Though the stride is not great, the steps are made with rapidity and a springy elasticity, and he will travel in this manner regardless of how tired he may become. The technical explanation for the distinctive appearance of his gaits is that powerful short muscles contract on the tremendous leverage of the limb, which is made possible by the extremely short lower leg. In the saddle we discover the comfort of the ride, the shorter stride and cushioning effect of the action making it unnecessary to post the trot, as in some other breeds. The Morgan is naturally a three-gaited animal and therefore is not usually able to perform the five gaits with the perfection of American Saddle Horse form.

In addition to being an easy keeper, the Morgan Horse does not require special attention. Because of his hardiness and durability he can be used as seldom as two or three times a week without special preparation to keep in form. The training methods for Morgans are no different than for other horses of similar gaits.

USES OF PRESENT-DAY MORGANS

Morgan breeders do not make unreasonable claims for their horses' ability in highly specialized fields. They admit that they do not compete with the Thoroughbreds as speed horses nor with the American Saddle Horses in gaited classes. However, few horses have the all-round versatility of the Morgan. They have been successful as hunters in the New England states and stock horses in the Western states. The principal field for Morgan horses is pleasure riding, trail riding, and on the ranges. Cool intelligence and surefootedness have made them popular with horsemen and horsewomen who like to ride rough mountain trails as well as the bridle paths of the parks.

Mr. Hill, who uses a great number of geldings, which he has bred on his large ranches in Nevada, likes them about 14 hands 3 inches for cow work. His standards are very exacting, but the Morgans he has developed for this purpose suit him better than any breed or combination of breeds he has tried.

On grueling endurance rides, the Morgan has always given a good account of himself. In recent years, the Green Mountain Horse Association has held 100-mile competitive rides over rugged Vermont roads and mountain trails. In competition with animals of almost all light breeds, Morgans have won these contests in the years 1937, 1939, 1941, 1942, 1943, 1944, 1945, and 1946.

The Morgan is an exceptionally fine drill and posse horse because of his tractability, beauty, trappy action, and smooth-riding qualities.

This remarkable breed is recommended for those who wish a horse of many qualities. Should you desire a mild-tempered horse which will work willingly under saddle, in light harness, on the range or trail, or, if need be, perform light draft duties, the proud progeny of old Justin Morgan will serve you.

Standard Bred Horse

Years of selective breeding have refined the Standard Bred so that it now more nearly resembles the Thoroughbred than any other breed. It differs mainly because of heavier bones. Muscles throughout are long and flat. One of the most durable horses produced by American horsemen.

Head lean and bones well defined. Face straight or convex in profile. Eyes show wisdom and determination.

Back medium long. Hip coupling sturdy to withstand powerful drive of hindquarters.

Long and cleanly muscled, top line of neck is straight with no considerable arch. Square juncture between ears where head and neck join.

Croup slopes; tail not set high. Long, flat muscles.

Good leg bones and strong tendons. Joints and pasterns well modeled and strong.

Depth through girth is considerable. Forequarters flexible and sheathed with customary long muscles.

8

Standard Bred Horses

Of all the breeds represented in this volume none is more typically American than the Standard Bred. The part this stanch, durable horse has played in the progress of the nation is immeasurable. His bone and fiber were cast in the mold of necessity. Without him the duties of the old-time drummer, the judge, the parson, and the country doctor would have been exceedingly difficult. Though his speed and scope were not as great, he served in the same way that the passenger automobile does today.

It was natural that the animal which was so necessary in workaday affairs should also be enlisted as a companion in recreation. The idea of speed in the light-harness horse developed simultaneously with his more practical use. As a result, he has been perhaps the most democratic of American equines. There was a day when a roadster stood in almost every man's stable, and the thrill of slapping the lines over the back of his fast stepper was as great a source of enjoyment to the crossroads storekeeper as it was to Commodore Cornelius Vanderbilt. Of a certainty, the subject of harness horses was a common ground for both.

Today, however, we think of the Standard Bred as being a horse which trots or paces in light harness to a cart or racing sulky. Though he is now rarely seen anywhere except on race tracks or in the roadster classes of horse shows, older generations remember the days when this type of horse was used in more practical ways. Alas! paved avenues and mechanical modes of travel have forever banished the rush of fast roadsters down main street in the contest of speed between friends.

There was a time still earlier in American history when pacing and trotting horses were raced under saddle instead of being driven to a vehicle. Men-

169

tion has already been made of the racing activities of the Narragansetts which paced under saddle. It is an interesting fact that the Standard Bred type was initially developed for riding rather than driving. At first, however, the trotter was not esteemed as a saddle animal so much as the pacer. The trotter, with his jolting gait, was a horse for the gentleman rider who could "take" the bounce. The pacer was favored by travelers to whom comfort was essential.

Though the utility of the harnessed trotter had long been recognized in England, the change from saddle to wheels did not take place in America until after the Revolution. The supplying of armies required much wheeled traffic, regardless of road conditions, and this pointed the way to better roads and suitable vehicles for transportation. As the harness horse's practical use developed, his value as a common carrier decreased. Though this change took place gradually, it brought about the development of speed in the trotter. Instead of being a necessity, the saddled trotter was now taken up as a luxury animal by the moneyed class of road riders and drivers.

Most of the first amateur matches were performed under saddle. At that time, the carriagemaker had not yet applied his skill to the construction of light sulkies and wagons. The avenues and strips over which the dauntless trotting enthusiasts matched their mounts were too narrow and rough to be suited to speed in harness. Furthermore, trotters under saddle were capable of greater speed than when driven to a vehicle, and for that reason the saddle matches were considered more spectacular. In fact, as late as 1828, when the Philadelphia Hunting Park Association was formed, its by-laws stipulated that all trotting matches should be under saddle. Harness races were allowed only by special consent of a majority of its members.

EARLY TROTTING RACER UNDER SADDLE

Tradition may also have played a part in the development of saddled trotting matches. For example, the galloping racers which had been imported previously were always run under saddle. It is also interesting to note that the saddle was not the only equipment borrowed from the running set; colorful silks, jockey caps, and other accouterments were adopted by the gentlemen riders of the trotting group.

The gait of the trotter was, of course, different from that of the runners. His rhythm, squareness, action, and stroke, the joy of trotting enthusiasts, blossomed and developed through the years. Admittedly, the blood of the trotter and the methods of training have been improved, but it is this same skillful cross-pattern gait and its rippling smoothness which intrigues the trotting man of today.

The use of light horses in harness, however, was catching on rapidly in areas where it was feasible to use them, and in such localities, the popularity of the trotter increased over the pacer. While the South and the frontier regions fostered the pacing saddler because of necessity, the trotter gained favor in the more populated areas of the North where roads and avenues were being improved. The cross-gaited animals were better suited to teaming, and, as the English had discovered earlier, the cross-pattern gait, though rough under the saddle, furnished smooth, ground-consuming locomotive power when harnessed to a vehicle. Animals without the instinct to trot were trained to do the gait, often aided by weighted shoes and other devices.

Rising almost simultaneously with this great movement toward harnessed trotters was another activity which was born of necessity. Because of the wholesale depletion of horse stock in America, brought about by the destructive processes of the Revolution, it was necessary to import breeding stock. The prewar trickle of imported horses, later to be known as "Thoroughbreds," now swelled to great volume. Such horses had been developed as runners in England, but American horsemen confidently believed that they would produce good, usable horses when crossed on their own stock. As we shall see later, the blooded English horses did much to improve the American harness horse, although in theory the two breeds have always been opposed because of their traveling gaits.

With the importation of running horses, it was natural that a war-weary nation should turn eagerly to the diversion of horse racing. It was just as natural that reform should attempt to throttle it. At the beginning of the nineteenth century, the reform movement swept in a great stifling wave over the Northern states, closing track after track. Not until it reached the thoroughly entrenched racing states of the South did it meet sufficient opposition to stop it.

Though the running horse was banished from the racing ovals, there were still horses on the roads and avenues—and these were light-harness horses. If at one time running horses were considered necessary "to improve the breed," who could now deny that the occasional testing of the speed of a horse in harness down main street was not just as necessary? If Lawyer Brown's road stallion could outdistance Storekeeper Jones's, then that stallion was superior from a breeding standpoint. How else could using horses be improved? The consensus was that "trotting was not racing"—a belief which persists in the minds of at least a few to the present day.

There is a paragraph in Dwight Aker's book *Drivers Up* which amusingly describes the people's thinking concerning running horses, as opposed to trotters, as late as 1850:

> Even the parsons, usually in the forefront of the opposition to racing, were not always armor-plated against a line of reasoning that allowed them, in a spirit of tolerance, to condone humanity's passion for fast horses. In the eighteen-fifties—a date that indicates the long persistence of the distinction between trotting and racing—John M. Clay, a distinguished Kentucky horseman, refused membership in a Lexington church because he kept race horses, called the pastor's attention to the good standing in church of another Lexington resident who kept a stable of them. "Yes," answered the careful shepherd, "but *his* horses are *trotting* horses; yours, Mr. Clay, are race horses. We have no objection to trotting horses in our church." "Your members, I suppose, then," responded the rejected candidate, "do not gallop but trot their way to heaven." It was over the broad highway laid down by another church that Mr. Clay jogged on through life.

Thus aided by reform, law, political and public opinion, plus necessity, the harness horse was given an impetus which eventually put him on the race tracks in great numbers and consequently improved his lines of speed and endurance.

Trotting matches, however, did not take place on the tracks which the galloping racers had abandoned. Instead, matches were held over famous old-time highways such as Third Avenue, leading from the Bowery, and Jamaica Road on Long Island. The first trotting race on a regulation track did not take place until after the antiracing laws had been liberalized and running horses were again permitted to race.

The first time that the American road horse appeared for competition under such circumstances was on the Union Course, Long Island, May 27, 1823. The feature of the day, however, was not trotting; it was the match race between the famous New York race horse Eclipse and the Southern favorite Henry. Realizing that the occasion would bring great crowds, Harry Coster and his trotting-horse colleagues seized upon this occasion to show their trotting speedsters to the race-going public. Through the New York Jockey Club, arrangements were made to offer as a side attraction a free-for-all trot, the race to be in 2-mile heats under saddle with a purse of $1,000.

Though this trotting event was overshadowed by the victory of runner Eclipse, the interest in track trotting, thus started, was not allowed to lapse. The New York Trotting Club was organized in 1825, and by 1826 the club's Centreville course was established near Jamaica Turnpike, about a mile below the Union Course. Thus, the Centreville course was not only America's first but also the first track in the world to be devoted exclusively to the racing of road breeds.

EARLY RACES AND HORSES

Contemporary with the inaugural days of trot racing was a horse whose fame will never be forgotten. Topgallant was his name, and his story contains the element of democracy which has usually accompanied the trotting circle. Though this grand old horse had at one time been a galloper of some repute, his trotting legend begins in later years after he had found his way into service as a hack horse in a Philadelphia livery stable.

His "discovery" came about in an unusual way. One day he and his teammate were left unattended outside a tavern. For some reason the pair was startled and ran away. A bystander was astonished when he noticed that though the polemate extended himself to a gallop, the bay stallion, Topgallant, trotted true and square beside him. This fact was reported to his owners and thus began his belated career as a trotting racer.

To Topgallant must go the credit for winning the first trotting race on a regulation track in America, for it was he who was the victor in the Union Course trot in 1823. It is a remarkable fact that at this time he had reached the venerable age of fifteen.

One of "Old Top's" outstanding assets was his durability. He trotted both in harness and under saddle, mostly in the latter category, in conformity with the fashion of his times. It has been said that he held up well under the 150-pound saddle weight at great speed and for long distances. Twelve to 16 miles of racing were not an uncommon afternoon's activity for the hardy old veteran.

One of the greatest tests of Topgallant's endurance occurred during his twenty-second year at a race in Philadelphia, in 1829. He and his opponent, Whalebone, a handsome blood bay, were to trot under saddle in 4-mile heats. Topgallant won the first heat, Whalebone the second; the third was a dead heat; but the fourth and final clash saw Topgallant emerge victorious.

Topgallant's time, when totaled, was 45 minutes 44 seconds for the 16 miles of this race. In a day when three-minute trotters for a single mile were phenomenal, old Topgallant had averaged 2:58½ per mile for the entire distance!

Six years after Topgallant's race at Philadelphia, a filly was foaled who was destined to become an important figure in trotting-horse history. Lady Suffolk was her name, and during her time the sport flowered and was acclaimed by the common people as a spectator sport.

Also during her career, harness and vehicles almost completely displaced the saddle. In sixteen years of racing, "The Lady" trotted fifty times under saddle and one hundred twelve in harness. Saddle racing had a few shining moments of revival in the years following her racing days, but Lady Suffolk's record of 2:26 under saddle was not broken until 1853.

Lady Suffolk has become a symbol of the breed of horses known as "Standard Bred." She was the first horse to trot an official mile in less than 2:30, first under saddle and later in harness. The two-and-a-half-minute mile was later regarded as the standard measure of performance for Standard Bred Horses and was made a condition of admission to the trotting register both for trotters and pacers. We now consider the saddled trotting horse a novelty, but it is an interesting fact that the fastest official time for trotters under saddle was set as recently as 1940 when Mrs. Frances Dodge Johnson rode the gelding Greyhound a mile in 2:01¾ at Lexington, Kentucky.

The reasons for the decline in saddle trotting were various. The business of training and racing trotters has always been one for men of experience. As such trainers grew older, they could no longer endure the jolting in the saddle so they took their places on wheels behind the animals. More important was the fact that the saddled horse was being surpassed by the speed of the harnessed horse. As carriagemakers turned their skill to the construction of lighter sulkies and wagons, they also lent wings to the feet of the trotters, until at last man's age-old craze for more and more speed spelled doom for the saddled trotters which had begun as playthings for amateur gentlemen. Simultaneous with this was the development of better surfaced tracks and avenues, permitting more speed to wheels and the flying hoofs which propelled them.

BREEDING OF STANDARD BRED HORSES

It is apparent from a study of the early bloodlines of almost all American horses that certain outstanding individuals have been common ancestors in the foundation stock of numerous breeds. It is also apparent that each breed is a composite of many such forebears, one breed having a different balance of such mixtures. For instance, the American Saddler through the Chief strain traces strongly to Messenger, a stallion who influenced the American Trotter quite considerably. Also the Morgans have left their stamp on three American breeds—the American Saddle Horse, the Standard Bred, and the Tennessee Walking Horse.

While it would be difficult to prove that there were clear-cut phases in the development of strains in the American Trotter, certain horses stand out as greatly influencing the breed. Such names as Messenger, Bellfounder, the Black Hawk Morgans, the American Stars, the Pilots, Clays, and Hambletonians are preeminent in the bloodlines of the Standard Bred Horse. It may appear that the blood of some of these great strains has been erased and lost, but a closer study will reveal that the breed is a composite of the blood of all, some lesser and some greater in their influence. Thus certain qualities of each have been retained and welded into a horse which has now become standardized with one breed name.

Along with Imported Bellfounder, a Norfolk trotter, Imported Messenger is generally accepted as the founder of the American Trotter, which was subsequently developed into the Standard Bred.

Messenger was foaled in 1780 in England and imported to America in 1788. This gray stallion in his younger days had been successful on the turf in England. His bloodlines were supported by royal horses—horses which were among those to found the English Thoroughbred. His pedigree was studded with sovereigns of many racing generations—Mambrino, Engineer, Sampson, Blaze, Flying Childers, and the original Darley's Arabian. It is remarkable that a horse which was bred and trained for running should found a type that excelled at the trotting gait.

That he would play such an important part in the development of fast road horses was not dreamed of the day he was landed on a Philadelphia dock. It was to be expected that a horse possessing his lineage, proudness, vigor, and speed would produce outstanding offspring for the running track. In this he did not fail; his progeny proved to be outstanding performers in that respect. Attesting to this success he was given a burial befitting a champion.

The ceremony, which occurred in 1808 on Long Island, is described by John H. Wallace as related to him by an eyewitness:

> News of the death of the old patriarch spread with great rapidity. Soon the whole countryside was gathered to see the last of the king of horses and to assist at his burial. His grave was prepared at the foot of a chestnut tree and there he was deposited in his holiday clothing. In response to a consciousness that a hero was there laid away forever a military organization was extemporized and volley after volley was fired over his grave.

When the reform movement began to hack at the breeders of runners, the sons of Messenger were put to mares of the more useful and sedate gaits. Not many years had passed before the trotting-horse enthusiasts realized that the fastest and most perfectly gaited trotters were issuing from the stables served by the sons of old Messenger. Only fifteen years after the death of the gray stallion, Topgallant, a grandson, held the spotlight of trotting fame. Other descendants followed to prove further Messenger's greatness; Betsey Baker, Dutchman, Lady Suffolk, Princess were only a few of the early ones.

In 1856, a Michigan horseman wrote: "Occasionally a horse can be met with that shows his breeding from Messenger all over. We almost reverence such an animal. The Messenger stock has indelibly stamped its excellence on most of our first class horses."

Today it would be extremely difficult to find a Standard Bred of any repute which does not trace to Messenger. It is to the everlasting credit of early American ingenuity that the strain of stamina and speed found in the offspring of old Messenger was perpetuated.

Because of their speed and endurance, the offspring of Messenger spread to all parts of America and into Canada. Two outstanding branches of the Messenger strain were the Mambrinos and the Bishop's Hambletonians.

Another family that rose to recognition was the Clays. This strain was started with the stallion Andrew Jackson and gained its name from his son, Henry Clay, a foremost horse of his times. This strain also brought forth such horses as Cassius M. Clay, Kemble Jackson, and George M. Patchen. The latter, though his line was criticized for lack of fight in the finishes, gave the champion mare Flora Temple more competition than any other horse she encountered during her racing career.

The Pilots were noted for their toughness of spirit, though at times they were considered headstrong and unpredictable. This Canadian strain, through Pilot, Jr., established the earliest Kentucky trotters, while up North in Orange County the American Star family was contributing its qualities to the trotters of the country almost entirely through the female lines.

The Morgan Horses, through the Black Hawk strain, gained great popularity as roadsters and racers. The climax of their greatness was reached after the middle of the nineteenth century, Ethan Allen being the top representative of the strain. His defeat by George Wilkes turned the tide in favor of the Hambletonian strain by disclosing the superior racing qualities of the offspring of Rysdyk's Hambletonian, who is considered the leading foundation sire of the Standard Bred Horse.

Hambletonian (10) was foaled in 1849. He was by Abdallah, by Mambrino, by Imported Messenger; his dam, the Charles Kent Mare, was by Imported Bellfounder; grandam One Eye by Bishop's Hambletonian; great grandam Silvertail by Imported Messenger. From the foregoing pedigree it will be observed that Hambletonian (10) was an inbred descendant of old Messenger.

As has been indicated, the point of crystallization of the Standard Bred occurred with the emergence of Rysdyk's Hambletonian as a sire preeminent. Upon this horse hangs a human-interest tale of utmost interest to people of democratic nature. It is a story of a crippled mare, an unwanted foal, and the rise to fame of a hired man. It is best told by Dwight Akers in his book *Drivers Up.*

It was by accident, but not altogether by accident, that the events which led to the development of a standard breed of trotting horses occurred in Orange County, New York. The accident was "a lucky nick" in breeding, a chance affair that was quite in the pattern of the hit-and-miss breeding methods of the time. Orange County, however, was just the spot where a flowing together of strains might be expected to produce a horse of superior quality. As far back as there is a history of the Orange County horse, that region above the Hudson Highlands had been a breeding ground for race horses and roadsters. . . .

The Agricultural Society in this "horsiest" of New York counties, did not, it seems, endorse horse racing at the fairs. "The fastest-trottenest" were required to do their racing in the streets or on the roads. There was, of course, a plowing match at the fair grounds and as usual premiums were awarded for prime specimens of every type of farm product, from the best bull calf to the best pound of butter and the most cleverly designed piece-quilt. In the class of three-year-old stallions William Rysdyk's Hambletonian, a bay horse with black legs and white hind ankles, was rated first on the judge's score card and the Society's prize of five dollars was duly awarded his owner. The local press in its report of the awards gave no description of the young stallion and did not announce his pedigree. Neither did the *Spirit of the Times* trumpet the news to the world of sport.

Bill Rysdyk, owner of the prize-winner, had been Jonas Seely's hired man. Seely was an Orange County farmer of the old school, a man of comfortable means, living on a large farm, in a good house, amid surroundings and furnishings that gave evidence of its owner's education, refinement and social standing. A country gentleman! Residents of the county who recall him today remember his portly figure and his ruddy face. A man of stamina, built to withstand all weathers! In winter time, when his neighbors stayed indoors or bundled themselves in heavy wraps to withstand the cold, "Uncle Jonas" was to be seen driving his horse to phaeton, road wagon or sleigh over the country roads under no other covering than a large gray shawl. He lived at Sugar Loaf, a tiny village six miles from Goshen, and was in the cattle business.

In 1844, Seely, returning to Sugar Loaf after the delivery of a drove of steers to the New York market, brought with him a bay mare that he had found in the stable of a New York butcher, Charles Kent. She limped along at the tail of his wagon—an Orange County Flora Temple of no great notoriety who had had her fling in the big city and was coming back to the farm the worse for wear. She was no stranger to Seely. She was, in fact, a daughter of One Eye, a mare that had belonged to Seely's father. Seely had found her in the butcher's stable suffering from injuries received in a runaway. For reasons of family sentiment or of humanity to the mare he had bought her for a small price and was bringing her home.

The crippled mare was a daughter of the imported horse Bellfounder who a decade before had spent a season in Orange County. On the maternal side she was inbred to Messenger. The gray stallion, after his Goshen season in 1801, had left in the hands of Jonas Seely, Sr., a brown filly, Silvertail. In 1814, one of the best of Messenger's sons, (Bishop's) Hambletonian, had been sent to Goshen and Silvertail had been bred to him. From this mating, she had produced One Eye, the dam of the Kent Mare. Of such notable stock were the Seely farm horses.

As the Kent Mare's injuries were of a permanent sort, there was no work for her. Bred as she was, however, there was reason to expect good colts from her. In 1846, Abdallah, the ungainly, rat-tailed son of Messenger's Mambrino and of Messenger's famous granddaughter, Amazonia, having in 1840 been rejected by Kentucky breeders and returned to his native Long Island, was sent up to Orange County. He spent three seasons at the village of Chester, a few miles from Sugar Loaf. In his younger days a great career had been prophesied for Abdallah as a sire of trotters. He had not fulfilled the prophecies. Both his looks and his personality were against him. Orange County farmers no more than Kentucky trotting-horse breeders cared to breed their mares to a stallion whose extraordinary ugliness was linked to an incorrigibly vicious disposition. Seely, however, having no other use for his crippled mare, bred her to Abdallah. The old horse was soon thereafter returned to Long Island and after a season or two sold to a fish peddler for what he would bring. The price paid was five dollars.

As a driving horse, no less than as a sire, Abdallah failed colossally. A horse that would not submit to harness, a horse that at the venerable age of twenty-eight years would kick his master's peddling cart to matchwood, was no fit horse for any kind of honest work. Abdallah's exasperated owner, finding him not worth the price of his feed, turned him loose on a sand beach in bitter November weather to forage for himself. There he starved to death—Abdallah No. 1!—a black sheep of Messenger's flock, a hardened sinner and a ne'er-do-well, reaping in human indifference to his necessities the reward of his misdemeanors and his failures.

In 1849, the Kent Mare—there was no other name for her—dropped her foal. If it was inbreeding that was spoiling the Orange County horse, surely this colt might be expected to be one of the rickety good-for-nothings. Four lines of his pedigree, through Silvertail, (Bishop's) Hambletonian, Amazonia and Mambrino, ran to a single source—Messenger. There is no evidence that Seely shared the notion that the Orange County stock was too closely inbred. Apparently, however, he entertained no extravagant opinion of the value of this small son of Abdallah. When his hired man, Bill Rysdyk, illiterate, penniless but ambitious, cast a wishful eye in the direction of the colt and offered to buy him, Seely accepted Bill's promise to pay and having no more use for the mother than the son sold the pair of them to Bill for one hundred and twenty-five dollars. The new owner led the dam and her suckling foal away to the nearby village of Chester and there he set himself up in the horse business.

Rysdyk himself, it appears, expected no very fruitful blossoming from this branch of old Abdallah's tree. At least he did not stress beyond need the parentage of the colt. In the choice of a name for him he passed over the line of Abdallah and copied the name of a highly reputable grandsire on the dam's side—Hambletonian.

Building a business from scratch is slow work. In 1852, Hambletonian won a prize as the best two-year-old stallion at the Orange County Fair. In 1853, he was awarded the premium of five dollars as the best three-year-old of his class. Three years later, the firstlings of the Hambletonian breed were exhibited at the fair, held that year in Newburgh. The fair was a gala event. In addition to the usual features, there was a parade of the Newburgh firemen, a rowing regatta on Newburgh bay, and trotting races. A review of the stallion show published in the Newburgh *Daily News* accorded the highest honors not to any horse of Hambletonian's get but to a representative of the line of Long Island Black Hawk. With impartial eye the reviewer appraised the Hambletonians as good but not too good. "Seely Edsall's Young Hamiltonian," said he, "(why don't people show more Yankee ingenuity in naming their horses?) has a handsome movement and fine color and is of much better form than most of the stallions exhibited, but he lacks, and that is a family failing, that muscular swelling of the thighs and steam-engine motion of the hocks which propel horses along over a distance of ground. Mr. Van Houten of Chester had a beautiful Hambletonian filly, three years old, which carried a better croup and tail and had better thighs than most of that stock. Mr. Thomas Ellison of New Windsor had two fine mares, a yearling Hambletonian and two Hambletonian sucklings. The yearling is pretty but a little more bracing muscle would improve her."

Orange County was testing out the horses bred at Bill Rysdyk's stable but it was not being swept off its feet by them. An Orange County man who set himself up as a judge of horses had not yet learned to spell the name of Orange County's first horse-citizen and had discovered as the "family failing" of the Hambletonians their lack of propelling power. The drivers in Harlem Lane and on the Long Island trotting tracks of course knew nothing about these goings on at the Orange County fairs. Rysdyk's stallion was a dozen years old before his sons and his daughters with speed that had never been excelled and a perfection of action such as had never been seen began their whirlwind career on the trotting turf.

By that time, however, the Hambletonians were already a numerous tribe in Orange County farm stables. Traveling the country roads, brushing on the village speedways, trotting at the country fairs! If Harlem Lane and later the trotting turn wanted colts of Hambletonian breeding it was in the pastures of Orange County it would have to look for them.

The continuation of the story of Hambletonian's rise to fame calls for an account of the accomplishments of one of his sons—Robert Fillingham, later named George Wilkes. To set the stage for the episode, it is sufficient to say that George Wilkes entered his career at a time when the Morgan trotters were considered supreme. Ethan Allen was the pride of New England—Black Hawk Morgan was in the height of his brilliant career. Few horses of the fifties were more admired than this handsome, stylish bay stallion. Though small, his combination of speed, manners, and appearance made the Black Hawk stand high in the appraisal of horsemen and racegoers. This, then, was the horse against which Robert Fillingham was matched on September 10, 1862, at the Fashion Course. It was to be more than a match between two individuals; actually it was a duel between two great strains—the Morgans and the Hambletonians.

According to the reports, anxiety and tenseness were high. The audience was large and the betting intense. It was estimated that $150,000 changed hands as a result of the outcome of this match.

Let us turn again to Dwight Akers to take us up into the stands so that we may relive this exciting race between two great horses and two great horse strains:

Before the race, the horses were paraded before the stand, Fillingham led by his devoted pal Bill Cunningham. "He plodded through the crowd," said the *Spirit of the Times,* "with the steady air of an old stager. He had something of the sedate, resolute look with which the trained elephant follows his mahout. His slow walk is curious for its staid dignity and deliberation and he looks at a man in the course of it as if he were about to put a pertinent question."

Bring out your horses! They come to score in their sulkies: Ethan Allen, top horse of the famous Black Hawk line, "Black Dan" Mace driving him; Robert Fillingham by Rysdyk's Hambletonian, a sire almost unknown to the New England trotting-horse men. New York, however, is backing the Rysdyk horse so heavily that the odds are in his favor. Fillingham is driven by his trainer, Horace Jones.

Ethan Allen gets away to the lead and in that dashing way of his, always so dazzlingly displayed at the beginning of a race, outraces his rival. Around the turn a shadow across the track alarms Fillingham. He shies and breaks. Allen is ten lengths ahead. Says John Morrissey to his friend Eph Simmons, who sits next to him: "Get up, you sucker, and see your horse beat!"

But Fillingham is trotting again. Allen is far ahead of him at the quarter post. He is still ahead at the half-mile, though Fillingham is closing the gap. Just beyond the three-quarter post, at the turn into the home-stretch, there is an old apple tree. It is by that tree that on training days Rube, the running horse, Fillingham's prompter, has been turned loose to force the fighting down the home stretch. To Fillingham the apple tree is a landmark, a signal. He sees it, gathers himself, and goes. And how he goes! He comes into the stretch at a slashing trot and passes the drawgate as if he traveled on air. Allen is trailing him now. Fillingham reaches the wire, a winner by two lengths.

The New England delegation whose admiration for the Black Hawk stallion is almost fanatical, cannot believe that Ethan Allen has been beaten by the unimpressive little horse that in the parade had trudged so lazily behind his groom. But the second heat and the third heat repeat the first. Fillingham, with memories of Rube to inspire him, remembers to release his speed at the apple-tree turn, where speed is needed. Ethan Allen, always a fast horse at the start of a race, has no reserves for the finish. In the final heat, Jones pulls Fillingham and drives across the line almost at a walk. Ethan Allen follows him like a horse in hobbles.

"Sulky," the lively reporter of the doings on Harlem Lane, had left his beat that day and journeyed to Long Island to see the trot. Ethan Allen, he reported to his readers in the *Spirit of the Times,* "can trot a quarter and go to the half mile pole like a whirlwind but he can't run a full mile out as fast as the Simmons horse can trot it and there are few horses that go on iron today who can. Ethan acted in his last trot in such a manner as to lead many to believe that a preference in the blood of horses as far as trotters is concerned will be from the Morgans to the Hambletonians, at least at present." "We understand," commented the *Spirit of the Times* editorially, "that the stallion (Robert Fillingham) can be backed against any horse, mare or gelding, in the world, mile heats, three in five, for any sum from five thousand to twenty-five thousand dollars a side. Is there any response to this spirited cartel?"

Thus, through the offspring of George Wilkes, sometimes referred to as the "second Hambletonian," and other sons of old Hambletonian such as Edsall's Hambletonian, renamed Alexander's Abdallah, and Electioneer, the Hambletonian strain moved into the spotlight of trotting history from which position it has never been banished.

TRACK RECORDS AND FAMOUS HORSES

It has been stated that it was the horse, not his master, who first turned the drudgery of harnesswork into the alluring pastime of speed racing. Those who understand the nature of a mettlesome horse will readily agree that "that horse is noblest whose dust is foremost upon the plain." From the moment the excitement of rivalry took hold of the beast, he found a willing collaborator in his master.

Proof that American citizens of nearly a century and a half ago were possessed with the speed craze is contained in a letter to the editor of the New York *Gazette* in 1810. The writer complained that the "gay young men" were endangering the lives of citizens by riding and driving through the streets at too reckless a rate of speed. To remedy this situation, the Common Council passed an ordinance to the effect that south of Grand and Vesey streets no rider or driver should proceed at a speed faster than a slow pace or trot, not to exceed 5 miles per hour, and that all horses should be slowed to a walk at street corners.

What, specifically, were the reckless rates of speed at which horses were being driven in those times?

In the year 1806, Yankey, a New Haven horse, trotted a mile in 2:59 at Harlem. He was the first horse in America to contest officially against time at the trot. Incidentally, this was believed to be the fastest performance in America up to that time.

Horses capable of this rate of speed apparently were uncommon, for in 1818 racing men of Manhattan were laying open wagers that "no horse could be found to trot a mile to a sulky in three minutes or faster." In answer to such challenges, a horse bred in New England and called Boston Blue was brought to the Jamaica Road where he surprised Manhattan betters by trotting a mile in less than three minutes. Though the exact time was not recorded, Boston Blue's performance was regarded in those early days of harness racing as the maximum speed of trotters in America.

In England, however, races against time had been recorded earlier, though today we would consider such performances endurance tests. Bishop's Mare trotted 16 miles in 68:30 on the Epsom Road; Ogden's Mare trotted 30 miles in two hours ten minutes; and in 1793, Crockett's Mare trotted 112 miles in eleven hours forty minutes.

In America, few official records of trotting speed were kept prior to the formation of the New York Trotting Club, in 1825. When in 1828 the Philadelphia Hunting Park Association was formed for the purpose of "improving the road horse," Americans began keeping more frequent records of the speed of their horses. Also at that time, American horses began to surpass their British cousins in trotting speed.

Reports of records of speed sent to England brought back insulting retorts from English sportsmen. When a Philadelphia correspondent wrote John Lawrence that an American trotting horse had gone a mile in 2:35, that English racing authority replied: "American miles must be shorter than English miles—no horse ever did, or ever would for that matter, trot an English mile in so short a space of time else the excessive rapidity and friction of his feet would strike fire and set him ablaze."

Finally, the superiority of American Trotters was proved when they were shipped to England. On February 2, 1829, the American horse Tom Thumb trotted, in harness, a 5-mile circuit on the Sunbury Common, covering a distance of 100 miles (English) in ten hours seven minutes. On April 25, 1829, another American horse, Rattler, was matched against the famous Welsh mare Miss Turner and under saddle won his race of 10 miles in 30:42. The feat was proclaimed by the *Sporting Magazine* as "unparalleled in the history of horseflesh in England."

So, to the long-deceased Mr. Lawrence we must raise our heads heavenward and say, " 'Never' is a long, long time; who knows how fast a horse can trot before his feet must strike fire and set him ablaze?" The hundred years of sweat and toil following his statement have witnessed carriage craftsmen, superb trainers, and grand horses lop more than half a minute off the record he thought impossible.

As the years rolled onward, new records were made, only to be broken. Each generation was rightfully proud of the superior qualities of its stock. It

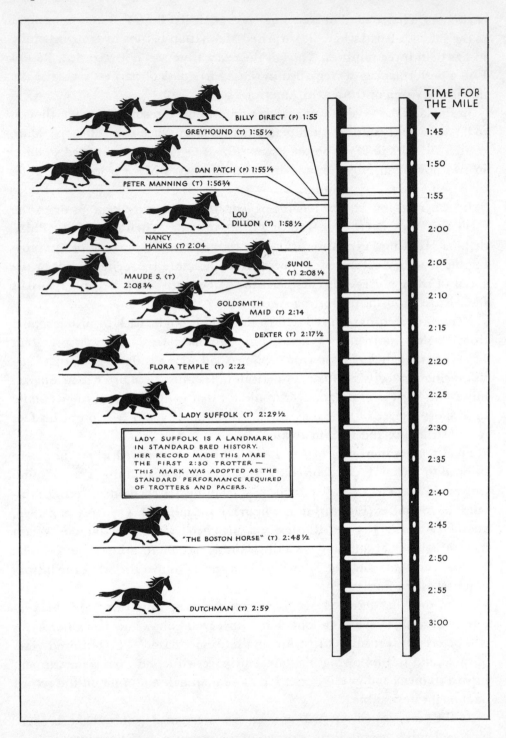

SPEED LADDER OF TROTTERS AND PACERS

is impossible to measure the worth of a horse of today against one of fifty or a hundred years ago. Unquestionably, Standard Bred Horses have improved through the years, but let us not overlook the fact that the great horses of early times labored harder to draw cumbersome vehicles as compared to our featherweight sulkies of today. Moreover, the tracks on which early horses performed were not like the elastic-surfaced courses of today. How many horses of the present sprint-racing days could stand up to old Topgallant who, in his twenty-second year, trotted 16 miles with only three brief rest intervals at an average speed of slightly more than 2:58?

To gain an understanding of the ever-increasing speed of trotters and pacers from the sport's beginning to the present time, let us picture a ladder with evenly spaced rungs. The bottom rung will represent a trotting speed of three minutes for the mile, and each rung, as we glance upward, will denote a speed of five seconds faster than the one immediately below it.

Dutchman

We have already noted that early in the nineteenth century, Yankey crossed the lowest rung of our ladder by going the mile in 2:59 and that later "The Boston Horse" moved on the difficult climb upward by trotting a mile in 2:48½. Then, for almost another twenty years, horses that were able to climb above the first rung of the speed ladder were uncommon.

In the 1830s, a bay gelding struggled upward to the next rungs of our ladder. This descendant of Messenger was called Dutchman, and his rise to fame was almost as phenomenal as Topgallant's.

Dutchman was raised in New Jersey and was transferred to a Philadelphia buyer for $120. As a young horse, he worked for a building contractor drawing menial loads. From such work he was finally promoted to roadwork, and it was in such service that his speed was discovered.

According to the records, Dutchman was a homely, rough animal. One of the writers of his time described him as "a great, ugly brown horse with a short hog neck—a fearful borer when going with his head down and his neck thrust out obstinately before him and the most ungainly goer and the most unpleasant horse I ever sat behind."

But it is apparent that what the Dutchman lacked in appearance he gained in qualities of bottom and endurance in sufficient quantity to make him a champion. When in 1838 "The Dray Horse," as Dutchman was sometimes called, trotted 3-mile heats in 7:50 under saddle, he was admitted to be the fastest trotter of his time. On July 4, 1839, when he beat Awful, his chief challenger in harness, he bettered his time by trotting 3-mile heats in 7:41.

During Dutchman's time, attention was given to the construction of lighter racing carts. In 1839, Dutchman and Awful were raced drawing 95 and 110 pounds respectively. Later that same season, these two horses were matched drawing vehicles that were lighter by many pounds; Dutchman's sulky weighed 82 pounds and Awful's weighed only 68 pounds.

"Wagon" races were common in those times, and the records involving such equipment were kept separate. Some such vehicles were mere skeletons, weighing as little as 70 pounds. Most race courses, however, ruled out wagons which weighed less than 250 pounds.

The date August 1, 1839, stands in importance beside Dutchman's name, for it was on that day that Hiram Woodruff rode him against time in a record-breaking 3-mile trot. The time was 7:32½. Although the time for each mile could not be officially recorded, the average for each mile was faster than the fastest single mile trotted by any horse. This record for 3 miles would not be bettered for thirty-three years—when Goldsmith's Huntress would go the 3 miles in 7:21¼. The middle mile was covered in 2:28, which unofficially made Dutchman the first horse to climb above the 2:30 rung of our ladder of speed.

We have already noted that Lady Suffolk was the first horse officially to cross the 2:30 rate of speed, with a record of 2:29½.

Flora Temple

As we glance upward on the ladder of trotting fame, we are attracted to a small bay mare with black mane and bobbed tail. She hails from Madison County, New York, and though we admire her fine quality and excellent conformation, we learn that she is willful and seemingly unbreakable to harness —a disappointing start for a contender in a world of champions. Flora Temple, in her early years, passed from the hands of many digusted owners; on one occasion she was sold for the insignificant sum of $13.

Flora Temple at last met her master in the person of George Perrin, and under his tutelage she became an apt scholar. Her bad manners and vices seemed to vanish into thin air and in less than four months she was winning races in competition with fast horses.

As a wagon puller this diminutive mare was unexcelled. When hitched to this heaviest of racing vehicles, Flora's extremely fine daintiness was contrasted to great advantage, causing her to be greatly admired by the ladies of her day.

Many good horses contested the supremacy of Flora Temple's trotting speed. In 1853, the mare Highland Maid pushed the champion mare to greater achievement; in one of these clashes the bobtail mare clipped three full seconds from the previous wagon record of 2:31.

In 1856, Flora Temple was matched against Tacony and trotted 2:24½, the fastest mile on record.

In her prime, the dainty Flora beat the best horses that could be found to race against her—Mac, Chicago Jack, Hero, Frank Forrester, Lancet, Ike Cook, Prince, Reindeer, and others.

The horse coming closest to putting an end to Flora Temple's career was the mare Princess, alias Topsy. Their first match, June 16, 1859, was 3-mile heats to wagon. In this encounter, Flora emerged victorious, but less than a week later, Princess turned the tables by winning a race of 2-mile heats with a time of 5:02 for the best heat.

It was not until August 6 of that year that Flora Temple recaptured her crown and downed her challenger. Yet to the grand mare Princess must go the credit for forcing the dashing little bobtail to greater heights of accomplishment. This time the two mares raced to sulky. The first heat saw Flora breast the wire first—the time: 2:23½, one second faster than the world's previous record. The second heat smashed the record of the first—2:22 flat! The third heat was raced in the same time as the first. Though Princess had failed to win, she had in her twelfth year forced the "little cricket" to trot all three heats in the fastest harness time the world had ever seen!

It was also to the fast tune of Princess's trotting hoofs that Flora Temple raced her speediest mile. In a match race at Kalamazoo, October 15, 1859, she breasted the wire at the end of the third heat in the record time of 2:19¾. This feat emblazoned her name on the records as the first 2:20 horse. It was at this mark that she rested.

That year and the next the dainty little champion encountered one of the greatest horses she ever contested. Though the bay stallion George M. Patchen never forced Flora to break her previous record against Princess, he did cause her to raise her average speed.

The last of Flora's famous victims was the Chestnut gelding John Morgan by Pilot, Jr. Unlike Princess and George M. Patchen, John Morgan did not once succeed in winning a race from the champion mare, but his speed pushed her to a new 2-mile harness record—4:52¼.

A short time later, Flora Temple was raced against a combination—the trotter Ethan Allen and his polemate Socks, a running horse. Though this odd pair beat Flora Temple on occasions, it never detracted from her honor as a champion. Shortly after these bouts, at the age of sixteen, Flora Temple, a veritable trotting freak for her time, was retired a champion. She had raced eleven seasons. Of the 103 times she raced, she had been beaten a mere 17.

Dexter

Dexter, the next champion on our ladder of fame, was, in a sense, the symbol of a new era in harness-horse breeding. This gelding was by Hambletonian out of the American Star (14) mare Clara. It is an interesting fact that from the moment this brown gelding broke Flora Temple's record, in 1867, the world's records have always remained in possession of Hambletonian-bred horses with the single exception of Alix (2:03¾), champion from 1894 to 1900. This mare carried Mambrino Chief blood, but had three close crosses to Hambletonian.

Dexter's training started when he was five, and his illustrious career extended from May 4, 1864, to September 7, 1867. He raced under saddle, to wagon, and to sulky at distances of 1, 2, and 3 miles. Out of a total of fifty-three races, he was beaten only four times.

Dexter's unusually energetic manner of going was called "the Dexter stroke." Trotting experts later came to realize that this efficiency of form and action was actually the budding greatness to emanate from the Hambletonian strain of horses.

At Buffalo, in 1866, Bud Doble rode Dexter a mile in 2:18. This, plus a world's record for the fastest time as a wagon horse, awaited only his harness record of 2:17¼, set at Buffalo on August 14, 1867, to make him the undisputed all-round champion of the world.

Goldsmith Maid

Somewhat similar to Flora Temple, Goldsmith Maid started her career late in life. First known as Nellie and later as Lady Goldsmith, she had at six been impossible to break to harness. Such adjectives as "graceful," "temperamental," "spirited," "nervous," "fine," and "alert" were used in descriptions of her by contemporary commentators.

This beautiful bay mare was foaled in New Jersey in 1857. She was by Edsall's Hambletonian out of an Abdallah mare. She was eight years old before being placed in her first race; and at the age of ten, she had not reached the heights that were to be hers, for on May 16, 1867, at Middletown, she lost three straight heats to the famous Dexter. At this time she was called Lady Goldsmith and was unsteady and flighty. As most horsemen will agree, a horse is no better than its trainer. It was fortunate fate that placed the unsteady mare in the competent hands of Budd Doble, who later bought her for $20,000. Under his guidance she bloomed and was launched upon the career that would establish her name as one of the greatest in trotting-horse history.

In 1868, she went a mile in 2:21½ and the next year in 2:19½, one of the first five horses to trot at 2:20. She defeated many good horses—George Palmer, George Wilkes, American Girl, to name but a few. At the age of fourteen, racing at Milwaukee, she beat Dexter's record by trotting a mile in 2:17. Like the great Flora Temple before her, she was a national idol, admired not only for her speed but also for her fineness, personality, and poise. Now a lady of aristocracy, she traveled in style in a private car coupled to a passenger train.

If she had started slowly, she finished like a whirlwind, apparently gathering momentum with age. At the venerable age of seventeen at the Mystic Park track in Boston, in 1874, she startled the world by going a record mile in 2:14. This was unbelievably fast and gave her the distinction of being the first 2:15 trotter. It was prophesied at that time, so great was her accomplishment, that no horse would ever be able to better such speed.

Though Goldsmith Maid's record has been laden with the dust of faster sulkies these many years, her mettle, courage, and loveliness can never be forgotten. Reflecting upon the records of this "trottin'est" mare in history who never raced until she was eight, in a day when 2:20 trotters could be counted upon the fingers of one hand, she trotted sixty-one heats in 2:20 or better, set a world's record at seventeen, raced until twenty, won more than $362,000, with only two purses over $10,000, and these things she accomplished carrying a 16-ounce shoe on each forefoot!

Maud S.

The next great trotter flashing upward on the ladder of speed was Maud S. She was by Harold, a son of Hambletonian, and out of the mare Miss Russell by Pilot, Jr.

The breeding of harness champions before the time of Maud S. was noted mainly for its hit-or-miss attempt to get horses with speed, regardless of bloodlines and without any concerted effort to study the breeding goal scientifically. Though of good fiber, many of the top horses were ill-tempered and coarse and were vastly varied in conformation. It was accidental that a few like Flora Temple and Goldsmith Maid were fine and handsomely conformed.

Maud S. marked the beginning of a new era in breeding to a goal. Her blood was purposely infused with the best qualities of two great strains—the Hambletonians and the Pilots. No longer would breeders be content with hit-or-miss methods. The yardstick of speed alone could not have succeeded in producing the fine trotting horses existing today. The freak Flora Temples and Goldsmith Maids could not occur often enough to compete with the caliber of colts which now crowd the racing ovals.

In 1880, at the beginning of her first season, Maude S. made a mark of 2:11¾. Later that year, at Chicago, she closed her season with a record of 2:10¾. In 1881, she lowered her record to 2:10½. After leaving the competitive field for a time, Maude S. was again exhibited in answer to a challenge from the owner of Jay-Eye-See, the horse who had beaten Maud S.'s time with a world's record of 2:10. On August 2, 1884, at the Cleveland track, Maud S. set a record of 2:09¾, thus becoming the first harness horse in the world to beat 2:10.

On November 11, 1884, at Lexington, she bettered her own mark and moved upward on the ladder by going the mile in 2:09¼. At Cleveland, on July 30, 1885, once more against time, she moved upward and rested with a world's record of 2:08¾—the mark which will forever remain as the fastest time on a regulation track for any horse to a high-wheeled sulky!

In closing the record of this great mare it is interesting to note that had it not been for the character of her shoes she probably would never have been able to trot at all. *Wallace's Monthly* reported that her gait was halfway between a rack and a trot. Only by using special toe weights behind was she enabled to trot true!

Sunol

The name Sunol appears next on our speed ladder. Opposite this horse's name is his mark—2:08¼. Sunol will be remembered as a symbol of revolutionary change in the sport of harness racing, the new idea which Leland Stanford had developed—the racing of colts.

By the middle 1880s, Stanford had established his huge farm in Santa Clara County, California, as the foremost trotting-horse stud in America. He injected science and aggressiveness into the raising and training of his horses. Just as he probed into the footfall pattern of horses' feet at the trotting gait, so did he delve into all the intricacies of horse breeding and training.

Looking at the sport with the eyes of a businessman, he felt that a colt was dormant, unrealized profit. To turn such a commodity into cash more quickly he believed that the colt should be trained at an early age, thereby quickening the liquidation of potentially profitable stock.

Among other things, he strongly advocated the use of more "running horse" blood, though he was condemned by many for this attitude. Colts had been raced previously but they had proved too slow to be of great interest. With an eye to early speed, Stanford introduced new methods of training along with a concerted study of breeding and developing fast bloodlines.

The Palo Alto colt's training was started from the time he was weaned. Though not actually broken to harness, he was handled at a tender age, thus cutting down the time usually taken later for gentling. Most of Stanford's colts did not know the meaning of unruliness.

Stanford also contended that weighted shoes and long strenuous workouts overtaxed the strength of a colt and wore down its natural spirit and eagerness for speed. Therefore, he abolished shoe weights and exercised his colts with short brushes at speed.

Fred Crocker, Hinda Rose, Wildflower, Manzanita, Chimes, and Palo Alto were among the earliest colts to carry Stanford's colors, and the records of some of these seemed to prove the worth of his revolutionary notions about colt training.

At the age of three, after a phenomenal kindergarten career, Sunol trotted a mile in 2:10½, short only 1¾ seconds of the world's record trotted by Maud S. when she was a mature track veteran. In 1891, as a five-year-old, Sunol moved up the ladder and trotted to the position of world's champion by going a mile in 2:08¼.

Nancy Hanks

Nancy Hanks is remembered in American harness-horse history because she was the first world's champion to draw a bike-wheeled sulky with pneumatic tires. With a record of 2:07½ trotted on a regulation track, this mare broke the records of both Maud S. (2:08¾, regulation track) and Sunol (2:08¼, kite track).

Though the newfangled sulkies undoubtedly enabled horses to go at greater rates of speed, nevertheless *Wallace's Monthly* thought Nancy Hanks was a great racing mare, as is evidenced by the following quotation: "I have heard oldtimers belittle the Chicago mile of Nancy Hanks in such a way as to make their uneducated auditors believe the sulky did it all and the mare herself was entitled to no credit."

It is, of course, a matter of record that many of the best horses of the day lowered their former marks as a result of the bike wheels. Nancy Hanks finally rested on her record of 2:04, made at Terre Haute, Indiana, in September, 1892.

Lou Dillon

The next champion on our speed ladder is a small chestnut mare foaled in 1898 at the Santa Rosa farm in Southern California. She is important because she represented almost a hundred years of harness-racing development, which started with Yankey's record trot of 2:59 in 1806. A hundred years of improvement in breeding, training, and equipage. A hundred years of endeavor. And the reward? A full minute clipped from the trotting record.

Purchased in 1903 by the colorful amateur sportsman C. K. G. Billings for the then modest sum of $12,500, Lou Dillon was destined for a nonprofit career that would symbolize her as the ultimate of achievement in the amateur movement which has always contributed so greatly to the sport of harness racing.

This great mare's career started in a whirlwind of success. Within the first few weeks of her public appearance in 1903, under the direction of Trainer Sanders, Lou Dillon had trotted a mile in two minutes flat. As if this record were not fantastic enough, on October 24 the same year at Memphis, she closed her season with the mark which stands beside her name—1:58½—the first horse in history to trot a mile in less than two minutes!

Dan Patch

Contemporary with the star Lou Dillon, but moving in his own galaxy, was the pacer Dan Patch. This brown stallion, foaled in 1896 in Indiana, was no "rags to riches" favorite. He was sired by the famous Joe Patchen, by Patchen Wilkes, by George Wilkes. He was out of Zelicka by Wilkesberry. Such royal blood made him a prince among Standard Breds.

Dan Patch thus was no freak, but, as his record proves, he was years ahead of his time. During his career, Dan Patch lowered world's records fourteen times. He is claimed to have paced 75 miles at an average speed of 1:59½. No horse since his time has equaled or approached his total number of astonishingly fast miles.

As a racing stallion, during the seasons of 1901 and 1902, he was raced fifty-six heats on the Grand Circuit and of these he lost only two. On August 29, 1902, at Providence, he paced a mile against time in 1:59½, only one-quarter second short of the world's record. The winter following, he was sold to

M. W. Savage of Minneapolis for the record price of $60,000. Not content with record prices, he paced a record mile, in 1903, at Brighton Beach, in 1:59. Later, at Memphis, on "Dan Patch Day," he astounded the world by pacing a mile in 1:56¼!

But his great struggle up the ladder of speed was not yet finished. At Lexington, in 1905, Dan Patch paced a mile in 1:55¼. This mark stands today as his official record—a monument to harness speed that endured for thirty-three years until the pacer Billy Direct paced a mile in 1:55.

But wait—1:55¼, though official, was not Dan Patch's fastest mile. At the Minnesota State Fair, in 1906, he paced a mile in 1:55 flat before a crowd of 93,000 people. This time was disallowed because of the newly formed ruling against Dan's method of racing against time with three front runners to pace him.

The fame of Dan Patch has become legend. He was idolized by the American men, women, and children of his time. Toys, sleds, horse feed, and even washing machines were named after him. Countless thousands of admirers filled the stands to see him wherever he appeared, and he traveled many thousands of miles during his years of exhibition. In 1904 alone, it is claimed, he journeyed 10,000 miles and entertained over 600,000 persons.

During his ten years of public appearances, his popularity never waned. Years after his retirement from the track, thousands of people visited the Savage farm to see and admire this great stallion. Living at the close of a period when road horses were a necessity, it appears that Dan Patch was unconsciously recognized as the ultimate of a breed of using horses—horses which the motor age was soon to obliterate forever.

The last rung on our speed ladder has almost been reached. There were many other great horses—champions and near-champions who spurred the ones we have mentioned to the heights they reached. It is regrettable that space is not adequate to record such great ones as Axtell, Allerton, Joe Patchen, Cresceus, Hamburg Belle, Native Belle, Bingen, Star Pointer, Directum I, Uhlan, Dean Hanover, Titan Hanover, and others. Our record, however, cannot omit the trio of champions whose speed performances hover at the last, and fourteenth, rung of our ladder.

Peter Manning

Peter Manning, a bay gelding, was foaled at Libertyville, Illinois, in 1916. Though he was by Azoff, by Peter the Great, he was not at first considered an outstanding candidate for fame. In fact, before he was placed in training, a buyer could not be found who would be willing to pay $150 for him.

His training was completed in 1919, when he was three, and that year he was entered in his first two races at Libertyville and the Wisconsin State Fair. He emerged from these encounters with the none-too-startling record of 2:17¼. However, when he was sent to Lexington in the fall, he upset the record for three-year-olds by going a mile in 2:06½. His stock immediately went up and he was sold for $21,000.

Unfortunately, through the illness of his trainer and the ups and downs of being kept out of training, his reputation suffered because of rumors that he was an "in-and-outer." It was against such odds that he was entered in the 1920 Transylvania. One of the outstanding horses against whom he was to compete was Nedda, the promising trotting mare by Atlantic Express, who was to climb high on the ladder of speed by setting a record of 1:58¼ in 1922, thereby making her the first trotting mare to beat the nineteen-year record of Lou Dillon.

Peter Manning won each heat of this hotly contested race. In so doing, he beat the record of Mabel Trask for the fastest time in three consecutive heats: 2:03 for the first, 2:02¾ for the second, and 2:02½ for the third. These marks, however, were far below the potentialities of Peter Manning, for in 1921 he was sent for a world's-record trotting mile of 1:57½. Finally, in 1922, this great gelding who could have been bought for $150 as a yearling broke his previous record by trotting a mile in 1:56¾—the mark which remains as his contribution to the ladder of speed, a mark which stood as the world's record for sixteen years.

Greyhound

The horse which topped Peter Manning's trotting mark was somewhat similar to him in that, as a youngster, he was not considered to have champion qualities. Greyhound, a gray gelding, was foaled in 1932. He was by Guy Abbey, by Guy Axworthy, and was out of the mare Elizabeth by Peter the Great. When sent to the sales ring at Indianapolis as a yearling, he did not impress the buyers. He seemed to be awkward and ungainly, and it was said he did not have a "good gait." At this sale, he passed from his original owner for a price of slightly more than $900.

Under the capable management of trainer Sep Palin, "The Silver Groomed Flyer," as he was later nicknamed, began to show promise. His coltish, ungainly way of going was polished into a powerful gait that measured a 27-foot stride.

Before long, this young gelding was adding record after record to his string of achievements, among which was the winning of the coveted Hambletonian, trotting classic for three-year-olds, in 1935.

Finally, at Lexington, September 29, 1938, as a six-year-old, he trotted his famous world's-record mile in 1:55¼, the mark which, up to the time of this writing, has never been bettered for trotting speed. It was also Greyhound who set the world's race record of 1:57¼. This has never been bettered by any trotter or pacer in an actual race.

Billy Direct

At last we look at the uppermost point on our ladder of speed and there find the horse which stands on the pinnacle of harness speed. Billy Direct was a bay colt foaled in 1934. He was by the pacing stallion Napoleon Direct by Walter Direct, and was out of the mare Gay Forbes by Malcolm Forbes.

Off to a whirlaway start, Billy Direct, at the age of three, paced the third heat of a race in 1:58. The records showed this to be the fastest mile ever paced by a three-year-old. Three-year-old Chief Counsel broke this record with a time of 1:57¾ in 1938, but Billy Direct's time remains the fastest third heat paced by a horse of any age up to the present time. Moreover, this record has never been bettered by any pacer in a race, though it is shared by two other great horses—Directum I and King's Counsel.

At Lexington, Kentucky, on September 28, 1938, one day previous to the record trotting mile by Greyhound, the stallion Billy Direct paced his momentous mile in the astounding time of 1:55 flat, a record which has stood not only as the fastest mile paced in history, but also as the fastest mile traveled by any harness horse.

At the age of thirteen, in 1947, the great Billy Direct died at the Hanover Shoe Farms in Pennsylvania after further contributing to the sport of harness racing by siring many famous colts, among them Ensign Hanover, Direct Express, Morgan Hanover, Deep Thoughts—all two-minute performers.

GOVERNING BODIES

One of the first and most diligent crusaders for the establishment of the Standard Bred type as we know it today was John N. Wallace. This tireless man devoted years to the attempt to inject fair practice into racing activities and procedure of registering trotting horses. A former secretary of the Iowa State Board of Agriculture, John Wallace, compiled with scholarly care and published his *American Stud Book.* In 1871, he published the first volume of *The American Trotting Register,* a second volume in 1874, and a third in 1879. Combined, these three volumes contained pedigrees of nearly ten thousand trotters.

All these animals represented were accepted by Mr. Wallace only after exhaustive research as to their true pedigrees. Thereafter, no animal was admitted to the *Register* unless it qualified under the Standard rules. Though the rules have varied considerably, this method of admittance has remained in force to the present time.

It is interesting to note that in the formative period, horses of any strain or breed were acceptable, provided they were able to trot the mile at 2:30 or better, or depending upon their degree of relationship to a Standard Horse. Though horses of today may still be registered as non-Standard, to all practical effect they are all traceable to blooded forebears.

Starting in 1875, *Wallace's Monthly* carried current summaries of all trotting races. By 1885, the volume of such compilations caused Wallace to publish these records in an annual volume called *Wallace's Yearbook.* This was augmented by *The Great Table* of Standard Horses listed under their sires. Because of the authenticity of such data, *Wallace's Yearbook* became the accepted record in harness-racing circles.

In 1876, the newly organized National Association of Trotting Horse Breeders appointed a board of censors to review Wallace's findings, and they were accepted as authoritative. As a result, the American Standard Bred Horse, as a breed, originated officially in 1879, when the National Association adopted its rules of admittance for individuals.

Through the years, other sponsoring groups were formed. Before 1938, the sport of harness racing was governed by the National Trotting Association, the American Trotting Association, and the United Trotting Association. Each group had its own rules and regulations, and owners and trainers were often not sure under which organization's rules they were racing.

To find a solution to this unwieldy situation a group of representative horsemen, who were members of one or the other of the three sponsoring bodies, gathered from various sections of the country. In 1938, the United States Trotting Association was organized, and in 1939 it was incorporated at Bellefontaine, Ohio.

Now all registrations and harness-racing activities in the United States and the Maritime Provinces of Canada are conducted and governed by the U.S.T.A. This composite group has furnished great impetus to the sport through efficient and centralized organization.

The organization's usefulness is varied and far-reaching. The effectiveness of its enforced insistence regarding fair practice in racing has made the sport one of the cleanest in the country. U.S.T.A. urges scientific advancement among producers of the racing stock itself. Such practices have returned immense rewards to the sport as well as to individual breeders.

Under the U.S.T.A., Standard Bred trotters and pacers can be registered "Standard" or "non-Standard." The Association's official application for registration is self-explanatory:

Section 1. Standard Bred.

Horses may be registered as Standard Bred with any of the following qualifications:

(a) The progeny of a registered Standard horse and a registered Standard mare.

(b) A stallion sired by a registered Standard horse, provided his dam and grandam were sired by registered Standard horses and he himself has a Standard record and is the sire of three performers with Standard records from different mares.

(c) A mare whose sire is a registered Standard horse and whose dam and grandam were sired by registered Standard horses, provided she herself has a Standard record.

(d) A mare sired by a registered Standard horse, provided she is the dam of two performers with Standard records.

(e) A mare or horse sired by a registered Standard horse, provided her first, second and third dams are each sired by a registered Standard horse.

(f) The Standing Committee on Registrations may register as Standard any horse which does not qualify under the above five rules, if in their opinion he or she should be registered Standard.

Note: Standard records are 2:20 or better for two-year-olds; 2:15 or better for older horses.

Section 2. Non-Standard Bred.

Any horse may be registered as Non-Standard upon filing application showing satisfactory statement of breeding.

Note: Every foal of 1937 and thereafter must be registered either Standard or Non-Standard to be eligible to race.

CONFORMATION AND TEMPERAMENT

The statement that the American Standard Bred is one of the most durable of all equines would not be disputed by any experienced horseman. Let us study a modern representative of the breed to gain firsthand knowledge of his physical conformation and temperament.

Of all American breeds, with the possible exception of certain individuals within the ranks of the Quarter Horse, the Standard Bred resembles the Thoroughbred more closely than others. If a word could be used to differentiate the two breeds, it might be said that the Standard Bred is more angular. Generally, the breed is also heavier of bone, though not coarse.

The height will usually be between 15.2 and 16 hands. The prevailing colors are bay, brown, and chestnut. Occasionally roans, grays, and blacks are observed. Extensive white markings are rare, most horses of this breed being solid color.

The bones in the head of a model Standard Bred are prominent and well formed. For instance, the muscular jaws which mark the Quarter Horse are not found in the Standard Bred. In many ways, the conformation of head is opposite in these two breeds. The whole head of the Standard Bred is longer and more slender, as also are the ears. The ideal faceline, when observed in profile, is straight and flat across the eyes. In a large number of individuals, the profile is convex, or "Roman-nosed," to use a horseman's term. It is exceptional when a Standard Bred face is dished.

Another general mark which distinguishes the Standard Bred from other breeds is the square angle formed at the top of the head where the neck adjoins it. In other words, if a straight line is drawn to represent the front of the face and another to represent the top line of the neck, the two form a square juncture at the point between the ears.

The fact that harness horses are able to go mile after mile at grueling speed is due to the long, flat muscles throughout their bodies. These are evident in the neck, which is rather straight, of good shape and medium length, being neither as thick as the Morgan's nor as slender as the Thoroughbred's.

It was an earlier belief that harness horses should have extreme body length to allow unobstructed play of the legs. Such conformation has been superseded by horses of shorter construction. Greyhound, the world's champion trotter, possesses a body 4 inches shorter than his height. However, for comparison it should be mentioned that the Standard Bred is not usually as short as the Arabian or the Morgan. He is not intended to be a weight carrier, and the usual argument in favor of a short back is in terms of its benefits for saddle purposes. Every model Standard Bred Horse has extremely good coupling at the point where the back attaches to the hips; otherwise it would be impossible for his structure to withstand the tremendous drive of his characteristically powerful hindquarters. Before completing our discussion of the top line, it is interesting to note a peculiarity of conformation in the frame of Hambletonian (10) which has been passed on to at least a few of his progeny. Quarter Horses are not the only ones which may be accused of "running downhill"; Hambletonian stood 2 inches taller at the hips than at the withers. This peculiarity came to be called the "trotting pitch."

Another feature noticeable in Standard Breds is the great length of the legs in so far as forearms and upper rear legs are concerned. When the way of going is considered, the reason for such structure is more easily understood. A galloping horse's length of stride relies considerably upon movement of the entire body and neck. Now picture a trotter or pacer; most of his forward propulsion is caused by the movement and action of his legs alone. The effort of lean, long muscles acting upon the leverage of long upper limbs affords great stroke and speed at the Standard Bred's specialized gaits.

Needless to say, the feet of this breed must be superior. When it is considered that at certain stages of training these horses may be shod and reshod frequently and that the hoofs pound mile after mile in strenuous workouts, it is obvious that faulty hoofs or bone structure within the foot could not measure up to such rigorous requirements.

A discussion of conformation would not be complete without mentioning road horses for show. The roadsters in horse-show classes are the same breed as the horses seen on harness-racing tracks, the only difference being that the racers are in lean racing form whereas the roadsters are in "show shape." Roadsters, however, must always be selected for their elegance of form. Fine heads, well-shaped bodies, and clean legs are all points to be considered in this type. Model specimens are constantly sought after for this phase of the sport. Road horses may be selected and trained from colthood for careers in the horse-show world, but there are numerous instances where successful track horses have been converted to the gentlemanly sport.

The long-lived Standard Bred Horse is richly endowed with intelligence and stability. Bred for utility in road work, such animals are tractable and steady. It is an accepted rule that horses containing all or part Standard blood are trustworthy and loyal in the uses to which they are put.

TRAINING

Standard Bred Horses are similar to horses of other breeds in that each one is an individual personality. The trainer must always realize that the animals in his care are varied in temperament and instincts and that each one presents a special problem.

In the old days before colt racing became so popular, it was the accepted practice to turn a colt out after his first few lessons and save him until he was three or four years of age. Nowadays most trainers start the young animal when he is a "long" yearling, from fourteen to eighteen months old. One trainer of my acquaintance groundbreaks the colt immediately after the fall sales are over and continues the training until race time.

The pupil is rigged in a bitting harness at first and is taught the use of lines and voice commands by ground-driving. The trainer ground-drives the colt until it is thoroughly bridle-wise. Then he hitches the colt every day to a light jogging cart and continues with the training. After a period of ninety days, the colt is started at 1 mile and is gradually increased to 6 or 8 miles daily. After this, the speed is increased.

The young animal should be worked slowly at first. This gives the trainer the opportunity to "tone" him up, study his temperament and gaits (at this early age he will show a tendency to trot or pace), and observe what he needs in the way of balance and stride through shoeing, etc.

If a trainer is to cash in on the opportunity afforded by today's harness-racing system, he must realize that the horse's greatest earning capacity is during his second and third years. There are sizable purses for two-year-olds at all the mutuel meetings. Even at the county fairs the two-year-old stakes rank with the top purses of the meetings.

The earning capacity of two-year-old trotters and pacers can best be shown by reviewing the results of the 1949 racing season. There were two two-year-old trotters which barely missed the $50,000 mark in their first year of racing. Lusty Song won $47,799.29 and Floricon won $47,604.14. During the same year in the pacing category, the two-year-old filly Our Time won $50,227.60 and Beryl Hanover won $24,840.93. The fact that two-year-olds can really race is proved by the World's Record Table which shows Titan Hanover at that age trotting a mile in 2:00 flat and Knight Dream racing 2:00⅖ in two-year form.

The same table shows three-year-old horses winning astounding sums. Among trotters, in 1949, Bangaway won nearly $75,000 while Miss Tilly was over the $48,000 mark. Among the pacers Good Time won nearly $59,000 and Stormyway nearly $32,000.

RACING PROCEDURE

As mentioned earlier in this chapter, vast changes have taken place in the system of harness racing. Fast-dash races have almost completely displaced heat racing.

The automatic starting gate, of which there are several types, was first introduced in 1942 at Roosevelt Raceway on Long Island. This device has been an extremely important factor in the upsurge of popularity which now attends the sport. One type favored by many tracks is constructed on an automobile which operates down the middle of the track, with the horses lined up abreast behind it. As the automobile with two long arms starts down the track at increasing speed, the horses follow. At the starter's signal, the arms are folded and the horses are off to a good start, thereby eliminating the earlier tedious method of starting which sometimes consumed as much as half an hour.

In harness racing, as in flat racing, the "pole" position next to the inside rail is preferred. Most top drivers attaining the pole position prefer to "cover up" their mounts by letting one or two horses pass them, going to the front to "break wind." Then, in the last quarter, if the breaks are with him, he will drive to win.

Top drivers will tell you that the average horse cannot be "pumped" (pushed at great sprinting speed) more than one-quarter of a mile and the best of horses not more than three-eighths of a mile. Another thing that experienced drivers know is that a horse has only one "brush" in a race. If he is allowed to brush on the backstretch, he cannot be pushed to a sprint at the finish.

A horse that switches gaits in a race—that is, from the trot to the pace or vice versa—is eliminated; but this is not too common an occurrence. Horses that break gait (going into a gallop from a trot or pace) are more common. Such a break does not eliminate a horse unless the officials decide the horse

TROTTING
RACERS

has bettered his position by the break. Usually the ground lost in pulling a horse back to gait loses the race for the contestant.

The training of roadsters for show purposes is started in much the same way as that of harness race horses. However, in the roadster, speed is not the only requirement. For a concise description of what the ideal roadster is and does we quote from the *American Horse Shows Association Rule Book:*

> The Roadster is a driving horse of good appearance, conformation and manners and standard color, who travels easily and at speed. To be 15.1 to 16 hands, weighing 1000 to 1150 pounds. Roadsters wear long tails, usually natural.
>
> Action should be free, easy, straight and balanced but excessive height of action not required. A fairly rapid road gait and speed when called for are essential, provided form is not sacrificed. A good walk is desirable. The trot is the usual gait although occasionally classes for pacers are provided.
>
> Good manners without severe bitting are requisite. Horses should be balanced and under control, take the turns without breaking their gait, be taken up at the turns or in the straightaway when necessary and come out of the turns fast. They should stand and back readily.
>
> Roadsters usually enter the ring clockwise at a jog or road gait then turn anti-clockwise first at a road gait and then at full speed. They should be able to go at full speed both ways of the ring. Roadsters may be shown to road wagons, to bike or under saddle.

ROADSTER

The championship, or "stake," class for road horses should be judged on performance, speed, presence, quality, conformation, and manners.

Standard Bred Horses and the events surrounding them have been a part of the warp and woof of America. For a sentimental glimpse of one of the few remaining fragments of such activity it would be necessary to journey to the Amish communities located in the eastern part of the United States. There the horse still reigns as a necessary part of everyday living, for the Amish religion does not permit the use of motorized equipment. While racing is not in accordance with the belief of these people, many Amish horses may be potential Flora Temples, Oxtells, or Lou Dillons. During the recent racing boom, quite a number of drivers scouted the Amish territory and came away with horses having good speed. One such horse was discovered pulling a milk wagon. Homer Butler purchased this three-year-old brown gelding in 1936. Today, Stoneridge Direct is listed as holding one of the world's records for four heats for pacers over a half-mile track.

Those who think that the golden era of harness horses is past need only take up the lines of one of the progeny of old Hambletonian (10) and feel the same exciting thrill that Judge Tompkins, Storekeeper Jones, or Commodore Vanderbilt felt in the nineteenth century, for the Standard Bred Horse is imbued with the same fine spirit now that he was then.

Tennessee Walking Horse

In addition to sturdy substance. the Tennessee Walking Horse has two outstanding attributes: intelligent, kindly temperament and ability to excel other breeds at the walking gait.

Back is short; ribs are well sprung; coupling at hips shows weight-carrying ability.

Average animal slopes at the croup. Tail less high than on most American Saddle Horses. Quarters outstandingly muscled.

Ample bone in legs. Pasterns medium long and springy. Often rear legs sickle slightly.

Most distinguishing feature of the head is the eye, the upper lid of which wrinkles peculiarly forward. Generally slightly convex face.

Neck is muscled, shapely, and medium long. Today's breeding is developing high-headed individuals.

Shoulder extremely sloping and flexible. Extreme muscular development of shoulder and breast required by animal's gaits. Considerable width of chest.

❧ 9 ❧

The Tennessee Walking Horse

"Dat am de walkin'est hoss I evah did see!" This statement of an old Negro trainer may be taken both literally and figuratively, for no other American breed has moved into the limelight of public popularity so rapidly as the Tennessee Walking Horse. In less than ten years after the Tennessee Walking Horse Breeders' Association of America held its first meeting at Lewisburg, Tennessee, on April 27, 1935, the Tennessee Walking Horse, hitherto little known outside its native state, gained recognition in far-flung circles. At the present time, there are over forty thousand Tennessee Walking Horses registered in the Association, and the breed has been recognized by the U.S. Department of Agriculture and the Canadian government as a separate and distinct breed of light horses. Recognition will undoubtedly soon come from other nations of the world.

It might be presumed that the Tennessee Walker is a comparatively recent development in the equine world. Such is not the case, for horses of this type have been "walking a hole in the ground" for well over a hundred years. When the first Tennessee settlers arrived across the mountains from Virginia and the Carolinas, carrying a rifle in one hand and a Bible in the other, they were mounted on horses that were stanch and enduring. As the new country was developed, the native Tennessee horses served their pioneer owners well. Reared to a life of versatility, they served in working the fields, as saddlers, and, on Sundays, as carriage horses.

In early times, the Tennessee horse was referred to as a "turn row" horse, the term coming from his use as a riding mount for inspecting the long crop rows. He was, and frequently still is, referred to as a "plantation horse." No

STANCH AND
ENDURING

other breed was so well suited to farm operations which required many long hours in the saddle. His amiable disposition and speedy walking gait were an ideal combination. A trotting or galloping horse would have been a threat to the comfort of the rider and to the growing plants underfoot.

It is natural that there should be many misconceptions about a breed which has so recently and suddenly come to public attention. I was greatly amused a few years ago when I was told that the Tennessee Walking Horse was half mule! The walking speed of the mule, my informant pointed out, was passed on to the breed.

Another common misbelief concerning Tennessee Walkers is that they are culls taken from the ranks of the American Saddle Bred. It is true that the two breeds are related; they were both based, in part, on the early easy-gaited native stock of the Southern states, and actual infusions of American Saddle blood later took place, but its importance is rated below the importance of at least two other American breeds.

A close study of Walking Horse bloodlines during the past century and more reveals the influence of many breeds. One compiler of pedigrees credits the influence from other American breeds in the following order of importance: Standard Bred, Morgan, American Saddle Bred.

The simple flow chart opposite illustrates the development of Walking Horse blood. The earliest taproot stock consisted of the easy-gaited horses brought into Tennessee by the pioneers. These riding horses, capable of transporting their riders in comfort and safety, undoubtedly contained the blood of the Narragansett pacers, from which easy-gaited stock in the Colonies sprang. Add to this the fact that Tennessee, late in the eighteenth and early in the nineteenth centuries, nurtured Thoroughbred racing horses, and it is easily deduced that the Thoroughbred was one of the first to add refinement to the breed we are discussing.

By the 1830s, Tennessee slightly outranked Kentucky as a blood-horse nursery. Running races were then to the Tennesseean what horse shows are to-day. Such running horses were more often referred to as "bred" or "blood" horses than "thoroughbred." Through the next thirty or forty years, there were two types of race horses—the "four-miler," which usually had a long pedigree, and the "short," or "quarter," horse, which was at least one-half Thoroughbred. The "distance" horses required regulation tracks, whereas the "short" racers supplied the bulk of the sport for "back-country" folk.

After the War between the States, quarter racing died out and was supplanted by racing pacers under saddle at a distance of a quarter mile or more, usually on a straight strip. Even earlier, about the middle of the century, pacing horses were raced in the saddle-horse ring; one ring was located at the old fairgrounds west of Columbia, Tennessee. The distance was approximately 300 yards around. Nolan's Copperbottom and Brooks were two of the famous old horses to contest with each other in this sport. McMeen's Traveler was another of this type, and his blood figures prominently in Tennessee Walking Horses. It is recorded that this famous old sire at the age of fifteen was taken North in Wilder's Raid in 1864. Unable to endure the severe travel, the old horse was found dead by the roadside near the Maury-Marshall line.

In the Tennessee counties where the walking saddle horse was developed —the ten counties comprising the watershed of the Tennessee River—both of the running-horse types mentioned above were used on native saddle stock to produce top-class easy-gaited riding horses. The "distance" horses supplied bottom and endurance while the "short" horses contributed speed and toughness. The following list of Thoroughbred stallions and their first year of serv-

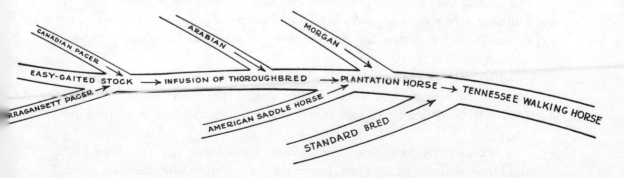

DEVELOPMENT OF THE TENNESSEE WALKING HORSE

ice in middle Tennessee gives us a clue to the Thoroughbred horses that had an early influence on the plantation saddlers as well as the period of their influence. The list, compiled by the late William J. Webster, Jr., was part of an article entitled "Origin of the Tennessee Pacer" which appeared originally in *The Trotter and Pacer*.

IMP. SOURCROUT	1791	IMP. BAGDAD	1824
BOWIE	1795	Sent by the Minister of England from Tripoli.	
WILDAIR	1798		
GRAY MEDLEY	1800	IMP. LEVIATHAN	1825
FITZ MEDLEY	1804	It appears that Leviathan was transferred to Maryland, Virginia, and Kentucky, later coming back to Tennessee.	
MCKINNEY'S ROAN	1805		
CELER	1806		
COEUR-DE-LION and ROYALIS	1807		
TRUXTON	1808		
WILKE'S WONDER, by DIOMED	1809	TIMOLEON	1826
IMP. BRIAN O'LINN	1810	Sire of Boston, sire of Lexington.	
IMP. DRAGON	1811		
IMP. BOASTER	1815	IMP. STOCKHOLDER	1826
SUWARROR	1818	IMP. LUZOBOROUGH	1834
SIR HAL	1821	IMP. AINDERBY	1849
COPPERBOTTOM	1823	IMP. ALBION	1850

From other records, Timoleon and Imported Leviathan seem to have been principal progenitors of "distance" blood to the Plantation horses, while such sires as Rock, Old Bowie, Sam Walker, and Johnnie Miller passed on their qualities from the "quarter" ranks.

Pedigrees, contemporary writing, and old sales reports and catalogues furnish proof that saddle horses containing 25 per cent or more Thoroughbred blood were numerous. The racing horses supplied stamina and finish, while the pacing saddle blood furnished aptitude for the saddle gaits—fox trot, running walk, stepping pace—as well as a quieter disposition. In those times, it was the opinion that horses containing as much as 50 per cent running blood were difficult to "gait."

In addition to the running blood, there were subsequent individual infusions of the Morgan and the breed now called the American Saddle Horse, for it will be remembered that this type was not established as a breed until 1891.

The breed most notable and recent in its influence on the Tennessee Walking Horse is the Standard Bred. Just as the American Saddle Horse recognized its founder in the Thoroughbred Denmark, the Tennessee Walking Horse acknowledged (Black) Allan (7623 A.T.R.) as its founder. From Volume One of the Association's *Register* we quote the following:

> This great horse [Allan] is at least the technical sole fountainhead of the strain he founded, as he has been the real head since its foundation. In the three years since the formation of this Association it has been fully demonstrated that no other horse was worthy to stand by his side as Recognized Deceased Sire. Proof of the statement is conclusively given in the First Volume of the *Register,* as the majority of horses entered in this Volume trace directly to Allan F-1.

Allan F-1 was a black trotting-bred pacer, bred by E. D. Herr, Lexington, Kentucky. This stallion, which was foaled in 1886 and died in 1910, was by Allandorf, by Onward, by George Wilkes; Onward's dam, Dolly, was by Mambrino Chief; Dolly's dam, by Potomac; Allandorf's dam, Alma Mater, by Mambrino Patchen, by Mambrino Chief; Mambrino Chief's dam, Lady Thorne; Alma Mater's dam, Estella, by Imported Australian.

Allan's dam, Maggie Marshall, was by Bradford's Telegraph, by Black Hawk, by Sherman Morgan.

It will be noticed that Allan F-1 was predominantly trotting-bred on the top line of his pedigree and Black Hawk Morgan strain on his maternal side.

The greatness of Allan F-1 was not fully recognized until his later years. In fact, as a younger horse, he was considered a failure both as harness racer and breeding stallion. As a result, he changed owners repeatedly, each time apparently lessening in value. From his breeder, Mr. Herr, Allan as a foal passed to the ownership of George F. Fly of Elyria, Ohio, along with his dam, Maggie Marshall. Upon being trained, Allan was found to have a passion for pacing. As Mr. Fly wanted trotters, not pacers, he returned him to Kentucky and consigned him for sale.

The Lexington *Morning Transcript* of February 12, 1891, listed Bransfield and Company's Public Sale of Thoroughbreds and Standard Breds for that day. Among the sales was listed Allan (Black) 5, by Allandorf, dam, Maggie Marshall, sold to John P. Mankin, Murfreesboro, Tennessee, for $355.

Placed in the hands of trainers, Allan was reported not to finish well in a hard drive. It is a matter of record that this was not due to lack of stamina but rather to the fact that he was a loose-gaited horse and knocked himself to pieces before the end of a race. It was possibly this loose-gaited feature which made him so important in producing good walkers. In any case, he was returned to Mr. Mankin's stable to be used as a breeding stallion.

About seven years later, the horse was started on a series of downward sales, first going to a neighbor of Mankin's, Mr. Bennett Goodlow, who owned him from 1898 until the winter of 1900. He was then purchased by Mr. West Orrin for $97.50. After using him during the breeding season of 1900, Orrin sold him to Mr. R. L. Ashley of Manchester, Tennessee; still going down in value, Allan was traded this time for a black yearling filly, a Jersey heifer, and $20 to boot—total value, approximately $80.

After use as a breeding stallion during the 1901 season, Allan was traded for a black jack to Dr. J. M. Price of Manchester. In the fall of 1901, he became the property of Mr. Ben Dunn in trade for a work mule and there he remained during the breeding season of 1902, after which he passed to the adjoining county and the ownership of J. H. Winton. A small black mare was taken by Dunn in the trade. This transaction occurred in March, 1903. After a few months, Winton sold him to J. A. McCulloch for the sum of $110, to be used in the lowly service of teaser for his jacks.

Within a week following this transaction, fate was shaping up a change in the affairs of the neglected little black stallion, a change that would eventually lift him from the ranks of the mediocre to a pedestal of everlasting fame. Mr. McCulloch offered a good jack to Mr. James R. Brantley for $400. At the same time, he priced Allan at $110.

Allan was apparently not a complete stranger to Mr. Brantley, who recalled certain statements made to him regarding the excellent bloodlines

A JACK $400
. . . ALLAN $110

of the stallion by R. L. Ashley, a relative and former owner. It is reported that Mr. Brantley was so interested in the pedigree of the black stallion that before buying the jack and Allan he rode almost a hundred miles to affirm what he had been told. Upon investigation, he discovered the original registration in the *American Trotting Registry*. Not only did the registration corroborate the words of Ashley but in addition there was a notation stating that Onward, Allan's grandsire, was the greatest stallion living or dead.

With such encouragement, Brantley harnessed his favorite mare Gertrude and, accompanied by a neighbor, journeyed by buggy to consummate the sale.

Then, as in later life, Allan was a horse of outstanding appearance. Smart ears set off a perfectly shaped head. Though not much over 15 hands in height, the small stallion's graceful neck and well-set tail gave him a beautiful carriage. Short back, long belly, smooth, well-coupled hips, well-sloped shoulders, and roomy breast combined to make his conformation nearly faultless. His legs were fine and smooth, with cordy muscles and clean, strong tendons.

His motion was described as extremely graceful and effortless. Old-time residents of Rutherford, Bedford, Coffee, Cannon, and Franklin counties, Tennessee, attest to the fact that Allan was a square-going walking horse with perfect gaits. J. A. McDonald, who handled Allan while he was owned by Mr. Mankin, stated that this stallion was one of the greatest walking horses he had ever seen and that in his running walk he slipped along as if gliding in snow.

It is no wonder that J. R. Brantley was convinced that his newly acquired stallion possessed qualities suiting a worthy sire of plantation horses. So great were his convictions that he bred Allan to his good walking mare Gertrude. From this union was produced one of the most noted and celebrated foundation sires of the Walking Horse breed—Roan Allen F-38, foaled in May, 1904. By the spring of 1910, Roan Allen was considered to be one of the best young stallions in the area. That year also marked the date of Allan's last change of ownership.

Mr. Albert Dement, a friend of Mr. Brantley, had become extremely interested in the stallion as a producer of fine saddle horses. In March, 1910, Allan passed into Mr. Dement's hands. Many years later, Mr. Brantley declared this to have been the greatest mistake of his horse-breeding career. It was the union of Allan to the celebrated Dement mare Nell which produced the grand champion mare Merry Legs, the only daughter of Allan to appear on the foundation list of Tennessee Walking Horses (Volume I).

The 1910 season was the last for Allan. At the age of twenty-nine, on September 16, 1910, the game little horse who had started out as a failure in life died. It is to the everlasting credit of horsemen in the Middle Basin area that the blood of Allan F–1 was allowed to nick with the good stock of that area to perpetuate the "Allen" strain of horses. (No one is able to explain the difference in spelling, though it is understandable that the change could have been made through misunderstanding of the original spelling of "Allan.")

The most famous sons of old Allan were Roan Allen F–38, Hunter's Allen F–10, Red Allen F–33, and King Allen F–34. His noted daughters, among others, included Merry Legs F–4, Birdie Messick, Bedford Dutch, and Hiles Minnie.

It is important to note that although Allan was "accidentally" discovered by Mr. Brantley in his quest for a quality jack, the products of his mating were far from accidental. The Tennessee Walking Horse has always been bred and improved for a definite purpose, and his use on well-established Walking Horse mares was based on a plan to intensify the qualities of the type desired. The glory of Allan F–1 cannot be detracted from, but at the same time it should be remembered that Tennessee Walking Horses were being sired before this stallion was foaled, just as there were American Saddlers in the Southern states before Denmark was introduced. One individual seldom makes a breed. This point was explained in an editorial by the eminent sponsor of Tennessee Walking Horses, the late J. J. Murray, in the magazine the *Tennessee Walking Horse:*

> At this meeting Allan was offered as Foundation Sire Number One. This was a natural consequence because most of the splendid gentlemen assembled owned Allan blood. It has successfully blended with the older sires which built the backlog for his blood to successfully and accurately nick in reproducing the running walk.
>
> Had the McCrarys, McAdams, Woods, Gills, Lunas, Boones, Painters, Websters, Orrs, Frys, Overtons, Moores, Gears, Neils and Bufords been present, wouldn't it have been natural for this group to have named Tom Hal the Number One Foundation Sire instead of Number 20? As great as the blood of Allan F–1 has proven, there is no history, data, or sly approach that can possibly verify Allan F–1 as the founder of the Tennessee Walking Horse, when other sires, long before his day, were producing just as well then as now.
>
> The writer recalls seeing in 1887, a walking horse class at the Marshall County Fair, with fifty-seven entries. The judge was May Overton, of Nashville, who thirty years later stated many times in discussing the Pacers and the Walking Horses of Middle Tennessee, that on the occasion stated above, he saw more great walking horses than he had ever seen in any one contest. . . .

Tennessee Walking Horses, we repeat, are well and firmly established in tradition and accurate history for a period of one hundred years and more, and to brush away all of the great sires and dams that made the backlog to nick with the blood of Allan F–1, is approaching a supercilious attitude. We shall endeavor with this publication at least to keep in harmony with the actual history of the blood.

ROAN ALLEN F–38

One of the most spectacular sons of Allan F–1 was the foundation stallion Roan Allen F–38. As an individual performer and as a producer of successful blood he was without peer.

We have noted his background of bloodlines through his sire Allan. Roan Allen's heritage through his dam Gertrude F–84 was richly steeped in plantation-horse quality. In giving her pedigree, it will serve also to complete Roan Allen's. Gertrude F–84 was added to the list of Recognized Deceased Sires and Dams in Volume VI of the *Registry*. She was a red roan, four stockings, bald face, 15½ hands high, and weighed approximately 1,100 pounds.

This great matron was by Royal Denmark, by Artist, by Great King William, by Washington Denmark. Her dam was Ball II, by Bullet, Jr., by Tolbert Fanning's Vermont, by Gifford Morgan; second dam Ball, by Earnhearts Brooks F–25. It will be noted that Gertrude was strongly infused with American Saddle blood on her sire's side and predominantly Morgan plus Canadian Pacer through her dam.

J. R. Brantley, the owner of Gertrude, stated that she was the best flat-footed walker he had ever seen, and Ball II, her dam, was also a truly great Walking mare, with speed and style. It is reported that Ball II never produced a foal that was not a natural Walker. Gertrude was fine and of good conformation, the kind of mare that would be selected to nurture a champion horse.

Thus, through natural heritage, Roan Allen came from a line of sires and dams that were all a credit to his breed. This stallion was 15 hands 3 inches high, a roan with both hind stockings, fore socks, and a broad strip in face. He was foaled May 23, 1906, and died August, 1930.

Few horses have lived which could lay claim to his versatility in the show ring. Eyewitnesses say that he was capable of performing the flat walk, running walk, canter, a perfect square trot, fox trot, pace, and rack, thus making him one of the few seven-gaited horses the world has known.

In 1911 and 1912, Mr. W. H. Davis showed Roan Allen in the fair circuit at Murfreesboro, Tullahoma, Fayetteville, and Winchester, and at the Tennessee State Fair at Nashville. At this time he was five and six years old. Roan Allen met the best horses available in walking, fine-harness, and gaited classes. In the two latter divisions he often defeated Roe's Chief, an outstanding five-gaited horse. In the walking classes he competed with such good horses as Hunter's Allen, Little Dutch, Old Dutch, Frank Bullet, and Alline.

Old-timers who knew him say that Roan Allen was a beautiful individual with erect head, long, perfect neck, and a beautiful naturally set tail of flaxen color. Such features enhanced the pomp and style of his carriage and set off the speed and perfection of his traveling style. It is said that his fast, gliding stride was noted for an overstride of more than 3 feet.

Like most Tennessee Walking Horses, Roan Allen's disposition and manners were perfect; women and children were able to show him without difficulty.

Among the most noted sons of this great stallion were Wilson's Allen, Mitch F–5, Merry Boy, Brantley's Roan Allen, Jr., Major Bowes, Curlee's Spotted Allen, Hall Allen, and Wilson's Bullett F–65. The potency of the tribe of Roan Allen is illustrated in the 1949 stallion rating for this breed; every one of the top twenty-five stallions on the list is a direct male-line descendant of Roan Allen. Through his son Wilson's Allen, sixteen are accounted for; through Merry Boy, six; and through Brantley's Roan Allen, Jr., three. This great foundation sire now is, and undoubtedly will always remain, one of the greatest progenitors of top-class Tennessee Walking Horses.

HUNTER'S ALLEN F–10

Hunter's Allen F–10 is the only other son of Allan F–1 to show male progeny in the *Tennessee Walking Horse Register*. He was foaled in 1906 and died January 15, 1932. Bred by Mr. J. W. Black of Wartrace, Tennessee, he was known in Marshall County as Little Allen. His color was chestnut of golden hue, with a white off hind stocking and a star and snip. He was 15 hands 2 inches in height and weighed around eleven hundred pounds.

We have noted his top-line breeding through Allan F–1; his dam was Allis, by Pat, son of Cunningham's Copperbottom, by Imported Copperbottom. His second dam was Nell, by Mountain Slasher F–59, by Morril's

Copperbottom, by Imported Copperbottom. Mountain Slasher's dam was by a son of the famous old Thoroughbred Timoleon; his second dam was a daughter of Julius Caesar. Thus it will be seen that Hunter's Allen was a blending of the more recent Allan strain with the taproot stock containing Copperbottom blood, which together richly endowed him with good gaits, speed, and toughness.

It is said of Hunter's Allen that in his advanced years, after traveling thousands of miles, he had neither a blemish nor any unsoundness of limb. At twenty years of age, he was as supple and had as good wind as most horses of five, and was an excellent saddle animal.

First shown at the Tennessee State Fair in 1912, he won the class for best Tennessee Walking stallion, any age. This performance was repeated the following year. In 1916, he took the blue in the stallion class and then was proclaimed champion by winning the stake class. At the age of eleven, he won the stallion class at the Tennessee State Fair. This was his last showing until 1924, when he again won the same distinction at the State Fair. His last showing occurred when he was twenty, at the Bedford County Fair, Shelbyville, Tennessee. Those who witnessed this event say it was one of the greatest stallion classes ever shown. Hunter's Allen was up against top young horses, among them his own famous son Brown Allen; also Bud Allen, one of the best. The old champion proved his fiber that day when he seemed to sense that he must show up the younger generation. The records show that he "walked up a storm" and carried off the championship in spite of the stiff competition.

Those who remember Hunter's Allen describe him as a stylish going stallion with great rhythm and speed, all executed in perfect form.

The get of this famous foundation sire will long be remembered. His sons and daughters won the Tennessee Walking Horse stakes at the Tennessee State Fair in 1920, 1921, 1922, 1925, 1927, 1928, 1929, 1932, and 1933, an enviable record of achievement for a single stallion.

Brown Allen was one of the most outstanding sons of Hunter's Allen. Other famous progeny were the show mare Mary Allen, as well as Old Hunter, Springtime, and Lady Turner, who was the first mare ever to defeat Merry Legs. One of the greatest Tennessee stallions ever produced was Last Chance, by Hunter's Allen, out of Merry Legs. The first stallion ever to win the coveted championship at the Tennessee Walking Horse National Celebration was Midnight Sun, a great-grandson through his dam, by Dement's Allen, by Hunter's Allen.

CONFORMATION

Individuals within this breed vary considerably in their physical make-up, and it is apparent that Tennessee Walking Horses are not yet as set in type as some of the other breeds. They can be described as more nearly resembling the American Saddle Horse, perhaps because of the same general-utility purposes required of the two breeds plus the fact that remote blood strains were channeled from similar sources.

The following brief descriptions of outstanding individuals illustrate the contrasting types:

BROWN ALLEN (350156)
Black horse, near hind, off fore fetlocks, star, snip, foaled 1924.
Sire, Hunter's Allen F–10.
Dam, Mary McDaniel.
Roundly conformed horse of excellent proportions. Alert ears, good eyes, flat face, medium long, muscular neck, good chest and barrel, extremely short back, slight slope to croup, muscular shoulders and hips. Fine but sturdy bone.

BLACK ANGEL (391118). Originally registered as Black Girl.
Black mare, foaled April 27, 1939.
Sire, Merry Boy.
Dam, Nell Bramlett.
Good ears set well forward, good eyes, Roman nose, well-muscled neck and fairly thick, deep shoulders, sloping croup, medium fine legs.

MIDNIGHT SUN (410751). Originally registered as Joe Lewis Wilson.
Black horse, foaled June 8, 1940.
Sire, Wilson's Allen.
Dam, Ramsey's Rena.
Large, powerfully built horse. Slightly convex head, good ears and eyes. Neck heavy but not short, enormous chest, medium short back, very slight slope to croup, muscular fore and aft, large bones, though well modeled.

MERRY-GO-BOY (431336)
Black horse, near hind sock, star, foaled May 4, 1943.
Sire, Merry Boy.
Dam, Wiser's Dimples.
Beautifully conformed horse of rather short proportions, flat face, good eyes, sharp, alert ears, neck a little short but well shaped and carried erect, short back, very little slope to croup, muscular throughout, fine but sturdy bone.

HONEY GOLD (451147). Originally registered as Rosy O'Grady.
Sorrel mare, near hind sock, strip, flax mane and tail, foaled May 30, 1944.
Sire, Rhoda Allen.
Dam, Hilda Ann.
Among the finest conformed Walking Horses to be observed. Good ears, good eyes, slightly dished face, long slender neck, extremely fine bone, medium flat croup.

MIDNIGHT MERRY (461829)
Roan mare, considerable white marking, mixed mane and tail, foaled May 5, 1946.
Sire, Midnight Sun.
Dam, Merry Giovanni.
Powerfully built mare of rather short proportions. Face almost flat but slightly convex, good ears, good eyes, short neck well carried, short back, roomy chest, powerful shoulders and hips, slightly sloping croup, ample bone.

Though these horses represent quite a wide variety of types within the breed, there are certain points of conformation typical of Tennessee Walking Horses which aid the discerning horseman in his recognition of the breed. Walkers today average 15 hands 2 inches in height and weigh from 1,000 to 1,200 pounds. Almost invariably their hide is thin and covered with silky-textured hair. Manes and tails are full and long. There is perhaps a wider variety of colors in Tennessee Walking Horses than in any other established breed. Sorrels, chestnuts, blacks, all kinds of roans, whites, bays, browns, grays, and yellows with both dark and light points are numerous. Many have large amounts of white markings—stars, blazes, snips, bald faces, coronets, socks and stockings, and underbody markings. Spotted horses of all colors occur, though most of these are seen among the roan-colored horses. I have observed that the majority of body-spotted horses are of the Overo pattern (see *pintos* in Chapter 11), with no sharply defined spots of the type occurring in the Tobiano pinto. Gaily contrasting manes and tails frequently vary from mixed to flaxen and pure white. Though eligible spotted horses are accepted for registration, the Breeders' Association frowns on horses with such markings, for these horses are suspected of containing pony blood.

The number of roans among Tennessee Walking Horses leads me to believe that this color may have come down through Roan Allen F–38 who, in turn, inherited the color from his dam Gertrude, a sorrel roan mare with mixed mane and tail. This does not mean that roans always occur in direct descendancy from roan parents—a common but mistaken belief. The *Ten-*

nessee Walking Horse Registry shows a large number of roan offspring from parents which were not roan.

One feature of Tennessee Walking Horses seems to be present in almost every individual of the breed; this is the character of the eye and the area surrounding it. Some horsemen describe it as an "old eye." The manner in which the upper lid wrinkles toward the front gives an expression of extreme contemplation and wisdom. Occasionally this characteristic may be noticed in other horses, but it is peculiar to the Walking Horse breed. Walkers also frequently show the whites of their eyes.

Usually, though not always and in varying degrees, the face of a Tennessee Walking Horse is convex. The great mares Black Angel, Melody's Heir, and Merry Wilson all show this feature. The extremely fine mare Honey Gold, of course, is an exception to this rule, though a few Tennessee Walkers do show a dished face similar to that of the Arabian horse.

The neck of the Tennessee Walking Horse aids him in his rhythmic way of traveling; therefore, it is most always muscular and well developed. At the same time, it is graceful and shapely, not usually as short as that of the Morgan. Many of the old-fashioned Walkers carried a low head, but the champions of today come into the show ring as high-headed as a Saddle Bred.

The Tennessee Walking Horse has a well-sloped shoulder, as do all good horses of the Saddle variety. Observed in action, however, it will be seen that these horses pull with their front legs and drive with their hind legs. The horse that is pulling and reaching for more ground will have a long and desirable stride in front. Therefore, more than any other type of horse, the Walker uses his front legs for part of his locomotion and consequently requires a muscular and extremely flexible shoulder. We frequently observe the Saddle Bred apparently working only his forearm, whereas the Walking Horse, in order to gain his great walking stride, must move the entire shoulder.

Almost without exception, these horses have short, sturdy backs, with good coupling at the loins. The chest is deep through the girth, and the ribs are well sprung.

The hips of nearly all Tennessee Walking Horses are extremely muscled, and this development extends downward toward the hocks.

Another feature usually observed is a sloping croup, a necessary adjunct to the extreme hind-walking stride. In this Saddle breed there is a slight tendency toward the sickle hock.

Almost without exception the joints of the hock and knee are square, well modeled, and strongly constructed. The limestone area in which Tennessee plantation horses originated has given them dense, strong bones and well-shaped, tough hoofs.

The Tennessee Walking Horse is most noted for his walking gait. It has long been my opinion that he has yet a greater point of value—his extremely amiable disposition. By nature, this horse is unequaled for his tranquillity. Bred for many years in an atmosphere of companionship, the animal is quiet and even-tempered. Always gentle, he is ideal for women, children, and inexperienced horsemen. The stallion Midnight Sun, twice Grand Champion of the World, typifies the agreeable nature of Tennessee Walking Horses. His owners declare that anyone can ride or handle him, and he has often been ridden by women and amateurs during his successful career.

GAITS

No subject has been the center of more controversy than the gaits of the Tennessee Walking Horse. There are several reasons for this.

1. No two horses appear exactly the same at their traveling gaits. One may have extreme head motion; another will attain great stride; still another may have considerable height of action.

2. Many owners outside the Tennessee area do not fully understand the true walking gait and confuse it with the stepping pace, the fox trot, and often the rack. Such persons invariably expect too much speed.

3. Most confusing of all is the ever-changing policy among top trainers as to how the show horse shall perform. The rule books state that a Tennessee Walking Horse must do a flat walk, a running walk, and a canter. However, we frequently hear the rumor that another gait has been added—the "show" gait.

That native Tennesseeans are concerned with the manner in which their horses are being shown is evidenced in an article in the *Tennessee Walking Horse* as recently as 1948. Entitled "Which Way Are We Going?" it was written by Burt Hunter, son of Mr. B. C. Hunter of Hunter's Allen fame:

> To begin with, I am a friend of all Walking Horse breeders and trainers, and am neither criticizing nor offering advice. . . .
> We, the Walking Horse enthusiasts, know that many of our top show horses have a lot of motion and can do the running walk fast and keep their form. . . . On the other hand, we have a few which have conformation, fineness, style, reach (at both ends), stride, and speed which constitute our top show horses; yet, it seems the tendency, even in Middle Tennessee, to over-ride them. In this section, of all places, riders should know better. . . .
> When the ringmaster gets a cue from the judge who wants to see the class do a flatfoot walk, do the horses then do a flatwalk or do they have their first

chance to do a true running walk? Are we going against tradition and say that a Tennessee Walking Horse now has four gaits which are a flatfoot walk, a running walk, a canter and the new gait which is described as a show horse gait? . . . It seems that the horses are doing or attempting to do these four gaits. However, it appears that some probably go a slow gait, some a rack, some amble. . . .

Now we come to the running walk, the gait of which the Tennessee Walking Horse has become famous. We are wondering just how this gait is performed. Is it a modified trot or is it a modified pace? Shall we accept the decision of a Walking Horse judge who would measure the overlap of the back track over the front and who would tie the horse which showed the most overlap (even if the horse might be pacing) over a horse that goes in proper form? Or, shall we choose the horse that goes a square walk and one which stays on all corners just as all true Walking Horses must? . . .

Now the canter. Who does not enjoy seeing a Walking Horse canter when the horse really does this gait right with that rocking horse movement, and one which counts (or gives that Walking Horse movement which is a very polite nod of the head) at every stride? A true canter goes at a height in comparison with the speed; in other words, a "rolling canter" which shows much motion. Did you know that in certain sections of our country a horse is criticized for showing motion while cantering? Shouldn't a canter be easy, with lots of spring and rhythm and just enough rise and fall to give the rider a thrill?

The Walking Horse gaits, speaking of those mentioned above, are natural to our well-bred Walking Horses. It is commonplace to see a foal, while following its dam in pasture, exhibit all the gaits of a trained Walking Horse. While these foals inherit the ability to go a running walk, they also inherit the ability to do just about every other gait. So, in order to improve and separate these gaits, rendering the young animal steady and teaching it to change from one to the other at the will of the rider, is the sole task which the trainer finds before him. . . .

Now a few words of advice to all Walking Horse owners and trainers: Let us ride our pleasure horse and, most important, ride our show horses exactly as they should be ridden and at the gaits they should go. . . .

We realize that all Walking Horse fanciers do not accept the same kind of running walk as being tops, but just talk to any of the old breeders and ask them if most of the Walking Horses are doing just what they did fifteen years ago. Which is best . . . a square walk which any inexperienced horseman can ride, or a gait that has been pervaded to the taste of the audience that wishes its four-legged favorites to be as far from nature as the good Lord would permit?

It is true that the manner in which plantation horses have been shown has undergone many changes. In 1887, the first great Tennessee Fair was held at Nashville. Divisions for Thoroughbreds, harness, and saddle horses were provided, and there were events for each of the three types. Among the classes for riding horses was one for "general saddle horse." Also in this division was a "walking ring" for the best stallion, mare, or gelding. For many years, the saddle classes were not as specialized as they are today. In the gaited classes, horses were shown at the rider's discretion, then by the judge's orders, and finally at the horse's favorite or best gait. As we have noted, horses of a few decades ago were more versatile than now, and it was not uncommon for the same horse to win in walking, gaited, and harness classes.

By 1910, the Tennessee State Fair offered classes for "plantation saddle horses." This class at times carried the voluminous title "Plantation Nodding Walk Saddle Horse"! By the year 1914, the class was called "Tennessee Plantation Saddle Horses," and the requirements for contestants were listed as follows: "Running walk or fox trot, soundness, manners, action, strength, stamina, ability to carry weight, ease of saddle gaits, and general adaptability to practical business saddle purposes."

According to those who remember, the fox-trot gait was acceptable until about twenty-five years ago. One of the reasons for the decline of the fox trot was that a square, rapid running walk was faster and also more rhythmical and interesting to watch. The late Jim Miller, one of the foremost trainers from 1915 until the late twenties, was quoted as saying, "A Tennessee Walking Horse needs just enough action to tip a baseball and keep it rolling."

As suggested by Mr. Burt Hunter, the running walk has been in a fluid state for some time. If it were possible to parade the champion Walkers of the past twelve years in chronological order, we would be startled by the development of speed and ever-increasing height of action in front.

The Tennessee Walking Horse Breeders' Association states the speed of the running walk to be between 6 and 8 miles per hour, yet it is apparent to those who have viewed recent championship classes that a horse traveling as slowly as 8 miles per hour would be sucked up in the draft of today's top show horses. In fairness to those who advocate perfect walking form, it should be added that after horses have traveled several miles, even the best ones cannot travel faster than 8 or 10 miles per hour and stay in form.

It would seem that part of the zeal for speed by modern trainers, and the concurrence by judges, has been brought about by public demand. Of course, if the Tennessee Walking Horse had remained a low-headed, slow traveler, it is unlikely that he would have gained so much ground as a show horse throughout the country, but it is unfortunate that he has been forced beyond his natural speed. It is to be hoped that the public will soon come to appreciate the four-beat symphony of action, stride, and squareness of the true-gaited Walker lest he be driven into the realm of the five-gaited horse where he will become a "nobody."

We must remember that the Tennessee Walking Horse is unique in that he is the only breed generally capable of learning *all* the gaits executed by *all* the varied horses in this country. Thus we will readily realize why it is so easy to ruin a Walking Horse. The running walk is a delicately balanced gait, easily thrown off balance.

A letter from the late J. J. Murray contains the following excellent advice to amateur owners:

> The most serious trouble today is the fact that owners bring their horses out of the stall, mount them and start them off entirely too fast in order to keep up with other trail riders. This develops the rack, slow gait or a stepping pace. Walking Horses should always be started in a flat walk, and if you are riding trail or bridle path and the speed of the other horses is beyond the running walk, the canter of the Walking Horse should be substituted instead of the gaits mentioned above.

It has been my observation that young Tennessee Walking Horses will inherit either a trotting tendency or a pacing tendency. As noted in Chapter 3, on gaits, there are many gradations between the flat walk and the trot, as well as between the flat walk and the pace. The difficulty, for many amateurs, is that when their horse speeds up, they do not realize that he is beginning to verge toward the trot or pace.

In my opinion, there is one test that is nearly infallible. If the horse is ridden on hard ground and is doing a true walk or running walk, the sound pattern is heard in four *evenly* spaced beats. If two beats are closer together, the animal is getting out of the four-cornered walking gait. Or, if the head ceases to nod, even though the beat may sound square, beware!

In order to understand the walking gait better, observe horses of other breeds when they walk. They do the walk more slowly, and it is easier to detect their movements. There is no essential difference in the footfall pattern; the only difference is in the rapidity of movement and the greater stride of the Walking Horse. Any horse, regardless of breed, will nod its head at the walk. When he ceases nodding, he is no longer walking. Horses that rack or slow-gait maintain a nearly true four-beat gait, but the nod is absent.

Let us assume that we believe that the animal is tending toward the pace or stepping pace. It is an error to watch the feet. In a stepping pace, the feet may strike the ground at separate instances, but if we observe the shoulder and stifle we notice that these parts of the anatomy move in unison at the stepping pace. The reason the rear foot strikes before the front foot on the same side is that the backbone slopes lower from front to back thus bringing the rear foot in contact with the ground before the front foot strikes. Accompanying this gait is a climbing action in front. If the horse is walking flat and square, the shoulder and the stifle *do not* move in unison, the backbone remains *horizontal,* and there is no evidence of front climbing action. Often the near-pace is accompanied by a suggestion of sway or swing in the horse's rhythm. Also the rear lateral foot does not come very close to the front one before it leaves the ground. The hind foot of a true Walking Horse nearly touches the forefoot on the same side before that foot is removed.

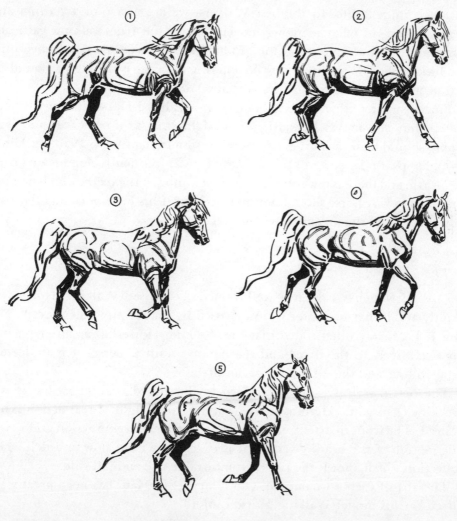

WALKING GAIT CYCLE

The easiest way to detect a tendency toward the trot is to observe the rear quarters. If there appears to be any bounce or jogging up and down, we may be certain that the horse is veering away from the true walk. A fox-trotting horse does not glide but instead moves forward in a choppy manner. Also, as we noted in Chapter 3, on gaits, the footfall pattern of the fox trot shows the rear foot striking the ground an instant before the diagonal fore.

The opposite is true in the walking gait. A horse that is walking gives no upward thrust to his body. If we observe the hind foot, we will see that at the beginning of the stride the sole is placed flat on the ground and remains so until the body leaves it so far behind that the heel is lifted from the ground and finally the toe. Of all the gaits, this is the one where height of hind action is undesirable. In the best Walkers, we are aware of a *pulling* and reaching instead of a springing movement. In the true walking gait, one front foot must *always* be on the ground, and the same is true concerning the hind pair. The only way for the opposite to occur is through a bounding action, and that never constitutes Walking Horse form.

Finally, we note that the backbone of the Walking Horse not only is horizontal, but also moves forward in a straight line, as do his feet and legs. There should be no winging, paddling, or spraddling. A top Walking Horse should appear relaxed at all times; hence he will frequently flop his ears back and forth, and there is not infrequently a snapping of the teeth, which denotes a relaxed jaw. A horse should not be ruled out if his head goes slightly from side to side with the up-and-down motion.

The Canter

Anyone who has ridden a well-trained Tennessee Walking Horse will readily admit that its canter is unsurpassed by that of any other breed. The late J. J. Murray often stated that the Walking Horse has a canter belonging exclusively to the breed and that among trained horses it is uniformly slow, rolling, and the easiest canter on earth.

The best descriptive phrase applied to this breed's canter is that it is a "rocking-chair gait." Here, as in the walking gait, height of rear action is not desired. The front quarters, however, demonstrate extreme action and rhythmic motion of the head. Over all, it is executed with a slow and deliberate collection which affords the rider a comfortable rise-and-fall ride.

The 1949 Reserve Champion, Old Glory's Big Man, has been greatly admired for his model Walking Horse canter.

TRAINING

It is my firm conviction that, regardless of pedigrees, a registered Tennessee Walking Horse is not a Walking Horse unless it can perform the gaits for which the breed is famous. If the animal is incapable of performing as he should, his most priceless quality has been lost and he is reduced to the status of any other saddle horse. We are told that horses of this breed are natural-born Walkers. Why, then, is it common to see many so-called "Walkers" incapable of performing the "free-and-easy" gaits proclaimed for their breed? Assuming that these animals are bred properly, it is apparent that such a situation is due to improper training.

The following remarks are addressed especially to the amateur owner and enthusiast who may be in need of constructive guidance in training problems.

A good bit of advice is contained in a booklet published by the Tennessee Walking Horse Breeders' Association: "Teach the young horse to do everything you want it to do and nothing you don't want it to do—then your worries are over, for the gaits come naturally."

To this should be added the admonition that it is absolutely necessary to know what is wanted of the horse before you begin its training.

Despite the fact that the running walk is a natural gait to this breed, I think it can be fairly asserted that the Walking Horse is one of the most difficult to train *properly* and requires the most considered judgment. This is not because individuals of the breed are difficult to teach but because they are potentially multiple-gaited horses.

Patience is a virtue when training a Walker. Do not be in a hurry; the horse that is not rushed will later prove to be more valuable. Three months of slow work may mean the difference between a real Walking Horse and one with only a pedigree.

In selecting a Walking colt, first consideration should be given his bloodlines. A fair idea of strong gait-producing strains has been discussed. Satisfied upon this point, we should select a sound, loose-going colt. By this it is meant that the colt, observed at liberty in the pasture, should evidence great flexibility of shoulders, stride, and a fair amount of overlap, along with head motion and rhythm. If he can unconcernedly cover ground rapidly and with little apparent expenditure of effort, he may be considered a likely prospect.

The young Tennessee Walking Horse, like the young of other breeds, should be introduced to primary training such as being gentled, haltered, and taught to follow when led. As the colt grows older, it should undergo a period of controlled leading. This is accomplished by attaching a lead shank to the halter and holding it at a point about 4 or 5 feet from the colt's head. This loose rein allows the colt to move in complete freedom. The colt should be led at a brisk flat walk; he should not be forced to go faster than a slow running walk. No attempt should be made to force head motion by taking hold of the halter.

When the colt is eighteen to twenty months old and has attained a weight of at least 700 pounds and a height nearing 15 hands, he is ready for a short period of schooling in a bitting harness. This will acquaint him with the bit, as well as accustom him to the girth and other restricting harnesses. He learns initial phases of obedience to the reins. He begins to learn that his head must be controlled. Daily sessions are short, and care is taken not to rein his head too high or exert much pressure upon his tender mouth.

The next step is the colt's saddle training. A bridle equipped with a snaffle bit is used. One trainer rides his colts a few days without a saddle until they outgrow their uneasiness about a man upon their back. During this procedure the young animals may be led by an attendant.

As with colts of any breed in the first few days with a rider up, the purpose is to teach response to the reins. Extreme care should be taken not to frighten the pupil by hurting his mouth. Such exercise should be performed at a flat-foot walk. Most trainers agree that a colt will not be thoroughly bridle-wise until he has been ridden from thirty to sixty days.

Every colt has a different way of going and a different "feel" to the rider. Most trainers start the colt slowly at this stage of training. Every hoofbeat should be felt, and the colt should be kept square, with an evenly spaced one-two-three-four beat.

Although some trainers deviate from this method, amateurs should follow the method of most old-time Walking Horse experts—riding the young horse at a flat walk with loose rein and snaffle bit until he begins to increase his speed and travels freely with absolute squareness and relaxation. He may be permitted to develop a slow running walk while wearing a snaffle.

Usually, at this point, the snaffle is exchanged for a curb bit with a mild chin strap to balance and collect the animal. He may now be pushed into more speed, but caution should be taken not to lose the "feel" of the four-cornered gait.

One trainer states that it is during the finishing stage that most Walkers are ruined in their gaits. Remember that the running walk is delicately balanced between the flat walk and the stepping pace or trot. The pattern of the gait must be gradually built up and fixed in the mind of the colt without confusion.

Whether a colt or a well-trained horse is being ridden, it should always be started at the flat walk for the first ten or fifteen minutes, being gradually allowed to speed up to the fast walk. The running walk should not be maintained for excessively long periods, and the young horse's daily lesson should not exceed thirty or forty minutes.

Many trainers believe that the canter should be taught simultaneously with the flat walk and running walk, arguing that the running walk can be improved through the colt's ability to canter. Others assert that the colt should not be confused by being taught the canter until he is fairly well set in the flat walk and running walk.

With either method, the young horse fresh off pasture will not at first understand that a slow canter is wanted. His inclination will be to gallop, and he must be slowed down gradually to the "rocking-chair" gait. The best place to teach the canter is on a gently rising slope where the horse will not be able to rush headlong. In your efforts to force the colt to go slowly, do not pull steadily upon the reins; rather give him his head, and as he generates too much speed, pull him back. The aids for teaching are the same as described earlier, except that most Walking Horses are taught to associate the touch of the rider's toe to their leading elbow as the cue to canter.

A colt, of course, should not be kept continuously standing in a stall. For proper development of muscles and tendons, the animal should be allowed daily exercise in an outdoor paddock or pasture. This also applies to mature trained horses.

SHOW HORSES

Nowadays, most Tennessee Walking Horses find themselves either in the category of show horse or pleasure horse. As a show horse, the Walker has made great strides in the past decade. Formerly concentrated in his native area, he has now been accepted in most areas in the United States where shows are presented, and audiences have come to appreciate the Tennessee show horse's rhythm, style, and beauty.

Show horses of this breed are groomed in the same manner as five-gaited show horses. Ribbons in stable colors are braided into forelock and first-mane lock behind the ears. The tail is full and usually artificially set. The mane is worn long. A flat show saddle and single-rein bridle with curb bit are used.

Riders wear riding suits with jodhpur breeches. Hats are soft, with snap brims.

The *American Horse Shows Association Rule Book* gives the following rules for the Tennessee Walking Horse Division:

SECTION 1. The Walking Horse should be between 15 and 16 hands high, of good bone, able to carry weight.

SECTION 2. (*a*) All horses shall enter the ring at the running walk, shall go to the right and continue running walk at will until ordered to change.

(*b*) Entire class shall be worked at least once around the ring at each gait, then reversed and worked at the discretion of the judge and in such manner as he deems advisable.

(*c*) Horses shall be lined up after preliminary workout, shall then be individually asked to back; and in champion classes shall have saddles removed and be judged for conformation and soundness. All saddles to remain off until riders are instructed to re-saddle. The judge shall penalize horses equipped with artificial appliances, except inconspicuously applied tail switch or brace.

SECTION 3. The qualifying gaits for Tennessee Walking Horses are as follows: flat-footed walk, running walk and canter.

(*a*) The flat-footed walk should be true, square and flat-footed.

(*b*) The running walk should be a smooth, gliding and overstepping four-cornered gait. The horse must have stride and head motion.

(*c*) The canter should be smooth, slow and straight on both leads, with a rolling motion with chin well tucked, comfortably in hand.

Classes may include those for junior horses, owner-amateur riders, championship stakes, and others. In amateur classes, top importance is placed on manners, whereas the stake classes are judged on performance, presence, quality, conformation, and manners.

Percentages for each gait are considered in this breed. The Tennessee Walking Horse Breeders' Association recommends the following: 20 per cent for flat-foot walk, 20 per cent for canter, 40 per cent for running walk, and 20 per cent for conformation. It will be noted that twice as much value is accorded the running walk. Owing to the importance of this gait, some judges accord 50 per cent to it and others consider it important enough to award as high as 60 per cent if it is perfect.

Tennessee Walking Horses, more than any other saddle breed, can be enjoyed for show purposes by people of all ages. Their fine dispositions and ease of gaits make them safe for elderly people or riders of questionable athletic ability. Many persons who are no longer able to show jumpers or gaited Saddlers are gaining much satisfaction from showing their Walkers.

PLEASURE HORSES

As a pleasure mount, the Tennessee Walking Horse is unsurpassed. Through natural heritage, horses within this breed are intelligent, kindly disposed, and not easily excited. The timid and inexperienced horse fancier finds no problem in handling this "gentleman" among horses.

My experience with the Walker would not permit me to recommend him as a drill-team horse or for use with three-gaited horses, since the speed variances of his gaits do not coincide with those of other breeds. The vast majority of Walkers will pass other horses at the walk, whereas other breeds will pass the Walker when they trot. Some Walkers have been successfully used in posse drill teams where the movements were all executed at the lope or gallop. The speed of the canter is easily controlled to coincide with that of other horses.

The Tennessee Walking Horse excels in trail or cross-country riding. He is easily handled, and the comfort of his gaits permits many pleasurable hours in the saddle, which may be English or Western in type.

The Tennessee Walking Horse is ideal for people who keep horses in their own stable. He is safe and companionable when being groomed and handled. Those who sponsor the breed have a challenging slogan: "Ride one today, and you'll own one tomorrow." It is certain that if you have never ridden a Tennessee Walking Horse, there is a great thrill in store for you!

Thoroughbred Horse

Refined slenderness and length of body parts denote the typical Thoroughbred. Centuries of breeding for speed have produced a horse of immense stamina and courage.

Head tapers from widely set eyes to pliant nostrils capable of great dilation. Face usually dished.

Withers more pronounced than in most other breeds. Back proportionately long. Great depth from top to bottom through girth line.

Slight slope usual in croup. Muscles of quarters long, yet powerful. Great length from hip to hock is desirable.

Neck long and thin—not carried high. Windpipe large with ample clearance as it passes between the jawbones.

Legs straight with evidence of trim, dense bone and strong tendons. Long above knees and hocks, short through cannons, and long through pasterns.

Well-sloped shoulder with long, flat muscles allows great length and force of stride. Chest does not necessarily show great width.

❧ 10 ❧

The Thoroughbred Horse

"Thoroughbred"—magic word for speed in the horse kingdom. Since time immemorial, man has revered speed in a horse. Ancient man, no doubt, required fleetness in his horses as an aid in hunting and fighting; later, he developed this trait to a greater extent by selective breeding, for his very survival depended on it. Trials of speed by running horses have taken place from earliest recorded history. The Thoroughbred, however, is the only breed of horse developed solely for the purpose of racing under saddle. This is the product of the English horsemen's ingenuity for molding equine form and spirit for a definite purpose. Bred primarily as a speed runner, racing performance being the standard, the Thoroughbred excels all other breeds in that capacity.

The designation "thoroughbred" means a distinct breed only when speaking of horses. Because of the literal meaning of the word, many people believe a Thoroughbred to be any pure-blooded horse. This is an error. For example, a registered American Saddle Horse is a purebred, but he should never be referred to as a "thoroughbred." Among horses there is only one Thoroughbred, and therefore, in discussion, we must heed the distinction between the terms "purebred" and "thoroughbred."

There has been some controversy as to why the name "Thoroughbred" was chosen to designate a breed of horses. Why were these horses not called "Race Bred," "Running Bred," or some other pertinent name? Some authorities say that the name "Thoroughbred" had its foundation in the Arab word *Kehilan* which, generically, meant a horse of "thorough" breeding or a purebred. Others state that it was the completeness of the product which caused

231

the English tongue first to call it "thorough-bred" and later "thoroughbred." A colt which was bred along lines of premeditated selection was referred to as being "thoroughly bred"; later, no doubt, this expression was abbreviated to the simpler "thoroughbred."

It is claimed that the word was not used as a descriptive name until after the breed had been introduced in the American Colonies, sometime after 1730. The first "bred" stallion imported to American soil was Bulle Rock, a son of the Darley Arabian, arriving in Virginia that year.

It is interesting to note that the Thoroughbred is the oldest breed for which a record of individual-line descent is kept. The Arab enthusiast may contest this statement. Admittedly, the high-type Arabians are pure in blood, but the individual lineage was not preserved, nor was it deemed necessary by the Arabs. A Thoroughbred colt foaled today, however, can be traced back through a maze of forebears in an unbroken pedigree of more than two hundred years to the progenitors of the breed.

ORIGIN OF THE BREED

"The Thoroughbred horse is the result of crossing Arabian stallions on the larger native English mares." This statement has caused so much controversy that it seems wise to follow the advice of Cicero who counseled all historians to remember that "it is the first law of history that the writer should neither dare to advance what is false, nor suppress what is true; that he should relate the facts with strict impartiality, free from ill will or favor."

There is no serious dispute concerning the male progenitors of the breed. The Byerly Turk, the Darley Arabian, and the Godolphin Barb, all Oriental horses, were imported to England in 1689, 1706, and 1724, respectively. Placed at the head of English racing studs, these sires undisputably laid the male foundation for the Thoroughbred.

But what about the dams which bore the new breed? Were they truly "native" mares, as some authorities assert, or were they mares of Eastern foreign blood, as others claim? There seems to be evidence to support both sides. William Harding Carter states that a number of Barb mares were imported into England from 1660 to 1685, during the reign of Charles II, that they were used in the royal stables, and that these and other selected stock were used when the three founding sires were established at the various studs.

Lady Wentworth, in her *Thoroughbred Racing Stock* and *The Authentic Arabian Horse,* refutes the notion that the taproot mares were native to England, but says, rather, that they were of Oriental breeding.

In addition to other evidence, she quotes from the *Sporting Magazine* of a hundred years previous which states that the Thoroughbred breed derived exclusively from foreign horses and mares, and *if* there had ever been a strain of native blood, it was so trifling as to have been bred out by the year 1700.

Further, she cites Weatherby's *General Stud Book* (Volume 1, Fifth Edition) as containing three lists pertaining to the earliest horses involved in the breed. The first shows 104 Arabians and other pure Orientals; the second lists 135 sires and mares of note prior to 1759; and the third, 43 others from 1759 to 1803. In the two latter lists, totaling 178 horses, which we must consider as not *purely* Orientals, Lady Wentworth states that there is only one horse or mare which cannot be traced back to Oriental blood and that that horse is Mr. Kettle's Diamond. She says that the balance of the animals listed are saturated with Arab Barb and Turk blood.

Lady Wentworth further stated that James I collected a racing stud at Turbury, headed by one of Mr. Markham's Arabians, much praised by Markham and disparaged by the Duke of Newcastle.

Though Gervase Markham, the importer of Arabs, evidently had much respect for that breed, he is reputed to have made the following statement: "What nation hath brought forth a horse that for swiftness hath exceeded the English?" and then to have related instances of English superiority over the Eastern breeds.

These words may take on a new meaning when we realize that they concern English race horses that existed in England prior to the reign of Charles II when the Thoroughbred groundwork was considered to be started. It is reasonable to believe that the blood of the English race horses lauded by Markham may have influenced, at least partially, the blood of the taproot mares which originated the Thoroughbred line.

Part of the idea that all foundation stock of the Thoroughbred Horse carried Oriental blood may have been caused by the fact that it was faddish or fashionable to own horses of Eastern flavor. Thus, many a truly native-blooded horse may have been described as, or by, So and So's Barb, Arabian, or Turk, which later was taken as fact by historians.

One of the strongest points in favor of the "native-mare" school of thought lies in the great size of some of the earliest Thoroughbreds. For instance, Matchem is reported to have stood 16 hands 3 inches in height, and he was a second-generation descendant of the Godolphin Barb who stood less than 14½ hands. Where did Matchem get such great height? It is true that Arabians, under a change of environment, often increase in size in succeeding generations. However, something over 8 inches is a tremendous increase in height to be attained in a mere two generations unless the blood of a larger horse is infused.

Perhaps the controversy involving the blood of the founding mares will never be solved to everyone's satisfaction. Both sides may be partly correct; perhaps the stock in question carried blood of both the Orientals and native English horses.

A BRIEF HISTORY OF ENGLISH RACING

When horse racing first began in England, the Thoroughbred was not to be a reality for several centuries. During and after the Roman occupancy, the race horses celebrated in Yorkshire were of light Oriental chariot variety, imported by the invaders.

The centuries which followed saw a gradual change in the weight of livestock as the necessity for different types arose. The change from chain to plate armor called for increasingly heavier horses, a demand which lasted up and into the fourteenth century. Such horses were imported in great numbers from the western European coast.

In the twelfth century, under the reign of Henry II, racing began as a part of the horse-trading business. The races at Smithfield were not held to entertain the spectators but to demonstrate the quality and durability of the horses to prospective buyers.

It was not long, however, until the Smithfield races became famous for reasons other than the sale of horses. Within the century, racing as a sport had England firmly within its grasp. The horses of the early Smithfield contests were not, of course, the light, spirited horses that we know today. Centuries would roll on and lumbering armor-bearing chargers would come and finally pass out of use before the beauty and fineness of Oriental horses would gain favor with the horsemen of the island kingdom.

At the beginning of the sixteenth century and the close of feudalism, Henry VIII took his place upon the throne of England. It has been said that there were at this time in England dwarf native horses under 12 hands as well as the larger type of chargers. That there were also medium sizes seems certain, for Henry, whose apparent interest lay in the larger variety, required his archbishops and dukes to keep at least seven race horses apiece, and these animals, he decreed, must stand at least 14 hands in height.

That Henry VIII was interested in horses is undisputed, for it was his desire to cause the entire world to look to England as a horse-loving nation. The question is: In what type of horse was Henry interested most? Some historians condemn him for massacring all but the heaviest horses in his realm. In order to give King Henry the benefit of the doubt and to allow the reader to draw his own conclusions, we reprint here the act which has caused considerable controversy:

By the 32 Henry VIII.c 13 it is enacted that no person shall put in any forest, chase, or moor, heath, common or waste (where mares and fillies are used to be kept) any stoned horse above the age of two years, not being fifteen hands high, within the shires and territories of [here follow the list of shires] on pain of forfeiting the same.

Any person may seize any horse of undersize, in the manner following [here followed detailed instructions as to the proper procedure for proving the animal undersized] and if he shall be found contrary to what is above expressed such person may take him for his own use.

All such commons and other places shall, within fifteen days after Michaelmas, yearly, be driven by the owners and keepers, or constables respectively, on pain of 40s., and if there shall be found in any of the said drafts any mare, filly, or foal, or gelding which shall not be thought able to bear foals of reasonable stature, or to do profitable labours, by the discretion of the drivers, or the greater number of them, they shall kill and bury them.

In addition, Henry VIII put into effect regulations which punished horse thieves and discouraged rampant breeding of scrubs.

While Elizabeth revived horse racing following its decline in Mary's reign, the "sport of kings" surged forward under the guidance of James I. Previously, while king of Scotland, James had championed light-horse racing until it was the national sport of that land. James I is important to modern-day racing because he was the first English ruler to advocate strongly the breeding of lighter horses. He also established the great horse-racing center at Newmarket. Prior to the breeding of race horses by James I and the importations of Arabians by the Markhams, the royal studs were composed largely of heavy horses. It is believed by some historians that the forerunners of all modern racing stock began in England not earlier than the rule of James I.

The period from 1649 to 1685 is particularly noteworthy because it was then that the Oriental-bred horses started flowing into England in great numbers. Oliver Cromwell was a light-horse enthusiast and made importations, though his puritanical philosophy did not allow for much progress in the affairs of horse racing. Following Cromwell's death, Charles II took control of England. The king was an ardent sportsman and truly loved the horse races conducted at Newmarket. He has been referred to as the "father of the British turf."

From 1660 to 1685, a number of Oriental mares were imported by Charles II and maintained in the royal studs. This marked the beginning of the real upsurge in favor of light horses, particularly the fine, fiery steeds of the East. The improvement of the sport grew almost fanatically until it assumed the firm and permanent foothold which has persisted to the present day.

The dawn of the English Thoroughbred was near at hand. As previously mentioned, the Byerly Turk was imported in 1689, which line in its fourth generation founded the great Thoroughbred sire Herod. The Darley Arabian, of the Arabian strain of Ras al-Fadawi, arrived on English soil in the year 1706. This line in its fourth generation produced Eclipse, thought by many to be the greatest Thoroughbred race horse of all time. In 1724, the Godolphin Barb was imported, and through his second generation was produced the great horse Matchem.

These three—Eclipse, Herod, and Matchem—are the principal male progenitors of all Thoroughbred lines.

Matchem

Foaled in 1748, Matchem was the first of the royal three to view the English countryside. Bred by a Mr. Holme of Carlisle, Cumberland, this bay colt was sired by Cade and was out of a daughter of Partner. Purchased at an early age by William Fenwick of Northcumberland, Matchem ran all his races under the colors of that owner.

The records of the past indicate that Matchem was a superb specimen, robust and standing 16 hands 3 inches at the wither when mature. His racing career began at the age of five, in the year 1753. Across the border of Cumberland at York he was entered in the Great Subscription purse. He won easily from Barforth Billy and Bold, who was also a son of Cade, the horse who had sired Matchem. The only other record of racing that year was when Matchem, in the Plate at Marpeth, defeated Blameless.

He started the season of 1754 by winning two hotly contested heats at the Ladies' Plate at York and likewise at the Ladies' Plate at Lincoln, where Martin ran second and Skim took the show. That season terminated with the local champion walking over the course for the Plate at Marpeth, there being no willing opposition.

Thus, by the year 1755 Matchem had attained wide repute and was taken farther afield—to the south at Newmarket—to test his ability. As a seven-year-old, he was entered in the £50 Plate over the Beacon Course. In this race, he was forced to display brilliant form and speed to take the race from the good horse Trajan. Many thought Trajan could have won had he been in better condition; nevertheless, Matchem covered the distance of 25 furlongs, 138 yards in seven minutes and twenty seconds.

The closeness of this race led to another which was discussed throughout the entire kingdom. The next year, William Fenwick offered to run Matchem for the "Whip" against any horse in the world. Still confident that Trajan, under the proper conditions, could beat the champion, his owner, Mr. Bowles, accepted the challenge, and the date, April 11, 1756, was looked forward to with a great deal of anticipation by the entire nation. The race was to be a sweepstakes of 200 guineas a side and the "Whip" was to be run over the old Beacon Course, each horse to carry 140 pounds.

Each horse was highly thought of, and the differences of opinion as to the outcome caused the wagering of tremendous amounts of money. As the starting signal was given, the great, impetuous Trajan leaped into the lead and opened a formidable gap between him and his contestant. The cool John Singleton up on Matchem bided his time, knowing the heart and fiber that were beneath his saddle; he was aware of the dazzling speed which awaited release when the proper moment arrived. As the two great horses swept along in this position wagering was five to one that Trajan would win. Then Singleton made his historic move and up came Matchem. The thundering stride of the big bay devoured the distance between him and the leading Trajan. Overtaking him at the turn of the course, Matchem easily won the encounter.

Though he tasted defeat at times, the gallant Matchem completed his racing career by winning the Plate at Scarborough. At the age of fifteen, he was retired to stud and soon became the leading sire in his locality. At the astonishing age of twenty-seven, he was still serving a limited number of mares.

Though the earnings of his get, £151,097, were less than that of either Eclipse or Herod, both of the latter had better opportunities. Further proof of the greatness of the Matchem line is the Solon branch in England and the American Fair Play family which has produced such great horses as Display and Man O' War. At the venerable age of thirty-three, the mortal part of Matchem died, but his quality and spirit will live on forever, perpetuated in his descendants.

Herod

Chronologically, Herod, or King Herod as he was originally called, was number two in the famous trio of Thoroughbred sires. Foaled in 1758, this bay colt was by Tartar and out of the mare Cypron. It is interesting to note that both he and Eclipse were bred by H. R. H. William, Duke of Cumberland, and that Herod was nursed in the same stables which, six years later, were to witness the arrival of the chestnut foal Eclipse.

Herod's trials had shown him to be a horse of great speed and stamina. Perhaps because of this and because he had reached five years, which was the customary age to start racing horses in those days, he was entered in a match race of 500 guineas with Roman, by Blank, owned by the Duke of Ancaster. The race was to be run at even weights over the Beacon Course. Herod subdued his opponent over the approximately 4½-mile course.

The following spring he was triumphant over a field of nine horses in a £300 sweepstakes in which Sir John Moore's Tartar was the runner-up.

At Ascot, he was entered in a match of 1,000 guineas a side for a distance of 4 miles against Lord Rockingham's Tom Tinker. Though he conceded 6 pounds, he defeated his rival.

Confident that his good horse Antinous was capable of challenging the champion, the Duke of Grafton arranged a match with Herod, the latter to concede 3 pounds to Antinous. The match took place in October at the Newmarket meet and was run over the Beacon Course. Although the Duke of Grafton's entry started favorite at six to four, Herod galloped triumphantly to the finish mark, winning his fourth straight victory.

The results did not convince the Duke of Grafton that Herod was the better horse, for he demanded a return match the following May. To back his enthusiasm, he placed 1,000 guineas on the side. This time Herod gave Antinous 9 pounds, and again Antinous was the favorite at seven to five, and again Herod romped triumphantly home!

But, alas, the champion was to know defeat. In the autumn of 1765, which was the third year of his career, Herod was beaten in a match race with the good horse Ascham, to whom he conceded 14 pounds over the Beacon Course.

At this point, at the death of his owner, the Duke of Cumberland, Herod passed into the hands of Sir John Moore. Sir John matched him to Turf, giving 6 pounds over the Beacon Course. Though backed to the tune of seven to four, Herod was again defeated.

Started in the Great Subscription Plate at York, he broke a blood vessel and was pulled up, allowing Bay Malton to go on to victory. At the age of nine, Herod again ran second to Bay Malton in a 500-guineas sweepstake over the old Beacon Course.

The old trouper's last race was a match with Ascham over the Beacon Course, in May, 1770. He won easily, and as one writer put it, "he thus closed his career on a note of triumph, which is the fitting thing for any hero to do."

Though perhaps not quite as spectacular in his racing career as his contemporary Eclipse, nevertheless he was more successful at stud, with his progeny winning £201,505.

It is of incidental importance, but many people believe that gray was the family color of the Herods. There were no grays within the immediate ancestry of Herod himself. The notion has come about as a result of the color produced through Le Sancy, a gray, who was seven or eight generations removed from old King Herod. Le Sancy received his color from his dam Gem of Gems.

Eclipse

Perhaps the most famous of the royal trio, Eclipse was foaled in 1764, the year of the great eclipse. The chestnut colt, bred by H. R. H. William, Duke of Cumberland, was sired by Marske, by Squirt, by Bartlett's Childers, who was a brother to the famous Flying Childers. His dam was Spiletta. At the death of the duke, the colt was acquired by a sheep dealer named Wildman. Captain Denis O'Kelley, who was intrigued by the possibilities of Eclipse, purchased a half interest in him for 600 guineas after his first race. He later acquired full ownership for 1,000 guineas.

Eclipse made his debut in a £50 Plate at Epsom Downs, in 1769. Suspicious of the heavy betting of O'Kelley prior to the race date, several gentlemen attempted a sneak preview of the trials but missed them and succeeded only in talking with an old woman who had evidently been present at the occasion. They gained little satisfaction, for the woman did not know whether she had seen a race or not. She related that the white-legged chestnut and another horse started down the course and that the white-legged one was "running away at a monstrous rate," continuing that if the other horse ran "to the end of the world" she was certain it would never catch up.

Even this story did not prepare the onlookers for what they were about to see on that May day at Epsom. The good field of horses there to contest the Plate included Gower, by Sweepstakes; Chance, by Young Cade; Plume, by Feather; Trial, by Blank; and the highly speculative Eclipse, about whom so much had been heard but little seen.

With five-year-olds carrying 108 pounds, six-year-olds 119 pounds, and aged horses 126 pounds, the Plate was to be run in 4-mile heats!

At the start, with John Oakley in the saddle, Eclipse was ahead of the field in a few tremendous bounds. As he hit his stride, the crowd knew that there was nothing mythical about the stories they had heard about this newcomer to the racing strips. Dominating the field with what seemed no more than a strong gallop, he brought John Oakley home.

While cooling out, the swaggering O'Kelley made his historic wager to the effect that he could place the whole lot in the next heat, which was "Eclipse first, the rest nowhere!" And so it turned out. Taking the bit and pulling his jockey out of the saddle, he again distanced all contenders.

That same year, undaunted by his arduous travel from track to track over the worst possible roads, he met all comers like a champion—at Winchester, Salisbury, Canterbury, Lewes, Richfield, a £50 Plate at Ascot, another at Newmarket.

The following year, the champion resumed his campaigning. He was matched with the great race horse Bucephalus over the Beacon Course, a distance of 4 miles, 1 furlong, and 138 yards. In all his career, this appears to have been the only time that Eclipse was really forced to gallop to put a contender behind.

His next race took place on the Round Course at Epsom, a distance of three miles, 4 furlongs, and 93 yards. This time, barely out of a canter, he beat the two good mares Penelope and Diana. In the second heat, it was wagered seven to four that he would distance Penelope, which he did with apparent ease.

Then, on the road again, he traveled triumphantly on a plate-gathering tour. "Champions fell before his all-conquering stride like nine-pins," said one writer.

After constant victories, he was finally entered in the King's Plate in October. No rival was considered equal to meet him, and he walked to victory, undefeated king of the racing world.

During his short career, he won $125,000, which would have been equal to one and one-half millions if earned today. Captain O'Kelley refused fabulous offers for the famous stallion. The only figure he would consider was $100,000 down and an additional $2,500 each year thereafter until he (the captain) died, plus the privilege of service for three mares each year.

Eclipse went to stud at Clay Hiss, near Epsom, at a service fee of 50 guineas.

His get won the sum £158,047. Though his active racing career lasted a mere seventeen months, his reputation and the fame of his strain have outlived him nearly two hundred years.

CONFORMATION

There is an old axiom among horsemen to the effect that "good race horses come in all shapes and sizes."

The Thoroughbred Horse, as with all breeds, has undergone physical changes of anatomy since its inception. Most notable is the gradual increase in size. The earliest individuals were more nearly the size of their Oriental sires, not many of them exceeding 14 hands 2 inches in height. It is estimated that Thoroughbreds increased in height an average of 1 inch each twenty-five years, from 1700 to 1850.

It is impossible to accept the earliest paintings of Thoroughbreds as factual, yet from observing them we must conclude that the earliest horses more closely resembled their Oriental ancestors than do modern representatives of the breed. While many such characteristics are retained, the modern Thoroughbred is an entirely different animal. In size, he now averages close to 16 hands, and some of 17 hands are at times encountered. A 15-hand Thoroughbred is considered exceedingly small.

Stallions in stud condition will at times weigh 1,400 pounds, whereas in racing form they will be a trim 1,000 pounds. The coloring of Thoroughbreds is usually the typically solid colors of bay, chestnut, black, or brown, with an occasional gray. White markings on legs and face occur. Pintos and palominos do not appear in this breed.

The Thoroughbred has shown greatest deviation from the Oriental in the fact that he has grown longer in all parts of his body, particularly in legs and neck. He retains much of the fineness, though he may have lost something of his ancestors' soundness, tractability, and docility. On the other hand, he has retained much of the endurance of his ancestors and has added greatly to his stamina and speed. The American record for the mile is 1:33⅗, made by Citation carrying 128 pounds in 1950. The conditions are not the same and therefore difficult to compare, but Flying Childers is said to have run the old Beacon Course at Newmarket, England, a distance of 4 miles, 1 furlong, and 138 yards, in seven and a half minutes.

Stanley Harrison's remarks in an article entitled "Sum of the Past," in the *Thoroughbred Record,* November 1, 1947, are interesting to consider at this point:

They say that the present is but a sum total of the past, and that nothing is greater than the roots it sprang from. Perhaps. Your commentator asks leave to doubt that the race horse of today is a noticeably finer individual than he was long yesterdays ago; a shade perchance, but no more. Training systems have changed and probably improved, as have the condition of the tracks, but the horses themselves may not have advanced in true class.

Leaving aside a giant such as Man O' War who lighted the turf like a meteor some three decades ago, we jump that much further back and have a humble feeling that such as Ormonde, Carbine and Hanover would still be kings in these boastful days of speedy idols and speedier iconoclasts.

The most successful trainers are down-to-earth businessmen, and there are only two items on which they can judge the young horse for potential speed and stamina: conformation and pedigree. The pedigree can be checked according to the beliefs, experience, and study of the trainer. To judge a horse's conformation involves, almost entirely, a visual study of body characteristics and outward "individuality." It is a severe test of a horseman's wisdom, especially in a situation where split seconds, courage, and gameness play such an important part.

Such men look for specific points which they consider necessary if the horse is to be in the winning class. Such terms as "well muscled down" or "a flat, powerful croup" have special meaning for them.

They like to see a head wide through the eyes and capacious above, for this denotes courage and intelligence. Lop ears are unattractive and seldom seen on a poor performer. Large, thin nostrils usually denote a good windpipe, and wide, deep jowls give room for the larynx from the head to the throat. The set of the head on the neck is important, as there must not be any interference with the breathing apparatus. In general, the head should have a tapering appearance from large, wide-set eyes to a fine, pliant muzzle. Many trainers look to the head, the expression of the eyes, the ears, and the nostrils, to ascertain the potential courage and gameness of the animal, much the same as they might look into the eyes and face of another person to fathom his character.

The experienced trainer will inspect the neck for its length and fineness. The juncture of head and neck should be lean, without coarseness or a heavy appearance. A long neck with a slight arch denotes flexibility and balance, which are important factors in the running horse. A spindly neck indicates lack of vigor, and a neck too short and bulky may result in a horse that bores on the bit.

A long, well-sloped shoulder is essential, for this feature forecasts the length and force of the stride. It should carry lean, flat, powerful muscles. A good shoulder is almost always topped by moderately pronounced withers running well back.

Great depth from top to bottom through the line of the girth is present in all good horses. It is particularly important in the running horse because of the spaciousness it allows for the heart and lungs. The ribs are rather flat immediately behind the shoulders, allowing unrestricted action of the fore-quarters, and are rounding and full back over the rib cage, allowing full advantage to the respiratory organs. The individual rib bones should be long.

The coupling at the loins should be well molded to the hips; a sloping croup, or "goose rump," is undesirable. Great length from hip to hock is extremely desirable. The quarters should show evidence of sufficient musculature inside and out.

The legs should be observed for straightness and clean modeling of knees and hocks. These joints, both fore and hind, should be low to the ground, with resulting short cannons. The forearms and gaskins should be powerful. The tendons of the legs should be parallel with the cannon bone and give the appearance of being chiseled and defined without being "tied in" below the knee or hock. The gaskin, or the section represented by the tibia and fibula leg bones lying between the stifle joint and the hock, perhaps more importantly in the Thoroughbred than in most other breeds, should not be crescent in shape. Usually a leg with such a fault will not appear straight up and down when the lower leg is viewed from hock to pastern but will incline forward from hock point to heel when the animal is standing motionless.

The feet, of course, must be sound with flinty hoof walls, straight-grained in texture. The heels should be wide, giving the track of the foot a circular shape.

Thoroughbreds fall into two general divisions—"sprinters" and "stayers." Ordinarily, though not always, the sprinters are built on blockier, more powerful proportions than the long-distance runners. A common saying among experienced horsemen is: "closely forked for stamina and wide-chested for sprinting." A powerfully muscled quarter is more often than not the sign of a sprinter. Likewise, the neck may be heavier and is powerfully attached at its juncture with the shoulders.

These are the outward aspects which meet the eye. There are other factors which could be discovered, but only by putting the horse in a laboratory test tube, which of course is impossible. Nonetheless, it is interesting to explore the reasons some horses are capable of great speed only for short distances while others are gifted with the capacity of going hard the full route. Perhaps through an understanding of such scientific facts horsemen will be enabled to understand better the capacities of their running horses and class them accordingly.

Movement starts in the brain. The message is carried from the brain to the muscles via nerve fibers and travels in the form of a wave. In common breeds, the waves travel from 200 to 400 feet per second. In the fastest Thoroughbreds, the waves may move at a rate of 800 feet per second; hence their ability to move faster.

SPRINTER   STAYER

Another factor affecting speed is how firmly the nerve fibers are attached to the muscles; they are firmer in the Thoroughbred than in a heavier breed.

The voluntary muscles, those which carry out movements of locomotion, are made up of thousands of cells and collectively form tissue. This muscular tissue converges at both ends, forming tendons which are in turn attached to the bony framework of the animal. Incidentally, the legs below the hocks and knees contain no actual muscle. Instead, the tendons are extremely long, running down into the feet. It is for this reason that the soundness of leg tendons is important. Many leg ailments are due to infirmities of the tendons.

The muscle fibers are intersected by an intricate network of blood vessels comprised of arteries, capillaries, and veins. While in all horses the blood vessels increase in size when strenuous action occurs, this increase seems greater in a stayer than in a sprinter.

However, in a sprinter, the muscle fibers are larger in size and less in number, sometimes being 400 to the square inch in section while those of a stayer may number as high as 500. It is believed that this accounts for the tremendous drive and superior short-distance speed of the blockier type of horse. At the same time, this possibly explains his inability to keep going, because the muscle cells possess less cell surface to be affected by the blood flow.

Fatigue in racing horses is caused by the building up of lactic acid. In order to function, the muscle is made up, in part, of sugar in the form of glycogen. The animal which is capable of storing the most glycogen is able to release more energy when the muscles are stimulated by the nerve waves.

When the muscle contracts, a portion of the glycogen becomes lactic acid. When the muscle is momentarily relaxed, a small quantity of the acid is neutralized by the alkali in the muscle fiber, some of it is transformed into liver glycogen, and the balance is oxidized and eliminated as carbon monoxide.

The ability to dispose of lactic acid is essential in the running horse. A fast-running animal, through its more forceful and greater number of muscle contractions, will build up an abundance of lactic acid. The ability to dispose of the lactic acid through its respiratory and circulatory systems then determines the animal's staying power, because the moment the muscle fibers become bound with the acid the action is retarded and finally completely stopped by what we know as "fatigue."

Compared to other breeds, the Thoroughbred is nervous and high-strung. His sensitivity may at times be construed as lack of intelligence, yet the reverse is often true.

I recall a case where an attempt was being made to load a five-year-old Thoroughbred for transport. This gelding was not a track-trained animal and had been loaded only two or three times in his life. The truck was backed to a regulation loading ramp with wings on both sides. It was dusk, and the darkness of the truck's interior made the gelding afraid to go in. Impatient with the hesitation, his handlers employed a rope around the animal's hindquarters to force him into the truck, but the rough handling only caused him to break away in fright.

When his handlers tried to lead him, the gelding would go willingly halfway up the ramp, but further efforts made him attempt to leap the side wings of the chute. Then suddenly, as if through his own reasoning, he seemed to make up his mind that further resistance was futile. Almost with the same degree of determination employed in refusing, he leaped into the truck and stood quietly.

The majority of Thoroughbreds are endowed with the competitive racing spirit. After all, that is the purpose for which they were originated and selected. Still, while a certain amount of fighting Thoroughbred spirit may be credited to pedigree, conformation, etc., these do not fully explain why a gallant horse like England's Humorist could win when, it was discovered after his death, he had but one lung; or why the courageous horse Black Gold struggled desperately but vainly toward the finish mark when he had snapped a leg bone coming into the home stretch.

TRAINING THE RACE HORSE

The earliest training of a Thoroughbred is similar to the kindergarten schooling of colts of most other breeds. One trainer has stated that yearlings are like small children. They are mischievous and playful. Merely to tease, they will do foolish things in much the same manner as their human counterparts.

Almost from the time the foal is born it is accustomed to the feel of men's hands. If handled and managed properly, almost all colts will develop gradually into well-behaved grownups who are aware of their manners and of race-track procedure. When only a few days old, the foal learns not to fear a halter; and not long afterward, it succumbs to the pull of a lead shank and the inevitability of the tie post.

Trainer John Ward stated it well when he said: "The principal thing about breaking a yearling is to manner him well. Then he can be trained with little trouble. A yearling should handle easily so as not to hurt himself or other people's horses on the track."

All Thoroughbreds have a common birth date—the first day of January. Thus, if a foal is dropped in February, March, May, or any other month, he is considered to be one year old on the following January 1.

After his first birth date, he is considered to be a yearling. The time of breaking varies, though it usually occurs during his yearling season. If the colt is to be trained by his own breeder, he will most likely be started early in the summer. If he is sold through the yearling sales, his training may not begin until sometime in the fall.

Two things that are essential and to which the colt must become accustomed in training are a bit in his mouth and weight on his back. Some trainers may first bridle the colt with a simple snaffle and headpiece. This is most frequently done in the stall where he feels at home. Others may commence by placing a surcingle about his girth, taking care not to buckle it too tightly at first. A light saddle may next be introduced, but without stirrups, as they may frighten him by slapping him. The first time he feels the weight of a man on his back it may be with or without a saddle. In all instances, the rider is a light boy. All these initial steps seem to be more successful when introduced in his own stall.

Most trainers feel it is best to work yearlings in groups or a "set." In fact, one trainer has gone so far as to say: "The worst thing that can happen is for yearlings to be trained one at a time." They are less subject to fright when surrounded by their companions. During the first outside lessons, the yearlings may be led with a light boy up. Later, when they show no fear at the weight on their backs, they are taught the meaning of the bridle reins. At first, they will wind in all directions, but with patient instruction they soon learn to obey the pressure on the reins and will go in a straight line or turn as commanded.

Once they have become fairly bridle-wise, they may be trotted and later galloped slowly.

The training thus far is primary and, depending upon the ability of the trainer and his pupils, consumes from two weeks to a month. Most colts will give no great trouble during this period. It is important for the trainer to be patient and understanding and at the same time firm. Nearly all bad habits in horses are caused by the people who handle them. Once a vice is learned, it is exceedingly difficult to eradicate it from their memory.

From this point on, the colt's training is more specialized. At first, he is jogged around the track and later galloped. One of the factors which determines progress at this stage is the colt's fitness. If he shows signs of stress when galloped, it probably is a sign that he should be jogged longer.

Coinciding with this phase of training are lessons on backing straight, which is essential later when the colt is introduced to the starting gate. At this time, also, he is taught to travel straight and on the rail. Also, he must learn to pull away from the rail when commanded. He should, in fact, learn to work in any position, on the rail, on the outside, or between other colts. These are all situations which must be familiar to him when he first goes to the post.

When the yearling is thought to be fit, he may be galloped a half mile to begin with and gradually built up to around 2 miles. However, the 2-mile distance is not galloped in one stretch. Not all trainers condition their colts in the same routine; some may divide the 2-mile gallop into three or four parts by galloping a half mile, then walking or trotting a short distance before taking up the gallop again; others may divide it differently. It must be remembered that colts of this age are mere babies. Overwork at this point may have serious effects on them physically as well as psychologically.

When a yearling is capable of galloping 2 miles without blowing or sweating greatly, he is ready to breeze. At first, he may be worked for a short distance only at a "two-minute gait," and this may be done at intervals with two days of galloping in between. If the horse is fit under such work, he may be gradually stepped up in speed and distance of breezes until at last he may be breezed a quarter in twenty-four seconds and galloped out 3 furlongs in thirty-eight seconds or so each.

Assuming that the colt has been a model performer, the training thus far will probably have consumed slightly over four months. Most trainers at this stage give the yearling a three- or four-weeks' "turn out" to allow him to rest before again taking up the serious business of training for the track. There are, of course, exceptions to this procedure. If the yearling is to be entered in the winter season, he may be continued without the refresher period; or if his training did not commence until late in the fall, he may not be turned out.

The next phase of training is an intensification of past routine. His speed is again increased and he is worked at greater distance. He is a two-year-old now and may be capable of doing the half in forty-seven. He may have had several breezes at 5 furlongs and is ready to race that distance.

One of the most important phases of race-horse schooling involves the barrier, or starting gate. Races are frequently lost at this point. It is important that the colt be familiarized with the mechanism so that he will not lose an ounce of energy, if that is possible, in going in, and he must learn how to break from it as expeditiously as possible.

At first, the colt may be made to stand near the gate and later he will be placed in one of the stalls with the front gate open and then with it closed. Then he will be taught to step quietly out of the gate at a walk in company with other colts. After a few lessons, he will be allowed to break away at a gallop, with emphasis on a straight getaway rather than speed.

It has been said that schooling at the barrier never actually ends. The excitement of the first breakout and actual competition may cause a nervous colt to require further instruction.

Through the entire period of schooling, the competent trainer studies each animal in his charge. As is true in all types of horses, each Thoroughbred is an individual and is unlike the others. As surely as if he had his hand on the horse's pulse, the trainer must recognize weaknesses or capabilities in each one. This one is nervous, that one shows remote signs of lameness, another is not holding up well, and still another indicates a complete variation of routine and management.

A great deal of the trainer's problem is indicated in Mr. Fitz's oft-repeated remark: "It would be much easier to train horses if they could talk." But that also might cause further complications.

GREAT AMERICAN THOROUGHBREDS

Arguments occur from generation to generation in an effort to establish this or that horse as America's greatest Thoroughbred. It is difficult to make comparisons. Track conditions have changed through the years; distances have decreased, riding technique has been transformed; the handicappers take their toll; the high-money winners may not look so good when compared to winners of the past when the dollar bought more.

Each season has its favorite, yet a horse may diminish in importance as time rolls on and he is engulfed in the perspective of only a few short years. Perhaps once in each decade a truly great one flashes brilliantly but briefly past our vision. A list of champions in one man's book would be disputed in another, yet from the dim past, starting in the eighties, great names are recalled —Ben Brush, Hindoo, Salvator, Domino. The turn of the century started a procession—Sysonby, Colin, and others. Over thirty years ago, the indestructible Exterminator came up from the bottom and campaigned until 1924. Contemporary with him was the immortal Man O' War. Our memory begins to sharpen—Sarazen from 1923 to 1928; Gallant Fox, first horse to gain more than $300,000 as a three-year-old; Discovery between 1933 and 1936; and the great money winner Seabiscuit between 1935 and 1940. The next few years pass more quickly with War Admiral, Whirlaway, Alsab, Count Fleet, Twilight Tear, Busher, Assault, Armed, and Citation.

THOROUGHBRED RACERS

It is impossible to relate the history or racing achievements of all these giants of the turf, but a few of the facts are too interesting to pass over.

Hindoo was one of the most versatile, winning at both long and short distances. He won the half-mile Alexander Stakes in 1880 and was also victorious in 1882 when he ran 2½ miles for the Louisville Cup.

As two-year-olds, Domino and Sarazen were undefeated. Sysonby lost only one race in his lifetime. Colin was triumphant fifteen times in that many starts and was considered by many to be one of the best.

A few authorities have nominated Exterminator the greatest Thoroughbred to grace the American turf. Like all good geldings of any breed, he worked hard and long. Speed, courage, stamina, and intelligence were the

qualities with which this gelding was richly endowed. Beyond this, he seemed
to be possessed with limitless durability. His campaigns extended through
eight seasons. Out of the astounding number of 100 starts he had 51 wins,
17 seconds, and 17 thirds. It has been estimated that had Exterminator campaigned in recent years he would have earned more than $750,000.

It is said that he was a perfect gentleman at the post and never guilty of
bad behavior. Though he was ridden by many different jockeys, trained by
various trainers, shipped thousands of miles, raced on tracks good and bad,
his courage was always of the highest caliber.

If you were to step onto the street and ask the first passer-by, "What was
the most famous American race horse?" you would probably receive the
answer, "Man O' War." Many experts will go a step further and opine that
he was the greatest Thoroughbred America has ever seen.

It takes three things to make a horse truly great: he must be successful in
his career; he must be admired by his friends and the public; and last, though
not least, he must be able to perpetuate the qualities of his breed through his
progeny. "Big Red," as he was affectionately called, measured up well on all
these counts.

Though his blood was of the finest (he was sired by Fair Play, by Hastings
—Fairy Gold out of the mare Mahubah, by Rock Sand—Merry Token), he
has been considered one of the best bargains in Thoroughbred history. Purchased by Samuel D. Riddle at auction as a yearling for $5,000, he won
$249,465 in his two seasons of racing. Later he was reputed to have com-
manded a stud fee of $5,000, the same as his purchase price. In later years,
Riddle was reported to have turned down an offer of $1,000,000 for Man
O' War. He was admittedly worth more than $3,000,000 as a stallion.

The chestnut colt was launched on his racing career in 1919 as a two-year-
old, and after he had won his first six starts the racing circle began to take
notice of him. The only defeat he suffered was during his first season, when
a horse named Upset led him to the wire by half a length. He was laden with
130 pounds. He went on to finish the season with three more wins.

In his second year, his brilliance continued. It was considered foolhardy to
bet against him, and the odds were often so short that there was no wagering
at all.

Among his eleven winning starts in 1920 he chalked up the Preakness at
Pimlico; Withers, Belmont, Lawrence Realization and Jockey Club Stakes
at Belmont; Stuyvesant Handicap at Jamaica; Dwyer at Aqueduct; Miller
and Travers at Saratoga, and the Potomac Handicap at Havre de Grace.

Man O' War set five new records for speed—the Withers Mile in 1:35⅘, the mile and three-eighths of the Belmont in 2:14⅕, the mile and a half of the Jockey Club Stakes in 2:28⅘, the mile and five-eighths of the Lawrence Realization in 2:40⅘, and the mile and one-eighth of the Dwyer in 1:49⅕.

This latter race is considered by many old-timers to have been the greatest horse race in history. It was virtually a match between Man O' War and John P. Grier, a horse that had been groomed to beat the champion. "Big Red" went to the post carrying 126 pounds against John P. Grier's 108. The two colts broke together and ran neck and neck past the half, then the Whitney colt gradually drew away from the more heavily weighted Man O' War. The crowd thought the red horse had met his Waterloo that day, for the two horses sped thus to the final sixteenth pole. But the fighting spirit within Man O' War mustered a drive which carried him to the finish one and a half lengths ahead and going away from John P. Grier.

Unlike Exterminator, Man O' War was not content merely to nose out his rivals. It seemed that he was bent on putting as much distance between himself and his competition as possible. In the Jockey Club Stakes he won by fifteen lengths, in the Belmont by twenty, and in the Lawrence Realization he distanced all opposition by nearly a quarter of a mile.

The career of "Big Red" ended with the Gold Club match with the Kentucky Derby winner Sir Barton. Though the latter was expected to give him a run, the champion galloped to victory with a seven-length lead. His $80,000 winnings from this race made him the first horse to top the $200,000 mark.

Owner Riddle retired the champion to stud with the explanation that the handicappers had piled so much poundage on the horse, with the promise of more, that he could not stand to see the animal broken down. Man O' War had consistently carried more weight than most. He never carried less than 115 pounds and was weighted with 130 in six of his juvenile races.

As a sire, Man O' War's record was as imposing as his racing career had been. By the end of 1944, he had sired 386 foals. Of this amazing total, 44 were stakes winners, 112 winners, 111 nonstarters, and 119 nonwinners, collectively earning nearly $3,500,000. His great-grandson Stymie was top money winner, with total earnings of $816,060. Notwithstanding the fact that he never had more than twenty-five foals in any one year, he was once the leading United States sire. His daughters have ranked high as producers and his great strain may be passed on by two of his illustrious sons, War Admiral and War Relic. His line has been responsible for many good steeplechasers and jumpers.

On November 1, 1947, after a long, full, and fruitful life of almost thirty-one years, the noble spirit of "Big Red" passed on to join those of Herod,

Matchem, and Eclipse. His body rests near Lexington, Kentucky, where his grave is marked by a bronze horse cast in his likeness to serve as a reminder of a great and noble character.

As befitting a national hero, the old warrior was accorded military honors in Tokyo by the three thousand men of the First Cavalry Division who had previously made him an honorary colonel; two thousand friends attended the ceremony of his burial, which was broadcast and photographed for the news-reels; and at the hour of his interment, all operating race tracks in the nation paused for a moment of silent tribute.

You say he was only a horse? Maybe so, but in the beautifully expressive words of his faithful old groom, Will Harbut, spoken while he lived: "Folks, he is the mostest hoss in the world."

INFLUENCE ON OTHER BREEDS

As a world-wide influence on other light breeds, the Thoroughbred is second only to the Arab. Stallions have been used to cross on selected mares of various breeds and types to produce highly useful horses. The U.S. Army remount for years placed many Thoroughbred stallions to get cavalry stock. Most polo ponies carry strong infusions of Thoroughbred blood. We have already noted the influence of the breed through founding stock of both the Standard Bred and the American Saddle Horse. The blood of the Thorough-bred flows in the veins of the Morgan breed and has greatly influenced the Quarter Horse.

HUNTERS, JUMPERS, AND STEEPLECHASERS

Horses used as hunters and jumpers, of course, are not necessarily composed of any one breed. It is generally acknowledged, however, that a pure Thor-oughbred, if of good type, size, and bone, is excellent in the field. In fact, many of the larger horse shows hold hunter classes exclusively for Thorough-breds. There are exceptions; but, in the main, hunters carry at least half or more Thoroughbred blood. The Thoroughbred–Standard Bred cross has been highly successful in producing lightweight hunters. Other breeders are producing good hunter prospects by crossing Thoroughbreds on horses of American Saddle, Cleveland Bay, Hackney, and in some instances, draft breeding. The last cross is rather drastic in the first generation, but with the reinfusion of Thoroughbred blood the results have been extremely satisfac-tory in getting heavyweight hunters.

Various forms of hunting with horses have been practiced from periods of remotest antiquity. Hunting as we know it today probably originated in Ireland where the breeding of the hunting type of horse has been carried on for hundreds of years. The Irish had imported horses from the Mediterranean area, many of them Libyans, which were held in high esteem as hunters. When the Byerly Turk was imported in the late seventeenth century, there were mares in Ireland which nicked well with his blood to produce the Irish Thoroughbred horse. It has been said that this blood crossed on Irish cart mares produced hunters of great quality and character. Much of their good bone and substance is believed to have been produced by the limestone land which nourished the pastures.

The Irish horse, which has been sought after for more than two hundred years, is large when compared to the Thoroughbred, having a larger head, longer legs, and more angular hips. The quarters, loins, and legs are powerful. It was my privilege to know and observe an animal of this breed, and he conformed to these specifications very closely. Though he was rather old, this gelding was spirited, courageous, and apparently endowed with a love of jumping.

Bred primarily to carry a rider to hounds across country and to be capable of safely negotiating fences, ditches, and other obstacles, hunters are classified by their weight-carrying potential. According to the American Horse Shows Association rules, lightweight hunters are considered capable of carrying weight up to 165 pounds, middleweights up to 185 pounds, and heavyweights over 185 pounds.

In considering hunter conformation, his specialized function must be borne in mind. The head need not be exceptionally fine, though it should not be of such size that it will tend to throw the horse out of balance. The countenance should denote intelligence if we are to expect the horse to possess sufficient judgment for the work he is to perform. Fineness to the degree which suggests oversensitiveness or flightiness should be avoided.

The neck must be long, yet muscled sufficiently to permit varying movement in sustaining balance. Much of the element of balance is determined by the conformation of head and neck, and it cannot be overemphasized when discussing jumping horses of any type.

The shoulders, as in any good saddle animal, should be flat, well sloped, and flexible. The scapula, humerus, and bones of the foreleg, and the muscles serving them, must be near perfection if the animal is to fold properly, alight safely, and maintain stride.

Hunting and steeplechasing probably demand more stamina in horses than any other equine activity. It is necessary, therefore, that such horses have great depth of girth and an unusually capacious rib cage to house the heart and respiratory organs.

The backs of many horses used in jumping are longer than those of some other breeds. This may be due to the predominance of Thoroughbred blood. If we consider this a defect and if it exists in the horse we are inspecting, we should be doubly sure that he has strong loins with no dip at the juncture of the backbone and the pelvic region.

The hindquarters should be equipped with muscles sufficient for the specialized task of jumping, with great length from hips to hocks. Sickle-hocked horses are apt to be victims of hock ailments. However, a slight tendency in this direction may not be objectionable, since it affords a better opportunity for the animal to engage the legs forward, thus aiding at the fences where suppleness of body is extremely important.

There is an old saying, supposedly originated by the Indians: "No foot—no horse." A new phrase might be coined concerning hunters, jumpers, and 'chasers: "No bone—no horse." One point of paramount importance in this type of animal is that he must have a sturdy framework, particularly in the legs. The bone should be ample (averaging 7½ to 8¼ inches in the 16-hand horse), well shaped, and dense in texture. The tendons should be clean, strong, and well defined.

In looking at pictures of Grand National Steeplechase winners, you may think that there were some "mighty queer ones," but upon closer study it is apparent that good bone was present in all of them. In David Hoadley Munroe's book *The Grand National* is a description which summarizes concisely the jumper type of animal:

> Cloister was the *beau ideal* of the steeplechaser of the big powerful type— a dark bay gelding, with beautifully laid shoulders, great depth through the chest, a clearly defined jumping bone, and muscular quarters with remarkable length from great square hips to well-formed hocks. He was a big horse in every sense of the word, but had great freedom of action, and galloped and jumped with seeming absence of effort. He was a hard puller, but otherwise a thoroughly comfortable rider when one got used to his peculiar manner of jumping. He ran with his head very low, like most great stayers, and would keep it low until his jockey felt sure he would never get it up in time; just at the last moment, when he apparently had not seen the fence at all, up would come his head, and a big fence would be thrown behind him as lightly as a little hurdle.

Among the horses trained to jump are three divisions: horses which hunt to hounds across country (hunters); horses used solely for their contest jumping ability (jumpers); and race horses which traverse courses with jumps (steeplechasers). All three types are jumping horses, yet each is specialized in its own field.

Hunters

The sport of hunting to hounds, rich in tradition, originated in its present form in the British Isles. Although there are fewer packs of hounds in America than in England, the sport has become extremely popular here, particularly in the eastern part of the United States.

To be a good hunter, a horse must be a consistent jumper of obstacles up to 5 feet which would be encountered on cross-country runs. One of the most important qualifications of the hunter is his ability to maintain a hunting pace and safely negotiate the barriers. The manner of fencing and taking obstacles in stride is more important than an occasional tick or knockdown if such performance is not attributable to faulty style. It should be understood that a horse capable of winning a high-jump contest is not necessarily a safe cross-country horse.

Adjunctive to the hunt are contests for hunters known as "hunter trials" and "hunter events" in horse shows. Classes for hunters may be divided into three general divisions: conformation, working, and breeding. In the conformation division, we find open hunters listed. The requirements, according to the American Horse Shows Association, are: "Performance, manners, way of going, 60%; conformation, quality, substance and soundness, 40%."

In contrast, the working-hunter division is judged according to the following rules: "The judges are to pick the horses, apparently the most agreeable mounts to hounds, the main considerations being even hunting pace, manners, way of going and style of jumping. Ticks will not be scored, unless fault of bad jumping. Riders will be required to lead over one fence. Conformation will not be considered. Hunting soundness only required."

There are many classes within each of the divisions. In the conformation division, for example, are classes for Thoroughbreds, where emphasis is placed strongly on conformation; classes for other than Thoroughbreds, where substance is emphasized; classes for various ages; classes for green horses; classes for lightweight, middleweight, and heavyweight hunters; classes for hunt teams; and many others.

A point worth noting is that conformation hunters and working hunters are faulted identically in so far as performance is concerned. Also, safety in jumping is the paramount issue in such faulting. For instance, a "rear knockdown," one that is caused by contact with any part of the horse's body behind the stifle, is considered less serious than a front knockdown and is counted as only two faults, whereas a front knockdown counts four faults against the contestant. Light touches are not generally counted as faults except where the jumping might be considered in faulty style, because such ticks are not deemed serious in the hunting field.

Breed classes are shown in halter and are judged in much the same way as other kinds of horses. In classes where formal hunting appointments are counted, the exhibitor should know the proper attire for the rider and the correct tack appointments for the mount.

Jumpers

Jumpers are judged solely on their ability to clear obstacles, and in some instances time is an element. Conformation and style of jumping are not considered; the open jumper is apt to appear in any color or type, some extremely fine, others blocky and powerful.

The obstacles used in jump classes are usually higher and more novel than those in hunter events, and the course may be more difficult in its layout. For this reason, jumping contests are among the most spectacular and full of suspense of all horse-show events.

Formerly, a jumping horse was not required to perform at any set pace or gait, and much valuable time was lost by horses and riders who hesitated before each jump. Rules have now been put into effect to regulate the pace, stipulating that a jumper, upon entering the ring, must immediately and without loss of forward movement proceed to the first jump. It is permissible to make one circle, but thereafter any additional circle will be counted as a penalty. A canter or gallop must be maintained except where a runout or refusal occurs.

The unexplainable quality that makes a great jumping horse is rare. There are many unusual stories about horses that were "discovered" and went on to fame and fortune as jumpers. One that comes to mind was a black colt bought at a slaughtering pen; another was a colt which began life as a seemingly hopeless cripple with a clubfoot. The story of the inimitable little jumping mare Queen of Sports is familiar to many on Eastern show circuits. Frederick von Lombeck has been her owner and rider for almost twenty-five years; in fact, the boy and the filly grew up together. She was purchased as a yearling with the idea of training her as an ordinary saddle mount, but the day Fred put her at jump changed the picture. Since then, the mare Queen of Sports has won more than $25,000 in prizes.

How high do horses jump? In horse shows we see them put to jumps from 4 to 6 feet, or slightly over. But horses are able to jump higher than that. Great Heart, an eight-year-old Thoroughbred, set an all-time high on June 9, 1923, at the South Shore Country Club Horse Show in Chicago, clearing the bars at the astounding height of 8 feet $13\frac{}{16}$ inch. This broke the earlier record of 8 feet $\frac{1}{2}$ inch set by Confidence at Ottawa, Canada. Confidence was reputed to have jumped 8 feet 2 inches, though it was an unofficial record.

Steeplechasers

Steeplechasing is one of the severest tests to which horses can be put. The name implies the manner of its origin: it is said that steeplechasing began as a point-to-point race in which the distant church steeple, an easily discernible landmark, was the object of the chase.

Since its inception, courses with fixed obstacles have been laid out specifically for steeplechase racing, and in most instances rails have been placed to mark the course. A few such chases have become popular in America, Maryland being the scene of some of the best ones. The greatest steeplechase event in the world is the Grand National, held over the Aintree Course at Liverpool, England. Regardless of what a horse may accomplish before or after, if

STEEPLECHASERS

he wins the "National" he is assured a special place among the immortals of the turf.

The course at Aintree has undergone many changes from its beginning, but it has always been a forbidding challenge to the best of horses. The turf has gone through various conditions of plow, wheat, or seeds, and finally grass, as it now remains. The use of preliminary hurdles as a "warm up" before the running of the race was instituted about 1887 but was discontinued after twenty years. The fences have been altered as to position, type, and condition, and their height was increased gradually until 1885, since which time the course has remained quite as it is today with only a few changes. The distance, established in 1885, is 4 miles 856 yards.

The changes of the Aintree Course have affected the type of horse running in the National. The old-fashioned half-bred hunter type has gradually been displaced by the faster Thoroughbred type of racer. As the popularity of the sport increased, horses were bred specifically with the intention of training them over the fences, and it no longer became necessary to depend to any great extent on cast-off runners.

An interesting comparison has been drawn between the flat runners of the Epsom Derby and the jumping racers of the National. The Epsom Course is a mile and one-half in length. The average time of Derby winners from World War I to 1930 is a mile in one minute forty-five seconds by three-year-olds carrying nine stone.

The two circuits of the Aintree Course are more than 4 miles in length and consist of thirty stiff jumps. As calculated for the same period of time, the average rate of speed for a mile has been two minutes nine seconds by horses averaging over eight years of age and carrying more than eleven stone. This is a mile average of only twenty-four seconds slower than the Derby winners. If age and weight are considered, it is almost equal to the speed of the flat runners who travel only about one-third the distance. Considering the nature of the obstacles encountered by horses running the National, these figures attest to the quality of the steeplechasers.

A map of the Aintree Course shows a total of sixteen jumps, all of which are taken on the first circuit and all but the last two on the second circuit, making a total of thirty jumps. The finish is a flat run-in of 494 yards. The fences are as follows:

No. 1 and No. 17—Thorn, 4 feet 6 inches high.
No. 2 and No. 18—Gorse, 4 feet 7 inches high.
No. 3 and No. 19—Fir, 4 feet 11 inches high.
No. 4 and No. 20—Gorse, 4 feet 10 inches high.

No. 5 and No. 21—Gorse, 5 feet high.

No. 6 and No. 22—Fir ("Becher's Brook"), 4 feet 10 inches high.

No. 7 and No. 23—Gorse, 5 feet high.

No. 8 and No. 24—Fir ("Canal Turn"), 5 feet high.

No. 9 and No. 25—Spruce ("Valentine's Brook"). Height not shown on map. In 1885, this obstacle was described as being a 5-foot thorn fence with a 2-foot guard rail in front and a 5-foot brook on the landing side.

No. 10 and No. 26—Gorse, 5 feet high.

No. 11 and No. 27—Fir, 5 feet high.

No. 12 and No. 28—Gorse, 5 feet high.

No. 13 and No. 29—Fir, 4 feet 7 inches high.

No. 14 and No. 30—Spruce, 4 feet 6 inches high.

No. 15 —Spruce ("The Open Ditch"), 5 feet 2 inches high.

No. 16 —("Water Jump"), 15 feet wide over all, with spruce fence 2 feet 6 inches high.

Merely to give the heights of the obstacles is not sufficient to explain their challenge. For instance, "Becher's Brook" on the landing side includes a natural brook 9 feet 6 inches wide and 6 feet deep. The "Canal Turn" is particularly bad, the jump being placed at a point where the course makes a 90-degree turn so that the horses are forced to turn sharply left immediately on landing. This jump is made even more difficult because of a 2-foot guard rail and a 6-foot ditch immediately preceding the fence on the take-off side. The "Water Jump," while not high, is hazardous because of its breadth. The almost 13 feet of water has a 2-foot thorn fence on the take-off side.

We quoted earlier from David Hoadley Munroe's description of an ideal steeplechase mount; now let us look at his word picture of the race itself:

When you go to the National you are generally persuaded by your own curiosity, or by that of a more energetic companion, to go down to have a look at the fences, and possibly to walk part of the course. You stroll up to one of the fences and are amazed to find that even by standing on tip-toe you can hardly see over the top. You straightway go to wondering how a horse can be expected to get over such a huge obstacle, and how the jockey feels when he sees it looming up before him. When you see the course stretching away into the distance, one great fence after another, and realize that each fence is much like the one you have just examined, you suddenly feel that there is no other race course in the world like this one, and you go back to a place in the stands with a heightened sense of excitement and anticipation.

All about you is noise and bustle, talk of this horse and that; people mill back and forth below you in the enclosure, and the strident voices of the book-makers rise up from their posts on the rail. At length the sport begins with two flat races, but hovering in the back of your mind is the thought of those great jumps, and the events on the flat seem somehow tame and uninteresting. After they are done with, many people get up and go out to the paddock to see the National horses saddled, but the wise man hugs his seat, for in a few minutes the stand is filled to overflowing, and many who have left never get back again. Someone says: "There they are!" and necks are craned to watch the horses as they come out through a little gate to the right. If you were lucky enough to be there in 1929, you watched the scene in brilliant sunshine, and saw, as well, the largest number of horses, by more than twenty, that has ever taken part in the race.

A long line of horses files by, their jockeys clothed in brightly colored silks. One by one they pass in parade until the count has reached sixty-six. Up to the left of the stands they turn and come back, some cantering quietly, others pulling hard on their way to the bend in the course where the starter lines them up. For a wonder this huge cavalcade is quiet and well-behaved; a few break and dance about, but are quickly brought into line, the flag falls, and with a roll of thunder they are off into the country. There has been much speculation as to what will happen when this mighty wave of horses breaks over the first fence. Your heart beats quickly—and, amazingly, they are all over! Only two down at the next jump, but at the third someone refuses, and there is a mass of milling horses and kaleidoscopic colors. But don't watch the falls; the favorite is out in front, the brilliant chestnut is striding away into a terrific lead, and perched above those swinging shoulders is a jockey in pink with black and white striped sleeves. Round the bend at the Canal Turn he leads them, and comes running easily back toward the stands, sails over the Water Jump, and is away into the country again. Behind him come those that are left, but only twenty-two in all—double that number are out somewhere on the course, and will wander slowly home, to bear after their names that ambiguous phrase "did not finish."

The favorite is still leading at the Canal Turn in the second round, but at Valentine's Brook he spreads a plate, and as he does so another chestnut, a big powerful horse with a tangerine jacket on his back, bursts from the second group, and sets sail for the leader. The favorite is tiring under his big weight, and that loose shoe is bothering him, and the other creeps up. Only two more fences, and then the run in! The tangerine sweeps by, clears the last fence, and gallops home in front—and the Grand National has been won by a rank outsider, a 100–1 shot!

TRAINING JUMPING HORSES

Almost all jumping horses require a great deal more training than Cloister, who won the National in 1893; it has been said that this great horse required very little schooling of any kind, and did not have to be taught to jump!

Occasionally a horse is found that seems to take to jumping like a duck to water. However, I recall one trainer's saying that when a person comes to him excitedly with a story of a natural jumper in his stable—one which clears the paddock fence with no encouragement and comparative ease and enjoyment —he wants to see *how* the horse jumps before stating that the animal is a born jumper. If he finds that the animal uses judgment and stands back and fences properly, he is interested in trying to develop the ability with schooling.

Different trainers use different methods in teaching a horse to jump, but there are a few underlying principles which are paramount. All trainers agree that each horse is an individual and that to train him properly requires a careful study of his traits. Often a method which will work for one must be changed for another.

Confidence must be instilled in all horses. This is particularly true of jumping horses because of the courage and judgment required. They should not be forced to jump when they are afraid. An animal in whose mind fear is uppermost is prevented from using his own intuition at the fences. You may have heard the expression that "a rider lifts his horse over the jumps." This is as preposterous as saying that a man can lift himself with his own bootstraps. The most an intelligent rider can do is to rate his mount to the jump and then give the least interference possible.

Another precaution that is taken in training a young jumper is to avoid putting him over obstacles which are so high as to discourage him or make him feel that the task is useless. An occasional "bump" is good, for it will let him know it can hurt, but continued failure at the barrier will soon discourage any candidate.

For the schooling of jumpers, let us observe the methods of two different trainers. Trainer Number One starts the colt as a two-year-old. He bits him and teaches him to lead either off another horse or from the ground. Next, the pupil is taught to work on the gyp line in circles around the trainer. Then the colt is taught to obey certain cues while on the lunge; he learns such voice commands as "walk," "trot," "canter," "back up," and "whoa." Proper manipulation of the lunge line also helps teach him the commands. The trainer always goes to the colt instead of allowing him to come to the center when halted; thus, the animal does not learn the bad habit of going to the center of the ring each time he comes to a stop.

The next step is to train the horse to do these things when at liberty, naturally and without the use of a bitting rig.

When put to the first jump, the colt is at liberty. The jump is low, not more than 3 feet, so that he will not associate hard work with the game of jumping. Trainer Number One says that the colt's first jump is the most important in all his career. He must not be allowed to refuse it. If he stops, he must be forced over it. This trainer does not believe in using a take-off bar. He claims that when they are taken away the colt has to learn judgment of distance all over again.

After schooling the colt over low jumps for two to three months, the trainer turns him out until he is three years old. When the colt is again taken up, the same method is used for a while over jumps not exceeding 3 feet.

When the colt is three years old, he is broken to ride. Trainer Number One's advice is the same as that of trainers of other types of horses: "Ride him just to the point where he begins to tire, but not any more than that, for these lessons should not be a burden to him."

At this point, Trainer Number One gave us a number of ideas: "School him loose once a week and ride him the balance of the week. Let him learn to be natural in his way of going when under the saddle; if he is trained in this manner, anyone can ride him later. Never be in a hurry when schooling a jumper." With these things in mind, the next step is to proceed to the jumps with a rider on the colt's back and with the obstacles kept low.

Trainer Number One believes that a three-year-old colt should be shown only once or twice in green classes. Then in the fall he is ready for his first hunt, though care must be taken not to put him to the jumps too fast. In actual hunting, the trainer explains, the colt will be confronted with natural obstacles which are never in the same place as the ones set up in the training ring, and thus he will be prepared for all eventualities. He learns to clear different types of fences, hedges, stone walls, or anything that may be in his path. After hunting for a short season, this man again roughs the colt out to refresh himself during the winter.

In the spring, the horse should be able to come out with a great deal of jumping ability. He is now a four-year-old, and stronger. At this point, the jumps may be increased in height. He may be entered in stiffer competition and ridden in more strenuous hunts. This trainer gives a final piece of advice: "School a 'made' horse loose occasionally. In this way he will be more natural in his jumping and at the same time he will realize that when mistakes are made they may be his own fault."

Trainer Number Two likes to start with a three-year-old. If the animal has had any previous schooling, he prefers it to be stockbroken, feeling that this promotes handiness in the horse for both hunting and open jumping.

In starting the colt over the jumps, this man leads the colt up to the jump so that he can satisfy his curiosity regarding it or overcome any fear of it. The animal should be talked to and also petted to reassure him at this point.

The jump must be low, not exceeding 2 feet. At liberty, the colt is brought into it and if necessary is crowded over it. Here again the trainer considers the first jump extremely important.

Trainer Number Two has observed that some horses refuse to jump at liberty. In the belief that confidence rather than fear should be the governing factor, he may use a lunge line or a mounted rider.

Contrary to the method of Trainer Number One, this man believes in starting the prospect with a take-off bar, but he eliminates this device as soon as the judgment of the horse is sharpened. As the jumps are raised, the take-off bar is moved farther from the jump so that the jumping arc will be correct. Trainer Number Two believes that open jumpers as well as hunters should be taught to take the jumps in their stride with ease and without loss of forward movement or interruption of pace.

Another device that Trainer Number Two uses is a wing at the sides of the jump. This is to prevent the colt from acquiring the habit of running out. This trainer believes that an occasional touch or knockdown is excusable in a finished horse but that running out is generally the result of improper schooling in the beginning.

Liberty training is continued until the colt is able to clear an obstacle 3 feet 6 inches high with ease and confidence. The time consumed in the process will, of course, vary with the individual horse.

Trainer Number Two now assigns a rider to the prospect. The jumps are dropped back to their original 2 feet, for with the additional weight the horse must adjust his judgment accordingly. If he fails at the first jumps with the rider up, he may associate his failure with the fact that a man is on his back. The jumps, however, may be raised more rapidly at this period of schooling, as it is now a matter of judgment rather than physical ability.

Usually, it will be found that a green horse thinks he has to rush the jumps. This is where the rider can help by rating him. Once he understands he can take the jump at a slower speed, he will be willing to do it.

Trainer Number Two gives us some additional ideas: "After a horse has gained confidence in his ability to jump, yet is a little lazy or reluctant to fold properly, I will 'pole' him." This is done by touching the feet with a bamboo pole, the effect of which is noise rather than pain. Sometimes the top jump pole itself may be raised to touch the horse's hoofs as he clears the jump.

"I sometimes resort to the whip," continues Trainer Number Two, "but only to prevent the horse from learning to hesitate or refuse. Some horses gain the habit of hesitating while gathering for the fence. This is not desirable, particularly in the hunter where a smooth 'in the stride' jumping action is desired." For proper form a hunter should jump sparingly; in other words, he should go only high enough to clear the jump safely.

As we know, the pure Thoroughbred is unsurpassed as a speed runner. There have been instances where he has been suitable as an all-round pleasure animal. A strong rider will have no difficulty controlling him, though he may be too "hot" for general pleasure use by children and inexperienced riders.

On the other hand, the part-Thoroughbred horse is perhaps the greatest all-purpose pleasure horse in America. Certainly in numbers he surpasses all others where riders are using him to take them on comfortable trail or cross-country rides or for flat-saddle drill classes and in jumping events.

❦ 11 ❦

The Western Horse

The history of the Western horse is perhaps more romantic than that of any other type developed on the North American continent, partly because of the vastness and primitive ruggedness of the Western areas and partly because the winning of the West was virtually accomplished on horseback. Mere mention of the word "mustang" conjures up an exciting picture of Western history and folklore.

Perhaps not everyone realizes that the wild horse, the Spanish Barb, the Indian pony, the early cow horse, the ranger's mount, and even the deathless "white mustang" were one and the same. For those who think this is an exaggeration, let us go back almost four centuries so that we may see how close to the truth it really is.

The idea that the horses of Cortez populated the Western plains with wild stock has been fairly well exploded. That a few straying domesticated animals could have multiplied to the extent of populating the entire area, thus furnishing mounts for every Indian warrior, seems highly incredible. It is more likely that production of horses in great volume came through the later Spanish pioneers who settled the land.

Horses of the same type as those ridden by the Spanish adventurers, however, were the first to populate much of the area of what is now the United States. This foundation stock came from the West Indies or Mexico, entering at four points—Florida, New Mexico, Texas, and California, in that order. The majority of such horses were bred on the islands and were preferred to European importations because of their adaptability to the southern climate.

The horses that were brought into Florida around the middle of the six-

265

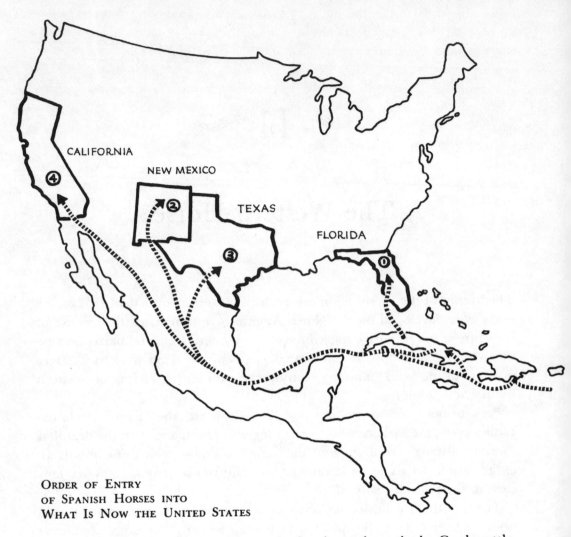

CALIFORNIA

NEW MEXICO

TEXAS

FLORIDA

ORDER OF ENTRY
OF SPANISH HORSES INTO
WHAT IS NOW THE UNITED STATES

teenth century were distributed over the Southeast through the Guale settlements. The next important point of entry was New Mexico, where at the close of the sixteenth century Juan de Oñate and a group of Spanish settlers established themselves a few miles northeast of the present site of Sante Fe. Horse and cattle breeding was the regular order of business. Incidentally, Oñate was the first white man to try to domesticate the North American buffalo, but attempts to rope or corral them were unsuccessful because of the obstinate character and strength of the animals. Unlike Spanish cattle, they could not be accurately herded or headed.

The first attempt to enter Texas was made by Azcué from Monterrey when he crossed the Rio Grande in 1665. Missions and ranches were established, only to be wiped out by the Janamberes Indian attacks in 1675. When Alonzo de León led his first expedition into Texas in 1687, he was surprised to discover mounted natives. The horses were the remnants and offspring of those captured twelve years earlier.

In spite of efforts of the Spanish to prevent the Indians from gaining possession of their stock (the Spanish Colonial administration repeatedly issued decrees forbidding the sale of horses to the Indians), it was inevitable that this would happen. This attitude of the Spanish authorities is easily understood when we realize that they were naturally jealous of their foothold in the rich new land. Furthermore, they knew from experience that horses and Indians were a combination to be feared. The eventual exchange of horses by Spaniards, Anglo-Americans, and Indians did more to spread horses throughout the North American continent than all the wild herds. It is believed by historians that the Indians began acquiring the offspring of Oñate's Barbs early in the 1600s. Within less than a century, Indians of the Iowa and Missouri tribes became well mounted, as reported by La Salle and Tonti; in fact, nearly all the tribes of the western half of the United States possessed horses.

As the pace of settling quickened, trails were established throughout the Southwest. The trail from Chihuahua to Sante Fe was worn deep at an early date. This was the route traveled by the first Spanish adventurers about 1540 and it was in continuous use until New Mexico became a part of the United States.

Sante Fe formed the hub from which radiated trails in all directions. The Old Spanish Trail meandered northwestward out of Santa Fe, up into south-

SPANISH CONQUISTADOR

ern Utah, across to Las Vegas, Nevada, and on westward into California. The famous Santa Fe Trail took a northeastward route into Kansas.

As most of the horses and mules emanated from Mexico, breeding ranches and horse-trading posts sprang up along the major Mexican trails. Horses were a fluid trading commodity. At the posts, worn-out animals were traded for fresh ones.

By 1812, there were three recognized zones of horse activity in the Southwest and in northeastern Mexico. The first area consisted of the plains country of the Arkansas River, where such horses were known as "Pawnee" or "Osage." The second zone lay between the Arkansas and Red rivers where the horses were owned by the tribes of Caddos, Wichitas, and Comanches. The largest area was south of the Red River, now known as Texas. These horses were owned by Texas Indians and Texas Spaniards.

Before this, in the 1750s, the French of western Louisiana and the Spanish of eastern Texas fraternized with each other, and many Spanish horses were traded for the New Orleans market. Though such animals were surplus on Spanish ranches, the Spanish government frowned on such transfers, and issued a royal decree ordering all settlers in the Los Adaes area to remove themselves and their stock westward to San Antonio.

The Pawnee tribes, inhabiting what is now Nebraska, were the first Indians in the north to use horses. About 1720, a Spanish military expedition, outfitted in Santa Fe and led by Villaspur, had reached the Platte River. At this point, the Spaniards were surprised by Pawnee warriors, and most of the Spaniards' horses fell into the hands of the Indians. Canadian French trappers taught the Pawnees what little they knew of horsemanship, and with this primary knowledge they developed a true type of Indian horsemanship. Their original stock was undoubtedly replenished by trade or raids to the south; the vast numbers of horses accumulated and other facts seem to indicate this. For instance, Patrick Henry sent traders to the Pawnee country for the "best and most pure Spanish breed," and many of the horses taken East actually carried Spanish brands.

The fact that the Pawnees had horses as well as firearms, the latter obtained from the French in return for furs, made them a powerful force on the northern plains.

It is believed that the Osages procured Pawnee horses through raids. That the French taught the Osages horsemanship is evident because of the similarity of the Osage style to that of the Pawnees. Pawnee-Osage horse handling, however, was much different from that of the Comanches, who were Spanish-trained. In controlling their horse herds the Comanches used a *reata* fashioned from selected cow rawhide that was closely braided and made pliable with applications of tallow. Their accuracy in throwing at a distance made it possible to catch up the best horses from the herds.

On the other hand, the northern Indians used what was called a "lariat." Loosely braided from spongy buffalo hide, it could not be thrown effectively. For catching a horse, a long pole was used to support the noose end of the lariat. Riding alongside the quarry, the Indian would attempt to place the loop over its head. The best range horses became increasingly difficult to catch because of these cumbersome methods, and horses among the northern Plains tribes eventually degenerated in quality.

INDIAN METHOD OF CAPTURING WILD HORSES

Another cause of the disappearance of many good northern Indian horses was the practice of "creasing" with a rifle bullet, invented and suggested by the French. The object was to graze the upper flesh of the neck, in front of the withers, momentarily stunning the animal. However, for every horse successfully captured in this way, a hundred others were killed. Although in 1830 the Plains Indians as a whole possessed more horses than at any other period in their history, by 1835 few good Indian horses existed in Missouri, Kansas, or Arkansas because of this useless killing of the wild herds.

Many attempts have been made to discredit the horses and horsemanship of the Indians. Actually, the North American primitives, during the Age of Horse Culture, revolutionized and improved their entire mode of life. The attitude of the Indian toward his horse made of him an excellent trainer, and his methods for subduing the animal were for the most part humane.

Two reasons have been given for the excellence of Indian horsemanship. First, the primitive had no saddle; he became "a part of his horse" or suffered serious consequences. Second, the Indian needed both hands free to handle his bow and arrows. Out of this necessity arose a technique of horsemanship peculiar to the Indian—that of guiding the mount with shifting weight and knee pressure.

During the Horse Wars, the Indian leaders devised military and fighting tactics unknown to any other race of people. The Plains Indians were credited by American generals with being the world's best cavalry soldiers. The life of every Indian, from the time of boyhood, was a continuous training period in cavalry procedure.

The Indians were perhaps the first to use the art of camouflage; by choosing the colored horse that blended best with seasonal and geographic background, they could make themselves less conspicuous. White horses were used when snow was on the ground; dun-coated horses were used in the fall to blend with dried prairies; blue roans effectively blended into sagebrush backgrounds; pintos and grays were favored more than all others because their body colors could be easily altered by smearing or dyeing to suit the surroundings.

Symbolic heraldry, consisting of elaborately painted patterns and insignia, was invented by the Indians and applied to their war horses and buffalo runners. Circles or stripes on the shoulders usually designated the side from which a kill had been made. The war horse of the brave was given credit for his assistance in taking a scalp or making a kill, by having a scalp talisman tied into the mane or forelock.

Like the Arab, the Indian never rode his war horse to the place of battle. To conserve its strength, the animal was led and mounted at the fighting spot. Indian horses were controlled partly by a lariat tied in a double knot around the lower jaw. Often an additional length of rope was allowed to trail behind so that if the Indian dismounted he could grasp the rope and prevent the escape of his horse.

The buffalo hunter was also given much care and devotion. This animal was often led to the scene of the hunt, though it was considered good luck to allow the huntsman's squaw to ride the animal. During the trek to the hunting grounds, she constantly implored it to show great bravery and allow her hunter to make many kills.

For the buffalo hunts, swift, maneuverable, well-trained horses were essential. The Indian hunters would ride swiftly alongside the quarry and let go the arrow to the one and only vulnerable spot behind the foreleg. Split-second judgment was required, for the animal had to be in extended action at the time of the arrow's impact. The moment the horse heard the twang of the bow he could swing away to avoid contact with the falling buffalo. If the buffalo was merely wounded, it became a deadly menace, which taxed the speed and agility of the horse in carrying his rider to safety.

The increase in horse stock and the extensive traffic in horses in the early 1800s eventually broke the grip fur "bosses" had on trappers in the northern country. Hearing tales of money to be had in horse trading, the trappers shifted southward. This undoubtedly had a more useful effect on the country as a whole because it stocked the frontiers with useful animals, making possible the settling of the land. Horses also helped to maintain communication with the outside, provided freight and pack lines, and eventually made possible the founding of the cattle industry.

With the opening of the Santa Fe Trail, in 1822, the life blood of the West began to pulse. Horses were largely responsible for this new era in American history, for the Western-bred plains horses could travel long distances and exist on native grasses. The horse that could be reined with one hand, so that the other was free to shoot or whirl a rope, was indeed a valuable asset.

An interesting fact is that in early times many Western horses went to the East but comparatively few Eastern-bred horses went West. The few attempts, where the large Conestoga horses were imported in the belief that they would be useful in drawing cumbersome loads, ended in dismal failure. Such horses, it was learned, could not subsist only on the grass that the land offered.

There were other reasons for the absence of imported Eastern horses. In the first place, most travel into the Southwest was by downriver boats and barges. Cumbersome upstream travel, on the other hand, was not indulged in. It was much simpler to purchase horses and thereby make better time. Many such horses were sold at Natchez.

Another fact to be considered is that there was an abundance of horses in the West but comparatively few in the East. With the difficulties of raising such stock and the great demand by settlers in the Eastern states, horses were scarce. The shortage of horses following the Revolutionary War has been noted before in this volume.

When the Revolutionary War closed, there was a great influx of new settlers into the backwoods areas. Some such pioneers became horse traders, acquiring Indian horses and driving them back to the East Coast towns. It is known that Daniel Boone moved to Missouri to trade for Indian horses. Early records show that he drove large bands of Western horses to Eastern markets.

It is a surprising fact that following the Louisiana Purchase, in 1803, the American army under General Wilkinson, organized for the purpose of settling boundary disputes, was mounted on horses of Spanish breeding. These mustangs had been brought up from San Antonio through Nacogdoches by the famous horse trader and Spanish-accused horse thief Philip Nolan. The soldiers had been brought down the rivers and outfitted with horses at river supply points.

In comparison with other Spanish colonies, Upper California was one of the last to be settled and receive horses. However, the fertility of the soil and favorable climatic conditions made it quickly the most important horse-producing area of the West.

Lower California had received its horses in the early 1700s. After 1735, horse breeding gained considerable impetus as a result of the Marques de Villapuente's sponsoring of the Pious Fund. This wealthy Mexican, owner of some of the largest horse and cattle herds, sent stock across northern Mexico and to the seven missions endowed by him. The offspring of these animals apparently became fixed and excellent in type, because of their good foundation and their selection for use.

The stock of Upper California sprang from that of the lower peninsula, and these horses remained excellent in type because of California's isolation until 1849. After that date, there appear to have been five recognized saddle-horse breeds existing in California: Spanish, California, American, Canadian, and English.

Five men are noted in connection with the earliest horses of California. Rivera, in 1769, drove the first horses, 140 in number, along with 200 cattle from Lower California to San Diego, the first of twenty-one missions built by the Franciscans; Anza, the first white man to cross the Sierras, in 1774, made two trips from Sonora with a total of 480 horses and 485 cattle (1773–1775); Neve, who replaced Rivera as governor of Upper California and was formerly governor of Lower California; Fages, who replaced Neve and penetrated north to the Sacramento Valley, was cofounder of the government horse-breeding scheme; and Father Campa, who remained in Lower California to gather horses for relaying to the Upper California settlements. Between 1769 and 1791, these men established all original horse stock in what is now the state of California.

From the time the Franciscan padres first entered California, in 1769, to the year 1800, the horse herds increased tremendously, numbering more than

HORSES OF CALIFORNIA MISSIONS

EARLY CALIFORNIANS ROPING A GRIZZLY BEAR

24,000 head. By 1840, California was reputed to be the most densely horse-populated section of the West, with more than 250,000 head.

The Spanish army maintained royal ranches for producing remounts at Salinas, San Diego, San Francisco, and later at Santa Barbara. Horsemanship in California at an early date reached a high point of organization. The militarists Neve and Fages and their able lieutenants Moraga, Ortega, Soler, and others originated the system which was designed to serve both demanding military use and ranchwork. Fages, the most exacting horseman of early California, was reputed to be one of the first men to rope grizzly bears from horseback.

In fact, the *reata* (Spanish word for rope) was a most effective tool in the hands of all early Spanish settlers in all sections. From the time of childhood the Californian prided himself in the expertness with which he used the *reata*. Roping contests and games which employed the rope were common at *fiestas*. Most of the California horsemen were so dexterous with a 60-foot rawhide *reata* that they could ensnare any one or all of the feet of a running steer. The variety of throws exhibited would probably astound rodeo fans of today; long or short throws, swing or toss, backhand to right or left, over the shoulder or flank, to horns or neck, and figure eights were all commonly used. There are stories to the effect that Californians used the rope instead of firearms in many instances.

At first, few early California horses were used by Indian tribes to the east. Though the padres were desirous of placing horse breeding in the hands of native Indians, the Army resisted on the grounds that they wanted no repetition of Arizona and Sonora days. However, by 1790, the Indians became well enough versed in horse handling to begin stealing from the Pueblo herds and trailing the animals into the interior.

Many persons erroneously believe that vast wild-horse herds roamed the Western plains from the earliest times. Few plains horses were wild in the true sense of the word. The Spanish method of horse raising was to allow the herds to graze at will on the natural grasslands. Such stock, as a rule, was not "forgotten" nor allowed to remain unattended for too long a period.

Some of the early traders made the mistake of claiming that such horses were wild, but the Spaniards argued differently and frequently backed up their arguments with killings. It was during one such altercation that the name "mustang," from the Spanish word *mesteño,* meaning wild, was put into use.

Fremont's accounts of his extensive expeditions make no mention of large numbers of wild horses anywhere except on the west bank of the San Joaquin in California. He infers that the bands he observed running at liberty were the property of Indians, trappers, mountain men, or traders.

One of the largest wild-horse herds of California resulted from a drought in the early part of the nineteenth century. The dry area extended from Mission San Jose to San Miguel, and several seasons were so severe that it became necessary to reduce domestic-horse herds. At first, many horses were killed, but the Californians sickened of the brutal method of running them over cliffs or sticking them with lances and decided upon a more humane way of dispersing the stock.

East of the Coast Range lay the great San Joaquin Valley, then called Tulare. The Californians drove hundreds of horses over the passes into this area, allowing them to forage for themselves. As they increased in number, food became scarce, particularly during dry seasons, and by the 1860s the Tulare mustangs began diminishing in size.

The horse and the mule were the tools by which the old West was won and operated. The horse industry was lively, and such old-time traders as Jed Smith, Jesus Villapando, Peg-leg Smith, Charlefoux, Ewing Young, and Sutter were historic figures in such traffic.

Ewing Young appears to have been responsible for the spread of California horses into many areas of the West. He was credited with opening the southern horse-and-mule trail from California to Taos and Santa Fe. One of his most noted enterprises, however, was the introduction of beef cattle and California horses into what is now the state of Oregon.

Apparently the Northwest Indians had acquired horses at an early date. In all probability, forerunners of such stock had come indirectly from that of Oñate's settlements. British trappers and American explorers and missionaries discovered the Nez Percés, Cayuses, and Wallawallas all to be exceptionally advanced horsemen and in possession of superior horses.

The appaloosa horses owned by the Nez Percé tribes were held in high esteem both by white men and Indians. The appaloosa horse was difficult to obtain, for under no circumstance would his Nez Percé owner sell him to a white man. Most tribesmen would trade several head of horses for a cow, horses being valued at $20 against $200 for a cow, but even a cow would not buy an appaloosa, as Fremont discovered to his disappointment.

All the horse-tribe Indians of the Northwest were reluctant to sell their mounts to the whites, and at first trading was with the less esteemed camp mares and pack horses. These made up the stock in use by trappers, farmers, and packers of the Northwest coastal region.

In general, horses and cattle in the Northwest were not of the California type. Cows were mainly the milking strains and were not handled by horsemen. Rail fences were built, and as the pasture was consumed the rails were moved to form another enclosure. The herds were driven from one point to another by men on foot. It is interesting to note that the Northwesterners were of the opinion that the few Spanish cattle they received by boat up the coast were the wildest ones from the California herds because they did not respond to such droving methods. They did not realize that the cattle would respect only a good working cow horse.

The farmers and the Hudson's Bay Company desired to accumulate larger herds of range cattle for the purpose of forming additional cargoes of hides and tallow for the fur ships sailing from the Northwest coast.

This, in brief, was the economic situation when Ewing Young arrived. He was a man who had hobnobbed with the Californians, was familiar with range-bred cattle, and knew that there was only one way to handle them— with well-reined cow horses.

The reason for Young's visit to the Northwest was horse trading. Aware of the shortage existing there, he contemplated selling or leasing a band of eighty-odd head of horses to Willamette farmers and the Hudson's Bay interests. Accompanying Young on this drive from California was Hall J. Kelley, a Bostonian with ideals. He intended to pave the way in the Oregon country for American settlers and prevent England from establishing her dominion there.

It was an unhappy coincidence that Young and Kelley fell in with a band of horse thieves who were traveling north with stolen horses. The governor of California dispatched a letter to Chief Factor McLaughlin at Fort Vancouver informing him that the horses in the band trailing north were stolen property. Though Ewing Young's animals were his own, the Factor had no way of knowing this and warned the Canadian farmers not to buy his stock. Consequently, Young was stranded in unfriendly territory, and Kelley fell ill and shipped East on the first ship out of Vancouver.

The enterprising Young, however, was not so easily defeated. A Tennesseean by birth, he was thoroughly familiar with whisky making. As a means of making money and perhaps also to take revenge on the Englishmen, he set up a still a short distance upriver. His operations disrupted the activity of the Hudson's Bay Company by thrusting upon it the curse of drunken Indian and Canadian trappers.

Meanwhile, Kelley had arrived in Boston, where he also wreaked vengeance, but in a much different manner. As a result of a pamphlet written by him condemning the Hudson's Bay Company's treatment of Americans in Oregon, the government in Washington sent a Mr. Slacum, attached to the Navy Department, to Oregon to investigate conditions there.

By the time Slacum arrived, Ewing Young had stirred up so much trouble that the Hudson's Bay authorities appealed to the Navy man to reason with Young. It is a matter of record that the intervention had more to do with cattle and stock horses than with stills and whisky.

As a result of the meeting, the Willamette Cattle Company was formed for the purpose of purchasing and driving a sizable herd of Spanish cattle into the Willamette Valley. American and Canadian settlers, with financial help from Slacum, pooled enough money to purchase about eight hundred head at the rate of $3 per head (f.o.b. California). The Puget Sound Company, a subsidiary of the Hudson's Bay Company, finally felt forced to come into the deal with $900 cash. Ewing Young's part of the plan was to organize a crew of Oregon drovers and purchase cattle in California. They were to drive the herd overland to Oregon.

Of all the party which sailed down the coast in Slacum's ship and landed at Bodega Bay, north of San Francisco, none except Ewing Young and a chap named George Gay had ever experienced a cattle drive using stock horses.

By August, 1836, Young had purchased 40 cow horses and 729 head of cows. These were assembled in the vicinity of San Jose. The ensuing drive must have been a nightmare to Drover Young and the cow horses. The inexperience of the Oregon riders was a tremendous handicap. From Mission San Jose to the San Joaquin River, the easiest part of the drive, 104 head of cattle were lost. Arriving at the river, the cows refused to swim across. A fence, open only on the river side, was built around the herd. This did not work. Rafts were built with which to tow them across. This also failed. At last the cattle broke for the hills. Horses were exhausted by the misuse of their green Oregonian riders.

At last, Ewing Young was forced to hire a couple of native *vaqueros,* and with their expert handling the scattered herd was rounded up and soon put across the river. Thus, the first great American cattle drive was started as the herd headed north up the Sacramento Valley and into the Oregon country.

After much hard work on the part of Young and his assistant, George Gay, 600 cattle straggled into the settlements on the lower Willamette. These were divided according to the amount each stockholder had paid in. The cowboys took cattle in trade for wages.

This trail herd of Ewing Young's was important to Oregon in more ways than one. First of all, it was the nucleus for a new industry in the frontier land. It helped break the monopoly of the Hudson's Bay Company by allowing the settlers to engage in something besides trapping. If McLaughlin had had sufficient foresight to hire Ewing Young to bring in cattle before the Willamette Cattle Company was formed, the story might have been much different.

For the first time, Oregon had true cow horses, for most of the 40 head used in the drive remained in the new land. Furthermore, George Gay was interested in the training of Western horsemanship as practiced by the early Californians, and he is noted in history as Oregon's first cowboy.

The Spanish mustang has frequently been maligned; but when it is realized that ranches covered from 6,000 to 30,000 acres, that there were no roads, and that everyone traveled on horseback, it is apparent that the Western horse was a remarkable animal.

Then, as now, the qualities most appreciated for stock work were intelligence, endurance, steadiness, sureness of foot, good saddle-carrying conformation, ease of traveling gaits, ambition, and ability to do a full day's work. The best horses of early times were of the same type as good cow horses of today.

The reader will remember that the mustang had its foundation in Spanish Barb stock. Records abound which attest to the qualities of the rugged offspring of such European animals. Native California horses were used successfully to draw the overland Butterfield stages. An Eastern passenger recorded his praise of these animals in the following words: "I have had long and great experience in horses, but had not the least possible idea in favor of the native California stock. They have been well selected, are of good size, not too heavy, strong and full of spirit, remarkably free travelers and possessing the most wonderful powers of endurance."

Kit Carson probably rode more horses in his lifetime than any other white man in the West. There is no record that he wished for any better transportation than the Spanish or Indian horse. In fact, it was Carson who introduced the Spanish horse to the famous trail blazer Fremont.

The usual assumption concerning Fremont's horses is that they were

Eastern-bred. Such was not the case. His first horses were purchased at Cyprian Chouteau's Indian trading post and they were Indian horses. The second expedition used Missouri-bred horses which proved unsatisfactory. Kit Carson, knowing that Eastern horses would not be serviceable until they had been acclimated to the West for a year, went to Taos and brought back California horses for the expedition. The American, or Eastern-bred, horses remaining in Fremont's party died on the trail at Green River, while the Western horses stanchly carried the party on into Indian territory.

Fremont never ceased in his praise of Indian horses. In helping prospective settlers, he advised, "These horses [Western], as ever in our journey we have occasion to remark, are valuable for hardihood and endurance."

A famous Western horse was Fremont's Sacramento. Purchased at Sutter's and reported to be a wild horse from the Tulare, this iron-gray California mustang was, in Fremont's own words, one of the finest horses he ever bestrode. Fremont rode him from the Sacramento Valley in California to Missouri. After wintering there, the durable horse carried his master West again on his third expedition.

In 1832, mounted units operating as rangers were organized in Oklahoma under the command of Captain Jesse Bean at Fort Gibson. To qualify, a recruit had to own his rifle and furnish his own horse. And of course these men owned Western horses.

Seven years later, the Dragoons were organized at Fort Gibson. Captain Eustice Trenor advertised locally for thirty sorrels for Company F; twenty-three bays for Company E; forty-five grays for Company C; and fifteen blacks for Company G. The requisitions were filled by local dealers in an area noted for Indian horse trading.

Theodore Roosevelt's writings contain many references to the hardiness and adaptability of the Western mustang. His confidence in these horses was expressed in a remark to a friend when he returned to the East after selling his Medora, North Dakota, ranch. He stated that "good fighting material existed in the cowboys of the West, who, mounted on their tough mustangs, would be a match for any cavalry in the world."

The history of the Western division of the Pony Express, though short, is a glowing tribute to the qualities of Western-reared horses. The eastern route of this fast mail service extended from St. Joseph, Missouri, to Salt Lake City and lay along an established stage line. Farther west, an almost new trail was used, with stations being built across the deserts and mountains to Sacramento. At first, the change stations were spaced 25 miles apart; later, this distance was reduced to 10 or 12 miles. Express ponies were required to run at full speed almost continuously. Those on the western end of the run had to be able to outrun hostile Indians and traverse exceedingly rugged terrain. At times, it was necessary for them to run lap after lap when stations were wiped out. One such heroic run was made by "Pony Bob" Haslem during the Paiute War when he rode 380 miles of hostile country, being in the saddle a total of thirty-six hours.

PONY EXPRESS

The ponies of the Western division were largely native Western stock. The job of obtaining the mounts for this division was entrusted to Major P. L. Solomon, United States Marshal for California, and he naturally turned to native stock as the horses best suited for the task. A few, however, were half-bred stock—blooded American horses crossed on Californians. Major Solomon showed his admiration for the Western horse by making the following toast at a gathering held in San Francisco to prepare a welcome for the first westbound Pony Express: "To the mustang ponies of California; they have done more for civilization, with California boys on their backs, than their mailed ancestors did in conquering the Montezumas."

As the result of a wager that mustangs were as enduring as blooded racers, an interesting event occurred in the year 1876. A number of unbroken California horses were selected from the Tulare area and were taken to Jersey City. The first race against time, to prove it was possible for them to run 300 miles in approximately thirty relays within fifteen hours, was started at the Fleetwood Park course. The event ended in failure because of bad weather and the inability of George Parker, the rider, to stay in the grueling test the full length of time required.

However, on May 25, Francisca Peralta, the Spanish-Californian assisting Parker, agreed to race 155 miles in seven hours, using twenty-five mustangs.

This was to be for a $10,000 stake. Peralta started the race at midday and had his share of difficulties. The sixth horse balked and reared. The thirty-sixth-mile horse proved to be stubborn; this animal bolted and ran off the course, down a bank and through trees and bushes, endeavoring to throw Peralta. On the sixty-first mile, another horse bolted straight through the rail. On one occasion, an attendant was knocked down and run over. In spite of these mishaps, Peralta finished the one hundred fifty-fifth mile two minutes ahead of the required time.

The first few paragraphs of an article by Dan Casement, which appeared originally in *La Hacienda*, entitled *"El indomable caballo cuarto de milla,"* admirably sum up the characteristics and historic importance of the mustang:

> Wherever cattle are handled commercially . . . they can be successfully managed only by men whose knowledge and experience have fitted them to comprehend perfectly bovine nature. But in the actual manual work of managing range cattle . . . such indispensable men are powerless unless mounted on swift and sensible horses whose understanding of bovine behavior perfectly matches their own. . . .
>
> When the mustang was first introduced to cow work he had already served his apprenticeship in running bison, reined by warriors of the Comanche tribe, the premier native horsemen of the plains. With hardy Texans in the saddle he took naturally to cows. On the trail no torrent was too turbulent for him to swim, no stampede too wild for him to head in the pitch blackness of a stormy night. At cutting in the herd he could out-smart the wildest and most agile steer and in roping he had speed to overhaul and knack to bust the biggest renegade. Almost equally with the great race of men who rode him this horse should share the glory of subduing the West to the uses of civilization. . . .
>
> A type of horse, therefore, exactly suited to this difficult and highly specialized undertaking must have in perfection the physical, mental and spiritual qualities essential to the proper performance of his job; those precise characteristics, in fact, which distinguished the old Spanish cow-horse.

It was inevitable that horses bred east of the Mississippi would eventually be brought West with the mass pioneer movements in that direction. It was just as inevitable that good horses would come with them and would in time blend their blood with that of the old-fashioned Spanish cow horse. The land became more crowded; the "longhorns" passed, giving way to improved breeds of beef cattle; railroads were constructed, making long cattle drives unnecessary; the vast pastures were segregated into smaller ones with barbed wire; the Indians were forced onto reservations. These were a few of the factors in the exodus of the Spanish cow horse and the Indian pony.

As the eighteenth century neared its final years, the blood of the mustang was being diluted by fancy driving and saddle horses and blooded runners. Like the famous Narragansett horse, the mustang became legend. To quote Robert Denhardt, " 'Appearance' and 'value' were almost synonymous. It was too much to expect a people used to tall, slender running horses or heavy draft horses to believe that an animal not much larger than a stocky pony could have the intelligence, stamina, and endurance to outwork on the cattle range half a dozen of their animals, to say nothing of one little feature called 'cow sense,' which the Eastern horses originally coming from northern Europe seemed to lack."

President Sam Houston was one of the first men to "import" blooded horses to the Texas area. Copperbottom, Rory O'Moore, and James O'Moore were brought out about 1839. It was Houston's idea to produce fine riding, buggy, and driving horses by crossing them on native mares.

As early as 1857, Vermont interests complained that the best Morgans were going West. Many of these proved to be good crosses on mustang blood in California and other localities.

In the belief that heavier horses might be more suitable in mountain pastures, Northwest cattlemen introduced Clydesdale, Percheron, and even Thoroughbred stallions. Such crosses produced greater size and, in some cases, greater speed, but, in general, each gain in weight seemed to subtract the important quality known as "cow sense."

The happiest union of Eastern and Western horses seemed to take place in the Texas area of the Southwest. Various strains of the Quarter Horse, quite similar in conformation and temperament to the Spanish cow horses, began reaching the plains country of Texas in the last half of the nineteenth century and were crossed on the native mustang. Undoubtedly the Barb blood, predominant in both, made a harmonious nick to produce cow horses with such outstanding qualities as quickly generated speed, cool intelligence, and cow "know-how."

CONFORMATION OF THE WESTERN
STOCK HORSE

It is comparatively easy to describe the conformation of a horse of established breed. As Western stock horses of today are not necessarily members of one particular breed and often are a composite of many, the task of describing them is less simple.

It has often been said that a good cow horse may possess any variety of physical qualities so long as he will watch a cow. It has also been observed that, regardless of breed, certain physical characteristics are common to all high-class cow horses of proved ability. There is an old saying that a top cow horse must have "a head and neck like a lady and the buttocks of a cook."

These generalities take on meaning when the function of the animal is considered. The work of handling stock requires a mount that is able to stop on its hocks, turn quickly, show a fast getaway, and exhibit short-distance speed. It is imperative that the working horse be perfectly balanced.

The usual procedure of describing conformation from fore to aft will be reversed here, since good hindquarters are of first importance. Extreme musculature is noted in this area. A medium croup, having neither extreme slope nor being exactly level, is desired. Heavy, bunched muscles are apparent all over and extending well down into the gaskins. The hips should be wide and long. The rear hocks and legs should be ample in bone content, but not coarse, and should be set somewhat forward under the body to show that much of the weight is supported at the rear.

To withstand the power of such hindquarters, the coupling through the loins should be full and broad. The back is short in order to carry weight. A barrel-like body is desired, with well-sprung ribs, depth of chest, and sufficient width between the forelegs.

As previously mentioned, the front end should be light as compared to the rear. The shoulders should have considerable slope to ensure stride and lift. The neck should emanate smoothly from the shoulders but should not rise upward like that of the American Saddler. The neck should be of medium length and not so thick as to prevent free movement.

Heads may show considerable variety, but it is preferable to select a cow horse with widespread jaws, thin muzzle with good nostrils, and a face with a flat profile. The eyes should be set wide apart and should show intelligence, ambition, and honesty. On a head of this type we usually find medium-small, alert ears which are set attentively, with considerable space between them.

This model may be any color, for good stock horses vary considerably.

The horse may be large or small, if balanced symmetry and proper proportion are present, but an average of 15 hands in height and weight between 900 and 1,100 pounds are preferred.

Finally, the horse should stand on medium-length legs; the feet, also, should be medium-sized and roundly constructed, with pasterns of medium length, not too straight and yet not too low.

TRAINING

Among all the horses of the world, I believe there is none which exhibits more artistry, as a result of proper training, than the Western stock horse. We need only observe a well-trained roper or a top-notch cutting horse to realize this fact.

Regardless of the specialized use to which they later will be put, all stock horses are started similarly in the first stages of training. Most modern trainers prefer to start the colt at the age of three, pointing out that at four he is having trouble with his teeth. Assuming that the young animal has been taken through the initial stages of gentling and has become acquainted with the saddle on his back, the next phase is reining.

Methods vary with trainers, but none of them starts the colt's reining with a curb bit. A few begin with a snaffle bit, and most of them introduce the hackamore in the first stages. One California trainer of my acquaintance puts the colt in a stall with a hackamore reined up to the saddle horn, but not too tightly. In this way the colt has an opportunity to study the meaning of the hackamore without becoming afraid of it. After this, he may drive the colt with long lines on a snaffle bit. Thus, the colt will learn to turn at a pull from the lines to left or right. Sometimes this particular trainer uses the snaffle bit before the hackamore or bridle is introduced. He often places a snaffle in the colt's mouth without reins attached at the same time the hackamore is being used. This is to accustom the colt to a bit in his mouth without any rein pressure. Later, reins may be attached but should be used only occasionally to aid in guiding the colt.

Neck-reining may be taught by the use of either the snaffle bit or the hackamore. The rein should be kept down and pulled toward the rider's knee. If, at the same time, the opposite rein is drawn across the colt's neck, an association will soon be set up so that he will no longer require the use of the direct rein. Guiding will thenceforth take place entirely with a loose rein drawn across the neck.

Many old-time horsemen believe that a horse should receive all his rein training while in the hackamore. It may require two years before the horse is capable of quick turns, backing, leaping immediately to a full run, setting up and stopping squarely, cutting out cattle and holding them on a rope. Such old-timers point out that a horse is no better reined the morning the curb bit is applied than he was the evening before when use of the hackamore was discontinued.

The bit, of course, is a means of applying pressure, in one way or another, upon the bars (or gums) of the lower jaw. The snaffle bit exerts a direct pull, whereas the curb exerts pressure through leverage.

The manner in which a hackamore works, however, is not so widely understood. The nose piece of hard rawhide bozal is placed properly when it strikes across the front of the nose at a point about one inch above the point where the cartilage joins the bone. The pressure of the nose button on the front of the nose and the knot under the chin are the controlling features. The colt is usually roughed the first time the hackamore is used in order to sensitize him to its pressure.

So important was reining to the old-time stock horses that *vaqueros* used to have a favorite saying: "Give me the three-legged horse with the rein." Though cattle are not so wild in these times, the well-reined horse is still necessary and greatly admired. When the colt is basically proficient in the art of reining, he is ready for specialized training.

Ropers

The method used by old-time *vaqueros* in training a rope horse was basic and similar to the methods employed today. The horse was started on a hackamore and ridden in the open, and a 3-foot length of hair rope was whirled by the *vaquero*, first on one side and then on the other. A hair rope was used because of its peculiar hissing sound.

When the colt was accustomed to this, the *reata* was used. At first a small loop would be whirled, then a larger loop was thrown to the ground ahead of the horse. When the horse no longer shied at this, the loop would be thrown on all sides of the horse as well as frontward and backward.

After this, the trainer would throw his loop on snags or light objects and back the colt each time to accustom him to the pull on the rope. Extreme patience was required. When the horse was finally worked on live animals, small calves were worked at first, but not for too long a period because the back of the horse became tender from live weight jerking the saddle. Graduation was made to heavier calves, and by the end of the year the pupil was usually able to hold mature animals, for by that time he had learned to brace and balance properly against the shocks.

It is imperative that the horse face the roped animal, keep out of the way of the rope, and keep it taut. An old-time method is sometimes used to teach these points. A yearling bull is roped and tied to the saddle horn about 25 or 30 feet from the horse. He is then placed in a corral and left alone.

After the horse is yanked, butted, and rope-burned a few times, he has learned the hard way to keep his eyes on the critter and face it at all times.

The essential difference between the roper and the bulldogging horse is that the dogger must not stop when his rider leaves the saddle. A well-trained horse of this type will run smoothly alongside the steer and pass it without stopping or veering away, lest his rider be caused to fall to the ground instead of to the horns of the steer.

Cutting Horses

The cutting horse, performing one of the most highly specialized jobs in ranchwork, is used for parting cattle from the main herd and holding them in the "cut." This horse must have an extra amount of "cow sense."

In making a cut, the horse is ridden quietly into the herd. When the rider has spotted the animal that is to be removed from the herd, he will "head," or "point," his horse toward it. The horse then proceeds slowly to work the cow to the edge of the herd, and when he reaches this point the critter is given a little rush to start him toward the cut. If the cow tries to return to the main herd, the horse's fast footwork comes into play and turns him back.

Most cutting horses show extreme intelligence, and the top-notchers work

CUTTING HORSE

with the utmost alertness. The best trained cutters will work without any signals from the rider from the time the cow is spotted until it is placed in the cut. This class of horse is termed a "self-worker." I have seen such horses demonstrate their skill by working without a bridle.

It would be impossible to relate all the ramifications of cutting-horse training in this chapter, but an article written by Wallace Reames, entitled "Cow

Sense Can Be Developed," in the May–June, 1945, issue of *The Western Horseman,* contains many valuable suggestions:

> The best way to teach cow sense is to always turn the colt's head toward the cow. This rule is so simple it doesn't seem sensible until given some thought. . . . Most horses will learn to turn a cow, and do it just as automatically as a human keeps to the right when driving. . . . It confuses a colt to turn him to the cow one time and away from the cow the next time. Never turn your colt's rump to the cow. The horse's eyes are in his head; he cannot watch a cow with his other end.
>
> Five minutes is long enough to ride a colt the first time. If he'll turn both ways a few times by plow-reining I'm satisfied. Probably on the second saddling I can gallop the colt along a fence and turn him by pulling his nose to the fence. He stops quickly, turns square around, and it doesn't make him limber-necked. The object isn't to stop the colt, but to turn and bring him back at a good clip, turn him the other way. This is called "double" or "doubling." Don't double your colt more than three times each way at one time.
>
> If you can double a colt, you can turn him to a cow. A good place to start is along a fence. When the cow is headed, double the colt to the cow. At first the cow will likely dodge behind you before you can turn the colt around, and continue in the same direction. The position reversed, you're between the cow and the fence. This is where riders who don't know how to teach cow sense fail. They know that when they turn the colt around they're still on the inside and the cow is already alongside, making tracks away from where they want her to go. It takes two or three seconds to turn the green colt so they figure it is better to skip the turn. The colt must be turned all the way if he's to learn. A few cows might get away at first, but it won't be long before the colt will begin to stop and turn of his own accord, and you'll be able to head the cow back along the fence.
>
> When your colt begins to watch a cow you start to cut on him. Don't cut in pairs, work your colt alone. Don't cut too many at first or try to cut on him if he's tired. You might make him limber-necked and switch-tailed, cause him to take a dislike to the work. Pet your colt if he does well. . . .
>
> It is better if the cows you work at first are not too fast. To pull a colt at high speed might make him cold-jawed. The idea isn't how soon you can head the cow but how quickly you can turn the colt. Regardless of how close the quarters or how advantageous it seems to turn the colt's rump to the cow, don't do it. If your colt passes a cow while driving the drag along a lane don't turn him away from the critter and circle around to get behind her. Pull him directly to the cow and he'll learn to work back and forth, and even go out to the fence for a critter that stops. A high-lifed horse will want to work fast when he begins to savvy. To hold him back too much will cause him to lose interest in the job.

As the colt progresses, the snaffle-bit reins can be handled with one hand. When he really gets to working I change the snaffle-bit for a light curb. . . . After the horse is worked with the curb for a while it is easy to put a fast rein on him by tapping him on the neck with a small stick. . . . A horse that does his work just as well as you would if you were in his place really loves the work. He gets as much kick out of putting a cow in her place as you do.

In addition to the working cow horses, there is still another Western type which takes its tradition from the same background. This is the parade and pleasure-type Western horse. Just as the *caballero* decked himself and his mount in splendorous riding equipment on *fiesta* days, so do the Sunday cowboys and girls of modern America. Such activity knows no geographical boundaries. Though some of the most colorful pageantry is observed in California towns around rodeo or *fiesta* time, Middle Western and Eastern areas have their share of Western riding clubs and sheriffs' posses. For instance, in 1947, there were more than sixty local saddle clubs of this type in the state of Indiana alone.

WESTERN SHOW HORSES

Most horse shows sponsor classes for horses and riders of this type. Horses used by these Western riders are of all shapes, sizes, and colors, though the horses most frequently used are of the parade type. They are usually larger than the working stock horse, and emphasis is placed on features not considered important by the average stock man.

The head should be refined, carried high, and balanced correctly on an upsweeping, arching neck. The shoulders should be obliquely slanted as in all good saddle horses. The chest should be massive, allowing good space between the forelegs. The body should contain a short back, with close coupling through the loins. The ribs should be well sprung and there should be extreme depth through the girth. The hindquarters should exhibit a naturally high-set tail, carried gaily. The slope of the croup should be imperceptible and the hips should carry heavy muscles. The legs should be sturdy but with beautifully modeled bones and tendons. The pasterns should be long enough to give spring to the horse's gait, but not so long as to break down in parade use. The feet, of course, should be round, sound, and of medium size.

Horses of the above conformation may be selected for parade work if they exhibit unusual beauty, vigor, and extreme style in action.

There are a number of show classes which include Western horses of all types. The American Horse Shows Association has recognized events for lightweight and heavyweight stock horses, green and advanced hackamore (jaquima) horses, trail horses, and parade horses. At the third annual convention of the California State Horsemen's Association, November 18–19, 1944, a comprehensive set of rules for judging and showing horses in Western events was drawn up.

Following is a résumé of the rules and requirements in the various classifications. They are given here because they have, in general, been accepted nationally, though minor points may vary from one locality to another.

Stock Horse Classes

1. Conformation 30 per cent, rein 50 per cent, manners 10 per cent, appointments 10 per cent.

2. Horses must be serviceably sound, in good condition, and of stock-horse type; blemishes on account of accident, such as wire cuts, not to be counted against horse. Entries to be open to stallion, mare, or gelding without discrimination. Height 14½ to 14 hands. Classes, light and heavy. Lightweight to be 850 to 1,100 pounds; heavyweight, 1,100 to 1,300 pounds. Horses to be passed for soundness and judged, stripped, for conformation before entering the ring.

3. Equipment: Horses to be shown with stock saddle and spade, half breed, or curb bit. No martingale or tiedown of any sort may be used. No wire, chain, or other metal device may be used alone or in conjunction with or as a part of a leather chin strap. No bozal, or nose band, shall be used.

4. Instructions to riders: One hand only shall be used while working, and hands shall not be changed while working. If any rider pulls or jerks his horse with one rein, whips his horse with quirt or romal while running or turning, he will be dismissed from class by the judge, and in no event shall spurs, romal, or quirt be used forward of the cinch, and at all times when horse is in motion the rider's hands shall be clear of horse and saddle.

5. Showing: Horses shall all enter arena at a walk, taking jog trot and slow lope when asked to do so. They shall then be lined up in the arena or retired therefrom at the discretion of the judge. Horses shall be worked one at a time, and no two horses shall ever be run out together.

The rider will start with a figure eight two or three times, of sufficient size to avoid short, choppy turns. The more smooth and even the gait, and the looser the rein, the greater credit to the horse. The horse will then be walked to the end of the arena, turned and run full length of the arena to a straight sliding stop, turned and run in the opposite direction the full length of the arena to a full sliding stop; turns to be made away from the rail. The horse will next be run to the center of the arena and brought to a square stop and immediately backed 10 to 15 feet. He will then be brought to face the judge and, with weight on his hindquarters and hind legs, shall be turned half a turn to the right and left as a stock horse would have to do in a gate working cattle. No spinning of the horse shall be asked or allowed.

After working as indicated above, the horse shall be worked on a sack weighing not less than 75 pounds. The sack is to be roped and the horse run from side to side, turning squarely back as the end of the rope is reached, with not more than 25 feet of rope out, the purpose being to show that the horse can work accurately and fast after an animal has been roped. The rope shall then be tied to saddle horn, with approximately 20 feet of rope out; the rider shall dismount, walk to the sack and place his foot on it; and the horse must hold the rope tight without indication from rider or aid from snubbing reins. Should horse run off with sack after rider dismounts, he may be disqualified, unless in the opinion of the judge the same resulted from accidental disturbance of the animal, in which event he may permit another trial.

6. Faults: Judges are asked to consider the following items as faults: switching of tail, bleeding of mouth, exaggerated opening of mouth, slackening of *reata* when holding sack, turning away or exhibiting lack of attention while holding sack, nervous throwing of head, lugging on bit, stargazing or improper position of head when restraint is applied to reins (a properly reined horse should bow his neck so that his forehead is approximately vertical when being worked), horse approaching rider in order to allow rope to be taken from sack, halting or hesitating when being shown, particularly when being run out, indicating anticipation of being set up, which is characteristic of an overtrained horse.

Stock Horses Worked on Cattle

A bunch of cows or steers, each animal having been conspicuously numbered, shall be held by riders as a herd of *parada* at some convenient place in the arena. At the direction of the judge, the contestants shall cut out a designated animal, take it to an indicated distance away from the herd, and work it as directed by the judge. Precision, ease, and speed with which the foregoing is accomplished shall be considered in rating the horse.

Hackamore Class

Entries not to be over six years old. To be shown with hackamore only; rider may use both hands and single-rein his horse but must not use quirt. The same procedure shall be followed as in the bridle class, except that the horse shall not be worked on a sack.

Trail Class

Performance 50 per cent, conformation 25 per cent, manners 10 per cent, appointments 15 per cent.

Horses to be shown on a reasonably loose rein, without undue restraint, at a walk, dogtrot, and lope, as directed by the judge, and over and through such obstacles as may be devised by the show management. It is recommended that a gate be used, as opening and closing gates is important in the education of a good trail horse.

Parade-Horse Class

Horses in this class are required to show only two gaits — the flat walk and the parade gait. So many exhibitors seem to have a misconception of the latter gait that it seems advisable to describe it. The *American Horse Shows Association Rule Book* specifies that the parade gait shall be "a high prancing trot but not a high school gait nor the slow gait of the five gaited horse. The parade gait shall not exceed four miles per hour."

Horses should be called upon to walk and parade alternately to determine the amount of control the rider exercises over them. Horses shall be faulted for sidewise motion, zigzagging, fighting the bit, carrying sour ears, and lack of manners.

Most parade classes of today exhibit the horse under stock saddle with silver, Mexican, or other type of colorful equipment. Horses should be shown with full mane and tail (not set). Horses are judged on appointments, performance, animation, manners, and conformation. (If it is a specialized class, such as for palomino or pinto, color and markings are given credit.)

A treatise on horses of the West would be incomplete if it did not include a few passages about the animals which have captured the popular fancy of Western riders because of their unusual color and markings. So great is this enthusiasm that associations have been formed to study, improve, and register palominos, pintos, albinos, and appaloosas.

PALOMINOS

Most people will agree that the palomino horse, with its golden body and snow-white mane and tail, is one of the most beautifully colored of all horses.

The history of palominos traces far back into antiquity. Many explanations have been given for the name "palomino," but nothing has ever been substantiated. Some say that Cortez introduced horses of palomino coloring to the New World. It is reputed that Queen Isabella of Spain used golden horses, called *palomilla,* in carriage service, and palominos were at one time referred to as "Isabellas." One school contends that in remote history palomino horses were a distinct breed and that through successive outcrossings the strain was lost.

There are variations within the color which should be noted. The *American Horse Shows Association Rule Book* gives the color qualifications as follows:

> A palomino should have the color of a newly coined U.S. gold coin. Purity of color and brightness of coat is important. The color may vary either lighter or darker than above specified but variations shall receive a lesser color score. Animals of extreme color variation may be eliminated at the discretion of the

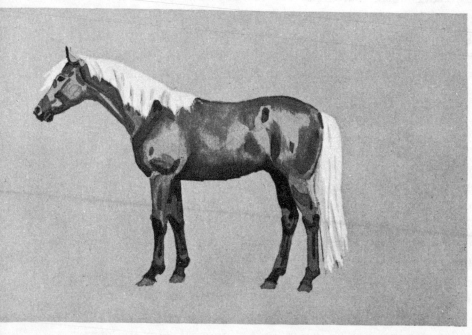

PALOMINO

judge. Mane and tail shall be white with not over 15 per cent dark or chestnut hair in either; the presence of dark hairs shall lower the color score. White markings on the face or white socks or stockings shall not be penalized but white markings above the knees or hocks shall receive a lesser color score. Horses with pinto markings, stripes on the legs, shoulders or down the back, or bleached mane or tail shall be disqualified. Eyes shall be dark or hazel and both the same color. Individuals with blue, moon, pink or glass eyes shall be disqualified.

Many problems now confront the breeder of palomino horses. Not many years ago, these horses were in such demand that little attention was paid to general quality so long as the matings produced the desired color. Buyers have become more discriminating and most of them now demand a good horse along with the rare coloring. The associations and most breeders are earnestly striving to meet this demand.

A great many people believe that when a palomino mare and a palomino stallion are mated, a palomino colt will be produced. This is not always the case, many such offspring being albinos. With a few exceptions, scientists believe that palominos contain in their genetic make-up a dilution factor. Some claim this factor to be dominant over normal color. If this theory is correct, it is evident that a "fix" on the palomino color may never be attained. Almost all breeders agree that the surest way to ensure palomino coloring is to cross sorrels and palominos. About 50 per cent of such matings will produce "golden horses." There are three types of mating which may produce palomino foals: (1) albino mated with chestnut; (2) palomino mated with palomino; (3) palomino mated with chestnut.

PINTOS

Most people speak of "pinto" as a color. Instead, it is a pattern marking which may occur in a horse of any color. Another common misconception is that it occurs as a result of mating, for instance, black horses with white horses. If this were the case, it is unlikely that there would exist today any horses of solid color.

The pinto has come to us in an unbroken line of descent from the remotest era of history. Some authorities believe that spots may have been the original marking of horses. The Bible contains references to spotted horses; cave drawings dating to the fifteenth century B.C. picture them; and history records that there were horses with spotted markings in the Iberian peninsula as early as A.D. 407–409. It is known that mounts of unusual color and markings were favored by the Spaniards, and pinto horses are said to have come to America with the early *conquistadores*. The pintos favored among the Indian tribes were of Spanish ancestry.

TOBIANO
PINTO

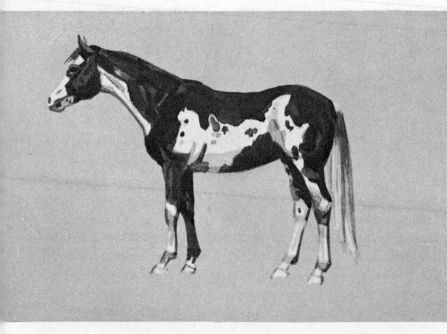

OVERO
PINTO

"Piebald," "skewbald," "calico," and "paint" are other terms which have been used to designate pintos of varying color and design. The word "pinto" probably has its origin in the Spanish words *pintado,* an adjective meaning painted or mottled, and *pintar,* a verb meaning to paint, color, or dapple. The Moslems in India and Arabia call the pinto *Kanhwa,* which means blotched with chestnut, white, and black. Also in India the word *Phulwari* is used to denote a white horse which "flowers" with black spots.

Perhaps because contrast is what interests pinto enthusiasts, the most prized are those of black-and-white coloring. Among pinto horses there are two distinct patterns, designated as "overo" and "tobiano." In the overo pattern, the white areas seem to originate on the underside of the horse and extend upward. As a rule, the back, mane, and tail are colored, though occasionally mixed manes and tails are observed. Horses within this category frequently have bald faces and glass eyes. Overo pintos are usually finer than the tobiano.

The outstanding characteristic of the tobiano is the manner in which the white areas seem to start at the top line of the animal and work down. As a rule, the tobiano's spots are larger and very sharply defined. Horses of this pattern frequently have head markings similar to those of horses of solid colors, with stars, strips, or snips. Tobianos occasionally have glass eyes but less frequently than in the overos.

None of the recognized American purebred associations, except the Tennessee Walking Horse Association, allow registration of pinto horses. On September 1, 1941, George Glendenning organized the Pinto Horse Society for the purpose of registering, preserving, perpetuating, improving, and developing pinto horses. This is the only American register for pinto horses.

Though pintos have been unpopular with many American horsemen, there are others who know that stanch spirits lie beneath the multicolored coats. One of the advocates would be Mr. A. F. Tschiffely who rode alternately two Argentine Criollos, one a pinto, from Buenos Aires to Washington, D.C., a distance of approximately ten thousand miles. The three companions made their way across vast plains, over cold barren mountains, through jungles, hot deserts, and swamps. Both animals arrived at their destination in good condition. After being shipped back to their native Argentina, the two animals lived many, many years.

Another would be Mr. Frank T. Hopkins, who owned the famous Hidalgo, a cream-and-white pinto stallion bred and raised near Laramie, Wyoming. When Mr. Hopkins was competing in the World's Fair in Paris, in 1899, he was requested to enter the 3,000-mile endurance race which had taken place in Arabia each year for a thousand successive years. The ride started at Aden,

Arabia, continued along the Gulf of Syria, then inland along the borders of the two countries. Though Hidalgo was competing with approximately one hundred crack desert Arab horses, over hot, dry country with a scarcity of water, he completed the race in sixty-eight days, the winner by thirty-three hours. The pinto Hidalgo thus won the distinction of being the only horse other than an Arab to win this historic race.

ALBINOS

Far too many people think of the pure-white horse as being Arabian. Fiction may be to blame, for it has often pictured the desert sheik galloping across the desert sands on a milk-white steed. Circuses frequently bill their white horses as "Arabian." It will be remembered from the discussion of Arab horses that few of them are true whites and that the desert tribes did not favor the color. Most of the Arabian horses which appear to be white are aged grays which have turned light. We also know that all Arabs have black skins—while albinos always have pink skins.

There are various grades of so-called "albinos." The two most common are: (1) the horses having a white coat, showing the merest traces of light cream or no color at all; the skin is pink and the eyes are pale blue or brown; and (2) the *cremellos*, albinos having a light cream-colored coat, pink skin, and china eyes with a bluish or brownish iris.

The American Albino Horse Club, established in 1937, sponsors the first grade described. Cal Thompson, the founder, has been actively engaged in producing and improving pure-white horses for more than thirty years. White Wings, the present herd sire, is a handsome pure-white stallion standing 16 hands high and weighing 1,100 pounds. The foundation sire of the Thompson horses was Old King, a milk-white stallion containing Arabian and Morgan bloodlines. Patoka, the blue-eyed stallion from the Thompson ranch, has delighted thousands of spectators with his dancing act.

Another American horse of pure-white color gained fame in a strange way. Sometime in 1937 or 1938, the Japanese military leaders, being familiar with the famous light-colored chargers of history, desired to obtain a snow white mount for their emperor. They instructed the Japanese consul in California to purchase a pure-white Arabian stallion. The consul discovered that such Arabian horses were extremely scarce. After much searching, an animal which seemed to meet all requirements was located, but, alas, he was not an Arabian, he had no pedigree, being the son of nonillustrious cow-horse parents. There was one point, however, which entitled Silver Tip, as he was then known, to registration papers. He was pure white and was thus admitted to the newly formed register of the American Albino Horse Club and assigned the number 330.

Cinderella was a piker compared to Silver Tip. Shipped to the island kingdom, he was received with impressive ceremony. In Japan, the little stallion, who stood a scant 14 hands 3 inches, was admired by the emperor and rechristened Fubuki, meaning snow.

When, during the recent conflict with Japan, Admiral William F. Halsey avowed his intention of riding Hirohito's favorite white horse through the streets of Tokyo, the Reno Chamber of Commerce set about fashioning a beautiful Western saddle for the purpose. We cannot help but wonder if Silver Tip, alias Fubuki, the little Western cow horse, would not have felt a twinge of homesickness when he felt the Bools and Butler saddle fork his snow-white back, had Admiral Halsey carried out his threat.

APPALOOSAS

The albino is noted for its complete absence of color or markings. The horse most noted for its riot of color markings is the appaloosa. Of all the color or pattern types, the appaloosa can lay greatest claim to being a distinct breed, at least in recent history.

Frequently called "polka-dot" or "leopard horses," the original stock came indirectly to the Nez Percé Indians from the early Spanish settlements. This Northwest tribe improved and fixed the pattern type, as well as certain desirable conformation characteristics. The Nez Percé race has thus been credited as being the only primitive people on the North American continent to practice animal husbandry to the extent of fixing a distinct type. It is recorded that these tribes, living along the Snake River and its tributaries as far south as the Wallowa Mountains, selected the best stallions as sires and castrated inferior and solid-colored colts over a period of approximately one hundred years. As a result, the appaloosas gained a commendable reputation among the early Western horsemen.

Dean Pollock's *Joseph, Chief of the Nez Percé,* gives an interesting account of the part played by the unusually marked war ponies when they served their masters in the final battles of that great tribe.

The often-explained manner in which these horses came by their present name bears repeating. From the name of the locality of their profuse breeding, the Palouse country, they were at first referred to as "a Palouse horse."

Later this was simply contracted to "apalouse," and through years of usage and misspelling, the word "appaloosa" emerged.

Actually, spotted horses of this pattern trace back to the very beginnings

BLANKET

SNOWSTORM
OR SNOWFLAKE

of horse lore. At least a few experts believe this pattern marking to have been the original coat coloring of prehistoric horses. In the earliest art they were depicted on stone, on horn engravings, and in early Chinese paintings. It is believed that a few such horses were ridden by invading Moslems across

LEOPARD OR
POLKA DOT

MOTTLED OR
MARBLEIZED

Africa and into Spain. Actually, there is little or no proof that appaloosa-marked horses did arrive from Africa. However, the existence of horses of such color in southern Austria and Hungary is an established fact. The known records of horse trading back and forth between those countries and the horse-raising establishments along the Guadalquivir in the vicinity of Cordova, Sevilla, and Cadiz seem to prove that the beautifully marked animals may have entered Spain via that route.

Regardless of how such horses were introduced into Spain, it is indisputable that they entered the New World ridden by the *conquistadores* and the Spanish settlers who followed.

Patterns of coloration rather than specific colors are typical of the appaloosa. Any color, or combination of colors, is acceptable in the typical appaloosa patterns described and illustrated below. While all of the "horse" colors occur among appaloosas, there are no solid-colored animals. The peculiar round, oval, or slightly elongated spots are always present. Among aged horses of lighter colors, such markings tend to fade. It has been observed that roans seem to predominate, while palominos and creams are the least numerous.

The four basic patterns may be described as follows:

1. *Blanket pattern:* A horse with roan or solid-colored foreparts and white over the loins and hips. The white area may or may not be punctuated with dark round or oval spots.

2. *Snowstorm or snowflake pattern:* A horse with roan- or solid-colored foreparts and with splashes, spots, or patches of white over the loins and hips.

3. *Leopard or polka-dot pattern:* A white, light-gray, or light-roan horse with dark spots over the entire body. The size and number of spots is immaterial, provided the round, oval, or slightly elongated shape is maintained. Frequently such spots are small at the foreparts and become increasingly larger at the hindparts.

4. *Mottled or marbleized pattern:* A roan horse, distinguished from the roans of other breeds by the peculiar round or oval concentrations of either darker or lighter color. The spots may be faint, giving the horse a mottled appearance, or they may be sharp, producing bold contrasts. This pattern should not be confused with dappled horses of the overo pinto type.

It should be understood that frequently there occur horses bearing combinations of the four basic patterns.

Thin manes and tails are common to many appaloosas, and most of them possess varicolored hoofs, lips, nostrils, and areas containing the reproductive organs.

The uses of the Western horse are more varied than of any other type in the United States. Such animals are serving for ranchwork, pleasure riding, show-horse classes, dude ranches, and rodeos.

Between 1910 and 1925, it was thought that the automobile might spell doom for the horse. Such a fate did not occur because it was the machine which gave man more time for leisure. Americans as a whole are horsemen by nature, instinct, and heritage. It was natural that more and more of them would turn to Western riding as a form of diversion growing out of that leisure; today, people of all ages and in all walks of life are finding relaxation and recreation in the sport.

In 1946, the commercial value of the horse industry in America was conservatively set at two billion dollars. Of this an overwhelming amount represented Western horses and feed and equipment for them. Interest in such animals was not confined to the West and no longer to any particular breed. Myriad Western saddle clubs continue to spring up in the Middle West and in the East, as well as in the West, where the tradition was founded.

And for those who think the working cow horse is a thing of the past, let's take a look at some figures. A survey which was made eight years ago will be extremely conservative today. At that time there were 25,457,000 beef cattle in the seventeen Western states. Considering that it takes an average of twenty saddle horses to handle each thousand head of cattle, 509,140 horses were needed. Sheep men alone needed another 27,000 mounts to handle their stock.

So long as there are vast stretches of Western range land, so long as there are rodeos and parades and people who like to ride, there will remain thousands of horses—and those horses will be "Western."

Index